FIELDWORK
FOR HUMAN
GEOGRAPHY

014594018 Liverpool Univ

D0537355

WITHDRAWN FROM STOCK

SAGE has been part of the global academic community since 1965, supporting high quality research and learning that transforms society and our understanding of individuals, groups and cultures. SAGE is the independent, innovative, natural home for authors, editors and societies who share our commitment and passion for the social sciences.

Find out more at: **www.sagepublications.com**

FIELDWORK
FOR HUMAN
GEOGRAPHY

RICHARD PHILLIPS AND JENNIFER JOHNS

Los Angeles | London | New Delhi
Singapore | Washington DC

© Richard Phillips and Jennifer Johns 2012

First published 2012
Reprinted 2013

Apart from any fair dealing for the purposes of research or private study, or
criticism or review, as permitted under the Copyright, Designs and Patents
Act, 1988, this publication may be reproduced, stored or transmitted in any
form, or by any means, only with the prior permission in writing of the
publishers, or in the case of reprographic reproduction, in accordance with
the terms of licences issued by the Copyright Licensing Agency. Enquiries
concerning reproduction outside those terms should be sent to the publishers.

SAGE Publications Ltd
1 Oliver's Yard
55 City Road
London EC1Y 1SP

SAGE Publications Inc.
2455 Teller Road
Thousand Oaks, California 91320

SAGE Publications India Pvt Ltd
B 1/I 1 Mohan Cooperative Industrial Area
Mathura Road, Post Bag 7
New Delhi 110 044

SAGE Publications Asia-Pacific Pte Ltd
3 Church Street
#10-04 Samsung Hub
Singapore 049483

Library of Congress Control Number: 2011932823

British Library Cataloguing in Publication data

A catalogue record for this book is available from the British Library

ISBN 978-0-85702-586-9
ISBN 978-0-85702-587-6 (pbk)

Typeset by C&M Digitals (P) Ltd, Chennai, India
Printed and bound in Great Britain by Ashford Colour Press Ltd
Printed on paper from sustainable resources

CONTENTS

ABOUT THE AUTHORS

Richard Phillips is Professor of Geography at Sheffield University, where he leads fieldwork classes and teaches cultural geography and postcolonial criticism. He is the author of *Mapping Men and Empire: A Geography of Adventure* (Routledge, 1996) and *Sex, Politics and Empire: A Postcolonial Geography* (Manchester University Press, 2006), as well as the editor for *Muslim Spaces of Hope: Geographies of Possibility in Britain and the West* (Zed, 2009). His current research investigates 'Geographies of Curiosity'.

Richard Phillips at a small dairy farm in Honduras

Jennifer Johns is an economic geographer teaching management and international business at the University of Liverpool Management School. She previously lectured at the Department of Geography, University of Liverpool and the School of Geography, University of Manchester and has taught on fieldtrips in the UK, France, US and Canada. Jennifer works on research issues of inter-disciplinary interest including globalisation, the agglomeration of economic activities, global trade and production networks.

Jennifer Johns in an Asian-themed shopping mall in Canada

OTHER CONTRIBUTORS

Joseph Assan is a Lecturer in Development Practice at Trinity College Dublin. He has extensive fieldwork experience in Africa. Joseph's research examines Political Ecology and the interaction between development policy and practice. He is the author of *Livelihoods and Development*, which will be published by Routledge.

Matt Baillie-Smith is a Reader in Sociology at Northumbria University. His research analyses development, NGOs, civil society and activism, particularly in relation to ideas of cosmopolitanism and citizenship. Recent work has explored international volunteering, activist biographies in South India, and NGOs and development education in the global North.

Alastair Bonnett is Professor of Social Geography at Newcastle University. His most recent book is *Left in the Past: Radicalism and the Politics of Nostalgia* (Continuum, 2010), a work that reflects a long-term interest in the paradoxes of modern radicalism. Alastair has pursued a vision of geography as the 'world discipline' and fieldwork as one of its core methodologies (in *What is Geography?* Sage, 2008).

Tim Bunnell is Associate Professor at the National University of Singapore, where he is jointly appointed in the Department of Geography and at the Asia Research Institute. Following doctoral and postdoctoral research in Malaysia, he has worked on Liverpool's historical connections to Southeast Asia and, more recently, on urban transformation in Indonesia.

Nick Clarke is Lecturer in Human Geography at the University of Southampton. His research and teaching focus on the cultural dimensions of globalisation. He loved fieldwork as a student and now leads a fieldcourse to Berlin, focusing on the production of urban space in twentieth-century Europe.

Bill Gould has been using fieldwork in teaching human geography and development studies since he taught A-level Geography in Uganda in the 1960s, and subsequently in the Department of Geography, Liverpool University, 1970–2007, with field classes with and for British and local students in Uganda, Kenya, Tanzania, Zimbabwe and South Africa.

Andrew Gregory graduated from the University of Manchester with a BSc in Geography and MA in Economy and Society. He has since developed a career as a management consultant, beginning his employment with Accenture in July 2004. He is currently a Manager in Products Life Sciences.

Jennifer Grehan graduated from the University of Liverpool with a BA in Geography. She attended a ten-day residential fieldtrip to Vancouver in 2009. Jennifer is now working in law, having gained a trainee position at a leading law firm in Canada.

Peter Hopkins is Reader in Social and Political Geography in the School of Geography, Politics and Sociology at Newcastle University, UK. His research tends to employ qualitative methods, including focus groups, interviews and participatory techniques focusing on issues relating to the geographies of youth, religion, race and masculinities.

Peter Jackson is Professor of Human Geography at the University of Sheffield. He is currently directing a project on 'Consumer culture in an age of anxiety', funded by the European Research Council (http://www.sheffield.ac.uk/conanx). He previously directed a multi-disciplinary research programme on 'Changing Families, Changing Food', funded by the Leverhulme Trust (http://www.sheffield.ac.uk/familiesandfood).

Mark Jayne is a Lecturer in Human Geography at the University of Manchester. His research interests include consumption, city cultures and cultural economies. He is the author of *Cities and Consumption* (Routledge, 2005) and co-author of *Alcohol, Drinking, Drunkenness: (Dis)Orderly Spaces* (Ashgate, 2011).

Innes M. Keighren is Lecturer in Human Geography at Royal Holloway, University of London. His research interests include historical geography, book history, and the history of science. He has recently published *Bringing Geography to Book: Ellen Semple and the Reception of Geographical Knowledge* (I.B. Tauris, 2010).

Brett Lashua is a Lecturer in the Carnegie Faculty at Leeds Metropolitan University. His research asks how young people make sense of their lives through arts, leisure and cultural practices, and how young people are 'made sense of' through particular representational and narrative strategies.

Kate Lloyd is Senior Lecturer in the Department of Environment and Geography at Macquarie University. As a development geographer her research and teaching focus on transitional economies within the Asia-Pacific Region and crossings and connections within Australia's Northern Borderlands. Kate uses experiential learning techniques to explore development issues within the Asia-Pacific region.

Sara Parker, who has provided numerous photographs for this book, lectures in Geography at Liverpool John Moores University. She has been working in Nepal for nearly twenty years, conducting research and supervising fieldwork in the village of Sikles in the Annapurna Conservation Area. A community project in this area is described in her edited book entitled Our Village Our Life: Sikles in Focus (http://www.sikles.org.np/).

Eric Pawson is Professor of Geography at the University of Canterbury, New Zealand. He is co-editor (with Mick Healey and Michael Solem) of *Active Learning and Student Engagement* (Routledge, 2010) and co-author (with Tom Brooking) of *Seeds of Empire: The Environmental Transformation of New Zealand* (I.B. Tauris, 2011).

Chris Ribchester is Programme Leader for Single Honours Geography and Deputy Head of the Department of Geography and Development Studies at the University of Chester. His primary research interests focus on pedagogy including, at the moment, projects exploring the impact of pre-induction social networking and the teaching of ethics.

Rachel Spronken-Smith has lectured in Geography at the University of Canterbury and is now Head of the Higher Education Development Centre at the University of Otago. Her research interests span climatology and higher education.

Mark Yaolin Wang is an Associate Professor of Human Geography in the Department of Resource Management and Geography at the University of Melbourne. His research interests include urbanisation, development and environmental issues in China and East Asia. He has coordinated and taught China Field Class for more than fifteen years.

INTRODUCTION

FIELDWORK FOR HUMAN GEOGRAPHERS

Fieldwork is central to geographical education and research as a core component of most undergraduate degrees in the subject, with large numbers of students embarking upon an overseas or non-local fieldtrip during their course. Many of them may have been attracted to fieldwork by visions of exotic settings and a break from the routine of lectures and exams rather than by an understanding of what fieldwork is, or what it is for, but these are indeed important considerations for you to take on board once you have signed up for a trip and are preparing to go into the field. This book is intended for any student who is considering or taking a human geography fieldtrip. Its aim is to help you as that student to get the most out of your fieldwork and to develop clear, critical ideas about what that fieldtrip is for and what it can do for you.

Fieldwork varies enormously, so there can be no simple formula for a book such as this. It is usually defined as supervised learning involving first-hand experience which takes place outside the classroom (Lonergan and Andersen 1988: 1; Gold et al. 1991: 23). This definition has been applied to *geographical* fieldwork, and more specifically as 'the opportunity for students to gain first-hand experience of geographical issues away from the classroom' (Livingstone et al. 1998: 3). Field classes can range from short trips during scheduled class time through to half-day and day site visits and up to the larger-scale residential field courses. Some fieldwork will involve close staff guidance and supervision; elsewhere students will be expected and encouraged to create and run projects independently. Fieldwork is also sometimes incorporated within study skills or substantive courses – on economic, social and cultural geography, for example – and sometimes delivered in free-standing modules. In addition field classes can take place in a wide range of settings: local and non-local; domestic and foreign; urban, suburban, rural and rugged; and so on. Some students will be set very specific tasks on fieldtrips, while a growing number will be expected to devise and conduct their own projects with support from their tutors. In reality, however, most students will undertake a mixture of directed and independent research. Moreover, most fieldtrips will have a number of things in common. Usually they will address broad themes which are fundamentally the same in different parts of the world. And their formats will be broadly the same, such that students on diverse fieldtrips will tend to face a common set of experiences and challenges. So whilst acknowledging the diversity of fieldwork experiences this book also addresses a number of generic themes and questions, most of which will be relevant to most students.

To answer the question of how you might do fieldwork, it helps to know why and how others have done it. This is partly a matter of understanding how research methods, which are more generally employed by geographers, have been applied to fieldwork. Methods relevant to fieldwork are explained in a wider literature on research methods for geographers and other social scientists and students of the humanities. Rather than reviewing and explaining these again in detail here, the emphasis of the most explicitly methodological section of this book will be upon the relationships between selected key methods and contexts. This book devotes a series of chapters to the research methods that are most commonly used in fieldwork in human geography. These approaches complement and overlap with each other. Though you will need to decide which are most relevant to your particular fieldwork projects you won't generally need to choose between them and will often be able to usefully deploy more than one technique. Doing so will allow you to spread your risk (in case one method doesn't work out or in case you're not very good at it) and enable you to triangulate your findings (cross-checking the findings of various methods).

Interviews and focus groups are examined in Chapter 7, while participatory approaches and participant observation can be found in Chapter 8. Nigel Thrift (2000) argues that human geographers have been too reliant on these particular methods, neglecting the wider range of methodological possibilities in our research and fieldwork. So this book also looks beyond the canonised to consider various other methods, some of which are more exploratory and less conventionally associated with the field. Chapter 6 is concerned with reading the landscape and with exploring sounds, images and texts, using emerging technologies where it is helpful to do so. Chapter 9 then asks more open-ended questions about 'how to be an explorer' and how to cultivate geographical curiosity. In each of these chapters, the relationships between methods and contexts are illustrated through case studies of particular field experiences. Experienced fieldtrip leaders from around the world have contributed these case studies – which we call 'postcards' – to illustrate what fieldwork can do and the problems and challenges fieldworkers face. We also include some student postcards, whose experiences provide another valuable perspective on fieldwork.

Before turning to field methods – the how of fieldwork – it is important to discuss some more fundamental questions about why you might want to do fieldwork. Chapter 1 frames the broad question of how you can get the best out of your time in the field, while the next chapter focuses on a specific question that many students have asked: how can fieldwork enhance the prospects for employment and improve students' skill sets? Chapter 3 then provides suggestions for how you can prepare yourself for fieldwork, by conducting preliminary research and developing fieldwork plans. The following chapters discuss the ethics of fieldwork and the social experience of travelling and working together. These discussions raise some challenging questions about how you, as a student fieldworker, can best position yourself in the field and work ethically and effectively when you are there. As in other chapters, we seek to raise issues and questions that you will want to answer as you plan and conduct fieldwork. Rather than answering these for you, our aim is to help you answer these for yourself. This is a pathway to conducting critical and imaginative fieldwork.

PART I

APPROACHING
THE FIELD

1

GETTING THE MOST OUT OF FIELDWORK

OVERVIEW

This introductory chapter addresses the following questions:

- How can you get the most out of fieldwork?
- What is fieldwork and why is it important in university level geography?
- What is meant by 'the field' and how can you engage with it?
- What are the key concerns and criticisms of fieldwork? These encompass the intellectual relevance of fieldwork; its practical value to you as a student; its financial and environmental costs; and its ethics.

The chapter invites you, as a student, to enjoy fieldwork but also to take it seriously, asking challenging questions about and through the field.

INTRODUCTION: FIELDWORK AND GEOGRAPHY

Fieldwork is compulsory for many geography students and a recommended option for most others because it occupies an important place within academic and professional geography. It has been suggested that fieldwork is to geographers what clinical practice is to medicine. For better or worse, fieldwork is often treated as an 'initiation ritual of the discipline' (Rose 1993: 69) and the field is 'depicted as the locus of becoming for the real geographer' (Powell 2002: 267). This is as true of undergraduate geographers as of their professors. As Felix Driver has noted, this commitment to fieldwork reflects the 'assumption ... that that the complete geographer is one who can conduct fieldwork according to certain standards – in other words, safely, skilfully and effectively' (2000: 268). Moreover, it is often suggested that fieldwork is what distinguishes genuine geographers from mere interlopers. Canadian geographer Cole Harris puts it this way:

> There are geographers who do not enjoy fieldwork. One of my colleagues in the late 1960s, an eminent spatial theorist, could not abide the world as it presented itself to the senses. It was too cluttered. He liked to be driven, and he would sit in the back seat of a large car with the blinds

down. At home he watched gangster films and adjusted his equations. But most of us are not such
purists. We are more inclined to take the world as it is – or as it seems to be – to get out into it,
look hard at it, ask questions about it, and grapple with the conundrums so presented. This usually
means fieldwork ... (2001: 329)

Having 'been there' is said to lend credibility not only to geographers themselves but also to
their research findings and claims, even though these truth claims have increasingly been interrogated and contested as we explain in subsequent chapters.

The importance of fieldwork in the geographical tradition reflects the influence of foundational geographers and geographical institutions, who defined modern geography as a field-
based discipline. Carl Sauer, who headed the Geography Department at the University of
California, Berkeley, and is often regarded as the father of North American Geography,
famously declared that 'the principal training of the geographer should come, wherever possible, by doing fieldwork' (Sauer 1956: 296). He practised what he preached: running weekend
fieldtrips in the local area and spending his summers and sabbaticals further afield, particularly
in Mexico (West 1979). In doing so he renewed a fieldwork tradition which he inherited from
and shared with others, including fellow American geographers such as William Morris Davis
(1850–1934) and institutions such as the Association of American Geographers (AAG), which
cohered around a shared interest in fieldwork and field-based data and convened annual field
conferences in the 1920s and 30s (Mathewson 2001; Rundstrom and Kenzer 1989). Fieldwork
was also important to geographers and geographical institutions outside the United States.
These included explorers: the most important geographical institution in the Victorian period,
the London-based Royal Geographical Society (RGS), committed itself to carrying out
'important Expeditions in every quarter of the Globe' (as its royal charter of 1859 put it) (*Times*
2009: 2). Fieldwork was promoted by educators too, with a 'cult of the field' in the early years
of British state schooling from 1870 onwards (Ploszajska 1998: 758). And when Geography
had become established in British universities the commitment to fieldwork continued, both
in the research activities of geographers and undergraduate curricula.

This commitment to fieldwork has been reaffirmed, both by geographers working broadly
in the tradition established by Sauer and by others with very different perspectives. Cole
Harris has reflected that for him, and indeed for 'many a geographer' he has known, 'the high
points of a working geographical life have been exhilarating experiences in the field' (2001:
329). His commitment to fieldwork is echoed by geographers from other traditions for whom
'the field' and fieldwork mean very different things. William Bunge, whose radical and creative
geographies both emerged from and challenged quantitative and analytical work within the
discipline in the 1960s, criticised what he saw as an emerging tendency to 'cite not sight'
(Bunge 1979: 171). He encouraged geographers to get into the field and find things out for
themselves, and he set an example for how they might do so that would involve members of
the public in the process (Chapter 9 explains how). More recently, others have reaffirmed the
commitment to fieldwork and the geographical tradition in which the field is accorded a

central place. David Stoddart introduced his inspired history of the discipline, *On Geography* (1986), as 'a book written from the field and not from the armchair' (p. xi), and fieldwork in all its forms is central to that book, which celebrates a world 'of great beauty and diversity, waiting for exploration' (p. x).

Fieldwork is not just an Anglo-American geographical tradition. It has also been important to geographical research and teaching in other parts of the world too. In Singapore, for example, it has flourished in the context of wider efforts by educators, supported by the Ministry of Education, to encourage independent, creative and critical learning (Chuan and Poh 2000). Similarly, in other countries from Argentina to Hong Kong, geographers have stressed the 'irreplaceable' role of fieldwork and successfully campaigned for its place on the curriculum (Kwan 2000; Ostuni 2000). So, to an extent, there seems to be a broad international consensus on the value and purpose of geographical fieldwork today.

Finally, we should add that the fieldwork tradition has not just been inherited and shaped by foundational figures – who were once called 'fathers of the discipline' and now increasingly will include 'mothers' too. Fieldwork also relies upon those who participate in and support it. These include workers who provide transportation and accommodation, ranging from guides and porters in nineteenth-century expeditions to flight attendants, drivers and cooks today. Ultimately, undergraduate fieldwork sinks or swims as a result of the ways in which students themselves engage with it. Pedagogical articles about fieldwork often quote favourable feedback from students, explaining how trips to the field brought course material to life – 'seeing how it mattered', as one student put it in a course evaluation (Hope 2009: 175) – and sometimes tracing forms and degrees of learning from and engagement with field projects. These surveys suggest – and when published are intended to suggest – that it is not only academic geographers who believe in fieldwork, willingly participating in the fieldwork tradition, but students as well. It will be necessary to revisit glossy claims such as these. For now, though, the point is that on some level the fieldwork tradition is alive and well and that students are playing their part in making it so.

On the other hand, fieldwork means different things in different times and places. The fieldwork tradition in geography is marked not only by continuity but also by change and diversity. Not just one tradition, it is comprised of a series of traditions which are variously performed and contested. We should not do fieldwork simply because others have done it. Rather, we must ask challenging questions about what fieldwork is and what it should be, and also about what the field in fieldwork is and should be.

WHAT IS FIELDWORK?

As noted in the introductory chapter, fieldwork means different things in different times and places, though it is usually understood as supervised learning that involves first-hand experience outside the classroom (Lonergan and Andersen 1988: 1; Gold et al. 1991: 23). This is not as straightforward as it first appears because different people have different understandings of 'geographical issues'. One textbook on fieldwork advises geography students not to 'become too interested in historical facts about towns or buildings' and to 'avoid biological information about the animals and plants you find' (Glynn 1988: 3). We prefer to define the geographical more inclusively however – not to exclude the historical or biological, for instance, but to regard these and other phenomena through geographical perspectives. We would also note that, while this book is concerned with fieldwork *for human geographers*, and while fieldwork is important in defining geography as a discipline – making it 'an identifiable subject in university and national academic regimes' (Pawson and Teather 2002: 275) – geographical fieldwork is closely related to and informed by fieldwork in other disciplines, such as anthropology and cultural studies.

Having started with a simple, general definition of fieldwork, it is now necessary to acknowledge that this has been conceived in many different ways: for example, as a means of teaching and learning specifically geographical concepts such as scale; of appreciating the 'glories of God's creation' (Marsden 2000: 17); of exchanging the stuffy and formal atmosphere of the classroom for the healthy and stimulating world outdoors (Geikie 1887; Knapp 1990); of inculcating values of patriotism and citizenship (Layton and White 1948); and even of advancing international peace and understanding (Marsden 2000). So fieldwork means different things to different people in different times and places. Gold et al. (1991) identify three distinct traditions of or approaches to fieldwork, which have their own histories but have also overlapped: 'the exploration tradition' which responds to 'the desire to go and see new places'; 'the regional tradition' which examines 'the interrelationship of physical and human phenomena in regional associations' (1991: 22); and 'observation and empiricism' which started from 'observable facts' and 'also contributed to an emphasis on active learning through fieldwork' (1991: 23). These traditions are not simply different; they are frequently at odds, with their visions of fieldwork contrasting and often conflicting. Fieldwork, they collectively suggest, is a diverse and contested set of practices: views are expressed about which kinds of fieldwork are better and the reasons for this.

The definition of fieldwork as learning out of doors is often qualified with reference to a distinction between fieldwork and tourism. The chapter on fieldwork in a manual on teaching geography in higher education begins with a dour warning: 'One should not ... confuse a fieldtrip in geography with picnics, outings or senior class excursions' (*Field Training in Geography* by P.F. Lewis, quoted by Gold et al. 1991: 21). Critics have dismissed fieldwork as 'academic tourism' (Mowforth and Munt 1998: 101) and condemned fieldwork that smacks of tourism, which is often presumed to be uncritical and neo-colonial. Indeed student fieldwork may sometimes be guilty of this. Dina Abbott (2006) felt uneasy about a fieldtrip to the Gambia in which British students were taken on a tour, which introduced to them the small West African country's history as a slave trading post. Tourists, and students among them, 'are welcomed with a potted history of enslavement and after they feel they have "done Gambia", return to the boat' (2006: 330). Her pessimistic conclusion is that these students are 'indistinguishable by local people from another set of "white" tourists' (2006: 335). More lighthearted, but otherwise similar claims are often made by the colleagues, friends and relatives of fieldworkers, who jokingly or otherwise accuse us of taking holidays at the expense of others.

Fieldtrip leaders reply to these charges by making a distinction between fieldwork and tourism, and also between more and less credible forms of fieldwork, by asserting that 'this is not a Cook's Tour'. Neil Coe and Fiona Smyth (2010: 126) put it this way:

> Many [geographers] will have had first-hand experience of a certain mode of field teaching in which the teacher/lecturer assumes the familiar role of knowledgeable expert. In this mode, students are treated to a carefully planned tour with the lecturer offering commentary, explanation, interpretation and leading discussion at, and between, the various sites of interest. In some instances local experts are also enrolled to offer their privileged knowledge on the topic at hand. Students are largely passive recipients, responding only to direct questions and taking notes on what is being said. The lecturer, in effect, assumes the role of 'tour guide'.

Coe and Smyth go on to describe more progressive, student-led fieldwork. Others have drawn similar distinctions. Yi Fu Tuan (2001: 42) expressed scepticism about fieldwork that may be 'little different from the rounds that tourists make', but suggested another model of fieldwork in which students played a more creative and active role. These distinctions between passive and active fieldwork are not always fair. On the one hand, it can be helpful to begin a fieldtrip with an orientation, in which students are given their bearings and introduced to the basics of life in a place that is new to them before they embark upon independent projects and explorations (Herrick 2010). On the other hand, student-centred fieldwork is not new. Previous generations of fieldworkers also tried to design fieldwork that was exciting and engaging for students. This commitment to active learning is widely accepted and has been for some time. As S.W. Wooldridge put it in more than half a century ago, 'proper fieldwork' was about 'doing' and not about students being told (1955: 79; quoted by Marsden 2000: 31). Bill Marsden generalises that 'fieldwork has always been associated with what might be called the progressive educational front of geography' (2000: 33).

The difference between tourism and fieldwork, and between passive and active forms of fieldwork, is not just something for the fieldtrip leaders to think about. As a student you can also take responsibility for your own learning, ensuring you play an active part in the field. When we asked students who had been with us on a fieldtrip to Vancouver to reflect on 'the difference between fieldwork and tourism', these were some of the things they said (in a survey conducted after the fieldtrip ended):

> Fieldwork incorporates a different level of interaction, as we studied areas and issues that most tourism would not fully understand or even want to engage with. (Hannah)

> You have to make sure that although you can have fun on the field trip, the primary reason is to work and gain skills. (Anthony)

Tourism is visiting a destination for recreational, leisure or business purposes and creates money for that destination, whereas fieldwork is research in that particular destination with a goal for a project in which study in this area is necessary. (Soraya)

I visited areas of Vancouver I wouldn't have on a tourist holiday. (Elizabeth)

Another thing, which these students might have added, is that fieldwork can be very hard work (Figure 1.1). This is particularly true of long-haul trips, in which lengthy flights cause fatigue and jet lag can limit the ability of both staff and students to 'hit the ground running' (Nairn et al. 2000). So a fieldtrip is not a holiday, and also a good student fieldworker is an active learner, always asking and seeking answers to questions. This is something that we would encourage every student reading this book and taking fieldtrips of their own, to reflect on.

Another way in which approaches to fieldwork have changed over time, prompting student fieldworkers to ask challenging questions about what fieldwork necessarily involves, has been

Figure 1.1 Though your friends might think you're off on holiday, international fieldwork can be hard work! (Photograph by Richard Phillips)

in their shift away from a traditional model of 'stout-booted' fieldwork. Gillian Rose (1993) influentially challenged the gendering of geographical fieldwork, calling upon geographers to move away from a set of practices that were closely associated with able-bodied men. While criticisms such as these may have turned some geographers off fieldwork entirely, they have nonetheless inspired others to rethink the ways in which they conduct fieldwork. Consequently, it is no longer fair to generalise that fieldwork is the preserve of 'men observing from on high'. Nowadays fieldwork is more diverse and inclusive, involving 'interviews and children, laptops and urban settings, local collaborators and researcher reflexivity – and of course *women*' (DeLyser and Starrs 2001: iv).

New approaches to fieldwork have been recognised not only by progressives but also by traditionalists as well, who have not always welcomed the changes. For example, in 2009 a number of critics argued that the RGS was losing touch with its roots, claiming it had 'not sent out a field research project for more than ten years'. 'Dr Livingstone', they regretted, had morphed into a field-shy 'Dr Livingroom' (*Times* 2009: 2; Maddrell 2010). These debates and disagreements are important to acknowledge here because they remind us that fieldwork is not simply a tradition to be inherited, but a complex, contested and changing set of practices. Students need not accept definitions or models of fieldwork handed down by generations past and various 'great' geographers – from Carl Sauer to Gillian Rose. On the contrary, you can ask challenging questions about fieldwork: why, where, and how it is done. This means taking responsibility for your own fieldwork, engaging critically with the debates about fieldwork that have been introduced here, and which will be explained in more detail in this book, and deciding for yourself how *you* will approach the field.

WHAT IS THE FIELD? WHERE DO YOU NEED TO GO TO DO FIELDWORK?

It has been said that 'the field' is to geography what 'the dig' is to archaeology, or 'the archive' to history: 'both a literal place and a key imaginary' (Kearns 2002: 76). But where or what is the field?

Fieldworkers have gravitated towards all sorts of of places. Sauer was not the first to be drawn to high points from which broad vistas were visible. An English educationist, writing in 1885, argued a similar point: that 'a pupil should receive first impressions of geography' from 'some commanding eminence' (Bain 1885: 273, quoted in Marsden 2000: 16). Others have taken a broader view of where fieldwork can be conducted. For some, the field can be anywhere outside the classroom and away from home: somewhere sufficiently far away from the surroundings they know and take for granted. Others, however, have argued that fieldwork can and should be conducted close to or in the home. Another English Victorian educationist argued that 'teaching, like charity, should begin at home' (Laurie 1888: 96-7, quoted in Marsden 2000: 16) and this has been followed up belatedly in geographical research on geographies of home

(Blunt and Dowling 2006). And for some researchers, particularly those interested in education, even the classroom can be a site for field research. Rose (1993) suggests that geographical fieldwork has traditionally paid excessive attention to the unfamiliar and that the field has been constructed as an exotic space. Others concur, complaining that it is too common for field-workers to gravitate towards 'special' sites at the expense of ordinary landscapes and everyday phenomena (Gold et al. 1991: 29). Indeed, familiar places such as the neighbourhood, home and classroom may be the most challenging in which to conduct fieldwork, precisely because they are so familiar, and therefore difficult to see afresh. Eric Pawson and Elizabeth Teather, teaching a fieldwork class in Canterbury, New Zealand, found that some of the greatest insights came closest to home:

> One student did not have to travel far in order to gain an excellent mark; he and his group analysed the tiny area around the petrol station where he worked part time, assessing the extent of landscape change over the last 4 years and the degree to which global brandholders are implicated in this. Student responses to the Canterbury expeditions indicate that learning to 'see' local places can offer rich delights in the short term – and the acquisition of analytical skills that lie in wait for that overseas trip when the opportunity arrives. (2002: 282)

The anthropologist James Clifford observed that 'when one speaks of working in the field, or going into the field, one draws on mental images of a distinct place with an inside and outside, reached by practices of physical movement' (1997: 54). And yet, as he goes on to argue, these assumptions are not always sound. We have already contested the assumption that the field is necessarily at a distance from home or the classroom. Now it is possible to correct another commonplace assumption about the field: that it is a tangible – discrete or material – place. Martin Dodge and Rob Kitchin (2006) describe 'fieldwork' involving the internet, not only as a medium for accessing information but also as an object of inquiry in its own right. And through his research among members of geographically-dispersed networks of Tibet nationals and activists, Andrew Davies (2009) reformulated 'the field' as a network of connected places rather than a single material place.

So, to return to the question of where we should look to find the field in fieldwork, the answer is this: anywhere and everywhere, far and near, in material and virtual spaces, within places and also between them. The diversity of field sites in contemporary geographical research is illustrated in Figures 1.2 and 1.3, in which fieldwork ranges from a group visit to an inner city to participatory research involving children in Nepal (the issues raised by these examples are discussed in this book: group dynamics in Chapter 5, participatory research and participant observation in Chapter 8).

The key to fieldwork is not really where we go but how we approach and justify the places we visit. In other words, the field is as much a way of seeing as it is a tangible place. Felix Driver explains that the field is not just 'there', it is space encountered in a particular way: 'produced and re-produced through both physical movement across a landscape and other sorts of cultural work in a variety of sites' (2000: 267). These encounters have a distinctive 'temporality': unlike most other classes, fieldwork is concentrated in a single block of time, in which learning is particularly intense and takes place in real time. These ingredients (the material and also the

Figure 1.2   Trevor Barnes leads fieldwork in Vancouver's Downtown Eastside. Photograph by Richard Phillips

Figure 1.3   Lucy Woods, a student from Liverpool John Moores University, helps run a workshop using images taken as part of a participatory photography project in Nepal. Photograph by Sara Parker

virtual geographies of the field; the disciplinary practices that constitute fieldwork; the particular group of students and field leaders involved; and the temporal concentration in a particular place) all establish the conditions of possibility for 'transformative' learning (Herrick 2010: 114). In other words, fieldwork is exciting because you never know quite what will happen.

THINKING CRITICALLY ABOUT FIELDWORK

While influential geographers have apparently lined up to endorse and celebrate the fieldwork tradition, and while some have followed words with actions, spending weekends and summers in the field, it is interesting to note that the field tradition is not quite as strong or as universal as it may first appear. To get the most out of fieldwork it is essential to pose challenging questions about this geographical tradition, to acknowledge and to ask why it is that not all geographers love fieldwork. This means facing up to concerns about the practical and intellectual problems associated with fieldwork.

While academic geographers assert the importance of fieldwork they don't always offer it to students or actually do fieldwork themselves – and when they do, students don't always elect to take it. In Hong Kong, Tammy Kwan observed a discrepancy between intention and practice in which lecturers and students agreed that fieldwork was a good idea but did not always do it (Kwan 2000). And in the United States, a survey conducted in 2000 found that, while fieldwork was a stable component of undergraduate geography, it was also a minority practice, accounting for 'only about 5% of the total annual enrolment in geography techniques courses and 15% of all undergraduate majors in geography' (Peterson and Earl 2000: 216). In other words, the majority of geography undergraduate majors did not take a field methods course. This may be symptomatic of a broader decline in fieldwork, which some observers have detected in academic research as well as teaching. Reporting 'the decline of fieldwork in human geography' over two decades ago, Robert Rundstrom and Martin Kenzer (1989: 294) argued that 'the use of on-site fieldwork component of primary data collection is at its lowest in almost 60 years and has declined sharply since the mid-1970s'. This pattern, if correctly observed, is not universal. In Britain, fieldwork has been transformed by the growth of long-haul travel and also by the apparent willingness of students to pay for their education, borrowing in order to do so where this is necessary. This has increased the range and scope of trips, and via various changes in teaching and learning approaches, has invited students to play a more active part in the fieldwork process.

There are some unfortunate reasons for the relatively modest role accorded to fieldwork in some places: universities declining to invest the time and resources involved in fieldwork; concerns about health and safety in the field; the perceived and real costs of dealing with litigious students and parents; academics failing to follow through on their assertions about the value of fieldwork; students being unable to take time away from the jobs they need to support their studies; fieldwork being costly; and so on (Herrick 2010). If you are student reading this book you will most likely have been offered the chance to go on a fieldtrip, so you may feel that these issues do not directly concern you. However, you should be interested to know some other – academic rather than simply practical or circumstantial – reasons why not all universities offer fieldwork, and/or why not all students take it when offered. By understanding these concerns about and criticisms of fieldwork, it is possible for you to develop a critical, robust approach to your own fieldwork: to insist on getting the most out of it. These concerns and criticisms define four sets of questions – regarding the intellectual relevance of fieldwork; its practical value to students; its financial and environmental costs; and its ethics – which are outlined in the following paragraphs and answered throughout the course of this book.

Is fieldwork relevant in the digital age?

Fieldwork was central to the discipline of geography during the heyday of regional geography, but the discipline has since moved on both technologically and theoretically and this raises questions about whether or not fieldwork has moved on with it. During the quantitative revolution of the 1960s, geographers turned increasingly to secondary numerical data (Rundstrom and Kenzer 1989). This seems to have accelerated even more in the digital age. A recent survey of heads of American geography departments showed that fieldwork had been displaced by 'technical-applied courses' in many cases (Gerber and Chuan 2000, 11; see also Peterson and Earl 2000). A minority of these respondents felt that field methods had become obsolete in an academic environment dominated by information technologies. This sceptical minority challenges the rest of us, who continue to believe in the value of fieldwork, to explain its ongoing relevance – in a discipline that has been transformed technologically.

But fieldwork need not be rendered obsolete through new technologies; it may be enriched through them and in turn it may mobilise and animate these technologies, exploring and exhibiting their possibilities. Indeed, the survey of American geography departments cited above found that some of the strongest fieldwork courses – including those that had proven most appealing to students – were the ones that absorbed new technologies. The authors found that successful fieldwork would bring together 'a blend of traditional skills and concepts with the purposeful application of new technology'. Fieldwork, they concluded, could facilitate an 'understanding of fundamental concepts in ways that classroom and digital laboratory instruction cannot' (Gerber and Chuan 2000: 11). The possibilities for embracing technologies within fieldwork are impossible to review exhaustively or keep pace with in a book such as this. A decade or so ago the emphasis was placed upon technologies such as GPS and GIS (Peterson and Earl 2000), and though these remain important today the cutting edge has moved on, with more attention – at the time of writing – being turned towards communication technologies such as Twitter, through which projects are managed and findings both produced and disseminated in real time. The result is that any 'how to' guide or survey of existing information and communication technologies would quickly become obsolete. But technological initiatives are nevertheless considered in every chapter, and these illustrate the spirit and some of the ways in which fieldwork may engage with the technological possibilities. Chapter 6, for example, discusses the use of visual and sound recording and manipulating technologies in fieldwork, and also the applications of internet and communications technologies in the field.

Is fieldwork an escape from theory?

It has sometimes been suggested that geographical fieldwork is an escape from theory and that by retracing the footsteps of 'great' geographers past there is a tendency for us to lose step with contemporary debates. Thus, while acknowledging Carl Sauer's influence and legacy, Peter Jackson has been critical of those who would seem to imitate his work, endlessly mapping 'the physical or material elements of culture' such as 'culture traits from log buildings to graveyards, barn styles to gasoline stations' (Jackson 1989: 19). In his groundbreaking work in the 'new cultural geography', he called for more attention to 'non-material or symbolic qualities of culture'(1989: 24). In other words, Jackson called for fieldwork to be renewed and re-engaged with theoretical debates, thereby ensuring that it led rather than followed these. This argument has been influential. Today, geography students undertaking fieldwork would generally now understand that fieldwork is no longer generally understood as regional geography, in the sense of being all about the place visited. Fieldwork is underpinned and engaged with theoretical debates (as discussed in Chapter 3). Contemporary students have increasingly turned to the sorts of places neglected by earlier generations of human geographers – to cities and contemporary culture rather than rural and historical cultural landscapes, for example (Burgess and Jackson 1992). This reflects a broader reinvention and reassertion of fieldwork within the discipline which has been going on for some time. Though one form of fieldwork-based regional geography has declined others have emerged. William Bunge, pioneering a new critical geography in the 1970s, reinvented fieldwork for an emerging radical geography. Shifting the locus of fieldwork from rural to urban settings and from historical to contemporary concerns, he ran large-scale projects in Toronto and Detroit which involved communities in research and participatory geographies (as discussed in Chapter 9). More recently, others have innovated with fieldwork within broader efforts to forge new regional and place-based geographies. Contesting claims about the death of fieldwork, David Wilson (1990: 219) identified a 'reconstructed regionalism' that 'uses critical social theory to revive field studies'. This movement began in the 1980s with the new regional geography of Allan Pred, which investigated 'the fusion of unique and broader forces' through detailed empirical and archival research and reasserted the importance of primary data collection (Wilson 1990: 220). And while these geographers have reinvented fieldwork by embracing new technologies and speaking to new theoretical debates, others have renewed the role of fieldwork in teaching and learning. They have asserted the importance of fieldwork to cutting edge pedagogical developments such as Problem Based Learning (PBL), in which students devise their own problems and the strategies for solving them and thus become more active and self-reliant (Marsden 2000: 32; see also Pawson and Teather 2002). These disparate developments illustrate the inventiveness of geographical fieldworkers and show how each new generation of geographers has reinvented and renewed fieldwork, thus making it relevant for their own times.

These theoretical and pedagogical arguments speak to fundamental questions which any geography student or researcher would do well to consider before planning fieldwork. What can you do in the field that you cannot do in front of a computer or in a library or classroom? What can you do in the field that does not simply retrace the footsteps of great field-based geographers, but advances contemporary debates as well as geographical knowledge? The bottom line must be that you can learn or illuminate something in the field that it will not be possible to achieve in the classroom. Peter Jackson illustrates this point in the following Postcard.

Postcard 1.1: Chicken Run. Peter Jackson, who is leading a research project on geographies of food, explains why it is important to get into the field, which in this case is a factory farm for chickens. As he explains: 'visiting the farm raised all kinds of issues that might have escaped me had I stayed in the office' and relied upon data collected by others.

My first visit to a broiler house, where intensively-reared chickens are 'grown' to their full slaughter weight in around 40 days from hatching, was a revelation. I was studying the development of the modern British chicken industry, tracing all the links in the supply chain 'from farm to fork' and, having interviewed the retailers and done some consumer focus groups, it was time to visit the broiler sheds. I went with my colleague Polly Russell to visit a farm in Dorset where Polly already knew the farmer quite well, having recorded her life history over a number of previous visits. From this and other interviews I knew that the farmer was well regarded in the industry as someone whose animal husbandry was considered a model of good practice. As we entered the first shed I was taken aback by the number of chickens, lined up in neat rows, with several thousand in each shed. I didn't find the conditions as shocking as battery farming, where chickens are kept in cages for their eggs, though animal rights campaigners object to the high stocking densities at which many broiler chickens are kept. What impressed me most was the matter-of-fact way that the farmer 'walked the sheds', using her expert eye to detect any problems with the heating, lighting and water supply, stopping to pick up any animals that were injured and, occasionally and abruptly, wringing the neck of any bird that was suffering and needed putting out of their misery. When we stepped outside, the dead birds were disposed of in a large metal incinerator.

(Continued)

(Continued)

The farmer clearly cared about the welfare of her birds, even though they were, to some extent, just a source of income. She said it was hard to feel emotionally attached to chickens, compared to the way she cared for her pet dog, for example. There were so many of them and the turnover was so rapid. But she could immediately sense when something was wrong as she walked the sheds several times a day: were they listless or flighty, noisy or unusually quiet?

As we talked it became clear that our farmer had no time for the 'modern housewife', blaming her for most food safety issues when chicken has been stored or cooked incorrectly. She felt a real sense of injustice that the 'poor ruddy grower' got the blame for outbreaks of Campylobacter and other foodborne diseases which would be drastically reduced if consumers had better culinary knowledge and skills. She blamed the supermarkets for relentlessly pushing down prices at the farm gate, and accused foreign growers of unfair competition, using antibiotic growth promoters and other methods that were outlawed in the UK or injecting poultry with water to increase their weight as has been reported elsewhere in the EU.

It was hard to come away from the sheds without some sympathy for the modern-day chicken grower as well as greater insight into the lives of the chickens themselves. Many of the consumers we talked to expressed a nostalgic longing for a lost 'golden age' of farming, wanting chicken to taste liked it used to in some imagined past. This may be understandable, given the rapid intensification of agriculture in recent years, but it ignores the fact that our mass consumption of chicken only became a reality in the last couple of generations (since the 1960s). Before then chicken was a treat for most families, to be enjoyed on high days and holidays, rather than the cheap and ubiquitous source of protein that it has become today.

Visiting the farm was a good 'reality check' for when consumers talked fondly of times past and when retailers employed rose-tinted images to sell intensively-reared birds. Being 'in the field' also served as a reminder, as one of our other informants told us, that there's a living thing at the end of the supply chain and that animals can't be treated just like any other commodity. We saw at first hand the way that nature can fight back, with chickens developing hock burn and other unsightly conditions when they are kept at too high a density or when the ratio of breast meat to leg strength means that they

(Continued)

(Continued)

'come off their legs'. For a city boy like me, visiting the farm raised all kinds of issues that might have escaped me had I stayed in the office and simply read the focus group and interview transcripts that Polly was recording. While our project focused on the way food is 'sold with a story', it was vitally important to combine our discursive and narrative methods with some direct observation 'in the field'.

Will fieldwork equip you for today's job market?

A survey of American students taking fieldwork courses found a mismatch between students' and professors' expectations of fieldwork. The survey found that, where there was some element of choice involved and students had actively opted for fieldwork, the most common attractions were practical, concerned mainly with enhancing skill sets and prospects for employment (Peterson and Earl 2000: 222). The top five reasons given by students taking field classes were:

1 The course was required for a degree programme.

2 To practise, learn and develop job-related skills.

3 To learn how to use equipment in the field.

4 To develop the skills required for conducting geographic research.

5 General enjoyment or appreciation of learning in an outdoor environment.

Interestingly, professors and lecturers running fieldtrips had different perceptions of student motivation, fondly imagining that students were driven by purer academic passions, as follows:

1 Fundamental scientific skills.

2 Geographic problem solving.

3 Applying geographic concepts in the field.

4 Acquiring skills with direct career applicability.

5 Applying new technologies.

This could be interpreted to mean that fieldwork does not always fulfil its potential and/or provide students with what they are looking for in their education. Arguing this point, Rundstrom and Kenzer (1989: 300) attribute some of the 'gradual elimination of the teaching of fieldwork' to 'increased student interest in acquiring "marketable" skills'. Another, more positive interpretation of the survey findings is possible though: that professors and students agree on the broad objectives of fieldwork – in developing learning skills, encouraging engagement with new technologies and/or techniques, and relating to debates about the contemporary world – but they have different ways of expressing this and different understandings of its importance. The challenge for you in taking fieldtrips is to understand how the skills you acquire on these trips can be listed on your *curriculum vitae* or *resumé*, mentioned in job interviews, and otherwise used to enhance your employment prospects. This is explained in Chapter 2, which shows how fieldwork fits into a geography degree as a whole, and helps you to see how fieldwork can provide you with the skills and experiences that will make you more employable.

Is fieldwork environmentally sustainable?

Long-haul fieldtrips make large carbon footprints. This raises some challenging questions. How, if at all, can students and universities justify and minimise these carbon footprints and the various other environmental impacts of fieldwork? What is the carbon footprint of any given trip and how can this be reduced? There are no easy answers to these questions, and the best answers – both verbal and practical – probably have yet to be thought of. Once again, we would pose this question and hand it over to you, the student, who must consider the potential environmental costs of your own fieldwork and make some decisions about how to reduce these and whether they can be justified at all. We can help with the first part of this, though, which is to get past simplistic statements about 'large carbon footprints' by specifically assessing the carbon budgets for fieldwork. This is a necessary first move in attempts to reduce and mitigate these environmental impacts. In Postcard 1.2, Chris Ribchester illustrates how the carbon budget for a fieldtrip can be assessed and provides some initial pointers on how fieldtrips can be redesigned to reduce their negative impact and envisage positive impacts. He explains how students at one English university monitored the carbon footprint of their fieldwork. The results proved surprising: for example, they found that an international expedition to Norway generated less carbon than a week on the English coast.

Postcard 1.2: The carbon footprint of fieldwork, by Chris Ribchester

A small team of students will take responsibility for monitoring the details of travel to and from a fieldwork location. This is just the start of a process of assessing and potentially mitigating the carbon footprint of fieldwork conducted through the University of Chester. Carbon counting does not stop with travel, but also considers energy used in other ways: from heating field centres to the production of food consumed in the field.

(Continued)

(Continued)

Responsibility for this lies partly with tutors as they contemplate new field courses or revise existing trips. But it is a joint responsibility and even if the general parameters of fieldwork are set by others students can influence the carbon footprint of fieldwork particularly when designing and carrying out independent research projects. As a simple example I am reminded of a group of three students, studying rural settlement change on a recent residential field course, who decided to walk between each of their eight study villages instead of taking the option of being transported by minibus or using the occasional service bus. Not only did they reduce the footprint of the trip by a few kilograms of carbon dioxide, they gained a much stronger insight into the day-to-day experience of living in an area of low population density and relative isolation.

We are bombarded with information about how to live a greener lifestyle and in many respects it is this same guidance which can be used to inform fieldwork design. This raises various questions: Where is the nearest place to study the phenomenon that you are interested in? Will the use of public transport to get there, or travel around when you are there, mitigate the footprint? What accommodation options do you have? Camping is a low energy activity, although all that processed, tinned food carries with it lots of embedded carbon. Field study centres offer the fundamental carbon-saving attribute of communal living and the sharing of resources. Moreover, it's now fairly unusual to find a field centre not committed to some form of eco-friendly action, for example recycling, or at least the partial use of renewable energy sources and the purchase of local foods for the kitchens.

While much of the information needed to make low-carbon fieldwork choices is now accessible, calculating the carbon footprint of a field course is more complex. However, a bespoke carbon footprint calculator for this purpose has been developed and is available for anyone to download: http://gees.ac.uk/resources/hosted/fwCO2/co2ftprnt.htm. It uses a spreadsheet with the opportunity to enter data on all the key elements of fieldwork (travel, energy use, food eaten, consumption and waste/recycling). As well as the overall footprint, the relative size of these different components is shown as part of the final output. More details about the calculator methodology are provided in Table 1.1.

We have used this tool now for a number of years, with students and tutors working together to collect the data and review the spreadsheet. We have shown that, in the right circumstances, fieldwork

(Continued)

(Continued)

can deliver a significantly lower carbon footprint when compared to a 'normal' lifestyle. So far our 'record' is a 60 per cent reduction for a residential field course based in and around the Centre for Alternative Technology, Machynlleth, in mid-Wales. However, the figures don't always turn out as you would expect: despite the lengthy journey from Chester to Norway, this summer campsite-based expedition tends to record a lower footprint than a winter field centre-based trip to the Devon coast, notwithstanding the extra jumpers that are worn.

Table 1.1 The carbon footprint calculator devised by Chris Ribchester (Postcard 1.2) processes the following variables

Calculator component	Key specific variables	Some considerations
1 General details of the trip	• Number of participants • Duration • Number of non-group members staying at the same accommodation	Knowing how many other people have used the same accommodation as you is particularly important as it allows the energy use figures to be weighted proportionally.
2 Transport (mode and distance travelled)	• By plane and ferry • By private transport, including minibus and coach • By public transport	The calculator utilises various freely available tools to assess transport emissions, although note that the outcome of air travel calculators does vary, dependant on the multiplier used to account for the greater damage caused by the release of greenhouse gases in the upper atmosphere.
3 Energy used	• Electricity • Mains gas • Liquid petroleum gas • Bottled gas (butane or propane) • Oil • Coal • Wood • Renewable	Something to watch out for here is how the electricity is generated – check for green tariffs, which will lower the carbon footprint to some extent. For the purposes of this calculator, the direct use of renewable sources (e.g. wind, water, solar) counts as zero emissions.
4 Food (diet)	• Number of meat eaters • Number of vegetarians • Number of vegans	The energy used in farming, processing and transporting food generally forms a significant proportion of personal carbon footprints, although this is affected to some extent by what you eat (generally a non-meat diet is more carbon-friendly!).

Table 1.1 *(Continued)*

Calculator component	Key specific variables	Some considerations
5 Other consumption and waste	• How much money spent on non-food items • Paper used • Waste produced (number of bin bags) • Proportion of items composted/recycled	The amount of embedded carbon in other forms of consumption is included in the calculator although, as with food, this is a notoriously complex exercise and tends to be based on general estimates. The carbon footprint of waste produced is weighted downwards on the basis of the proportion of kitchen/garden waste that is composted and other items that are recycled.

Is fieldwork ethical?

The environment is just one among a series of worries associated with non-local fieldwork. Others include the social consequences associated with intruding into the lives and geographies of others, through intellectual curiosity and in order to develop skills and conduct exercises rather than generally to immediately contribute to the people and places studied. Fieldtrips are often brief, asking quite a bit of the people encountered along the way, and potentially giving little or nothing back. This opens up a new and challenging question: what are the ethics of doing fieldwork and how, if at all, might the ethical challenges associated with entering, observing and representing someone else's world be overcome? These questions are elaborated on in Chapter 4, which explains that as a student you need to take responsibility for the ethical implications of your own fieldwork, and guides you in doing so.

Fieldwork also raises another set of ethical issues, which are concerned with the internal dynamics of the group of students and academic staff who travel into the field together. Fieldwork is almost always a social experience and the experiences of travelling and working together have not always been positive for all members of the group. Some students have been marginalised by field practices ranging from unnecessarily vigorous walks to heavy drinking in the evenings, to the extent that some geographers, looking back over their student experiences, shudder at the very mention of fieldwork and prefer to teach without it. These relationships are structured by gender and they have been brought to light through feminist critique of geographical traditions and practices, but they are also concerned with other aspects of identity and the body: these include age, differing forms and degrees of physical ability, and so on (Rose 1993). These issues are explained in Chapter 5, which concentrates on the challenging experiences of travelling and working together. We explain that, for many students, the strongest experiences and memories of fieldwork are shaped by the group dynamic: to go on a trip is to travel together, to plan and run projects together, to eat together, and often to sleep in the same rooms. Fieldwork is as much about getting along, working together, coping with conflicts, and conducting friendships, as it is about anything else. We would call upon students to come up with their own solutions to the challenges of travelling and working together, challenges that have not always been understood or solved by the academic staff leading fieldtrips. We have seen students facing up to and navigating these challenges so we believe you as an individual can do this too and we will provide with you some background and pointers to assist you in this.

By now, it should be clear that our approach is to raise issues and questions that you as a student fieldworker will want to answer as you plan and conduct fieldwork. Rather than answering these questions for you, our aim is to help you answer them for yourself. This is a pathway to conducting critical and imaginative fieldwork.

CONCLUSION

After reading this introduction you should have a clearer picture of how and why fieldwork is an important component in geographical education. It may have given you pause for thought regarding your own motivations for conducting fieldwork and encouraged you to think critically about your engagement with the field. The key points of this chapter were:

- The use of fieldwork in geography is not universally supported nor conducted. However, there are many reasons (including academic and life-long skills development) why you are being offered a fieldwork component as part of your degree. Chapter 2 discusses this in more detail.

- The ways in which geographers conduct fieldwork have evolved over time and continue to do so. Awareness of these developments has given each individual the opportunity to critically engage with the field and to think through what we study and why we study what we do, and also how we impact on those we observe and interact with. This chapter should have provided you with sufficient background and context to encourage you to think critically about your fieldwork. It may raise as many questions as it answers. If so, it has served the purpose of getting you thinking and these questions will be addressed in subsequent chapters.

- The decision to conduct fieldwork should not be taken lightly given the (often) substantial amounts of time and money that need to be invested. In addition, issues such as the environmental impact of fieldwork activities, its relevance in a digital age and its ethics need to be considered by each individual prior to signing up for fieldwork. As the following chapters will suggest, successful fieldwork requires each student to make informed decisions throughout the research process. Should you chose (or if you have already chosen) to conduct fieldwork, this is the first of many such decisions.

FURTHER READING/KEY TEXT(S)

- For a wider context and historiography of fieldwork, beyond the scope of this chapter, see D.R. Stoddart's *On Geography* (Blackwell, 1996). Though subjected to serious critique, the exuberance of this book together with its passion for doing geography still makes it worth reading today.

- Dydia DeLyser and Paul F. Starrs (eds) (2001) 'Doing Fieldwork', special double issue of *Geographical Review*, *91*(1-2): iv–viii, 1–508. Like most of the geographical literature on fieldwork this is aimed at lecturers and not students, but many of the essays may nevertheless be useful.

- Jacquelin Burgess and Peter Jackson (1992) 'Streetwork: an encounter with place', *Journal of Geography in Higher Education*, *16*(2): 151–157. This article describes an experimental fieldwork class, which introduces many of the themes and ideas that we elaborate in this book. Though addressed to teaching staff rather than students, it remains an excellent point of departure for critical and imaginative fieldwork in human geography.

2

JUSTIFYING THE COST: YOUR DEGREE AND YOUR JOB PROSPECTS

OVERVIEW

This chapter addresses the following questions:

- How can you make an informed decision about whether to do fieldwork?
- What kinds of academic skills can fieldwork help you to develop?
- In what ways can fieldwork help you to gain graduate employment?
- How can you better understand your own learning and processes of reflection and why is it important to do so?

This chapter is driven by what other students have said they want from fieldwork, and what you want to know about it. A survey of students taking fieldwork courses, discussed in Chapter 1, found that where there was some element of choice involved and students had actively opted for fieldwork, the most common considerations were practical, concerned with enhancing skill sets and prospects for employment. The most frequently cited reason for taking field classes was 'to practice, learn and develop job-related skills' and another was 'to develop skills required for conducting geographic research' (Peterson and Earl 2000: 222).

Fieldwork can be understood as an investment that can pay off by enhancing your degree and improving your job prospects. It is costly, both environmentally – as discussed in the previous chapter – and economically. Concerns related to the carbon-footprint of our activities as individuals, and indeed as institutions, have placed question marks over the necessity for international fieldwork. We hand this over to you, the student, to consider the carbon footprint and other potential environmental costs of your own fieldwork and make your own decisions about how to assess and reduce these and whether they can be justified at all. A narrower set of questions, which can be more adequately addressed in the context of this chapter, relates to the economic costs of fieldwork. These are usually borne both by students and universities. Hidden costs, paid for by universities, include staff time, safety management and administrative overheads. The heavy demands of fieldwork help to explain why some departments – particularly in the United States – are reluctant to continue residential undergraduate fieldwork. It also explains why there is increasing pressure to conduct fieldwork within walking distance and within manageable parcels of time that do not interfere with staff and student timetables (Foskett 1997: 200). Though you may not be interested in the financial debates that take place behind the scenes, you might wish to know why it is that many universities continue to run residential and non local fieldtrips. One reason is that fieldwork is often demand-led; departments offering exciting fieldtrips are more successful in attracting applicants. Another reason, which we explain in more detail below and in the next section, is that fieldwork is academically valuable and can therefore be central to a high quality education.

In most institutions, students contribute towards the costs of fieldwork and tend to have choices between more expensive long-haul and cheaper local fieldwork classes. These costs vary between universities and countries. Some students simply contribute towards the costs of subsistence (paying for meals and local travel) whereas others have to cover the full cost of the trip (most frequently for optional rather than compulsory courses). There can be indirect costs, too. You may have to take time off from paid employment and/or deal with an employer's complaints if you are delayed or jetlagged on your return. Or you may have to make arrangements for carers to accompany you on your fieldtrip if you have a disability or for childcare at home in your absence. These 'costs' can be financial and/or emotional and are discussed in more detail in Chapters 4 and 5. Additionally, you may well have lectures, seminars and assessments to prepare before the trip and work to be submitted after your return. So fieldwork is a real investment! But is it worth it? This is something you need to decide for yourself, by identifying the benefits of participating in fieldwork which you can set against the costs.

This chapter explains the two main benefits of fieldwork. It will therefore provide you with a rationale for opting into field classes and help you get the most out of fieldwork, ensuring that this enhances your degree results and your employment prospects. Having said all this, we know that your reasons for choosing fieldwork will not be quite so rational or instrumental! You may be attracted by the excitement of long-haul travel. Research on the motivations for international study certainly suggests this to be the case, with many students putting the glamour of exotic travel above more practical considerations (Attwood 2009), so you will probably choose a fieldtrip that goes somewhere appealing and exciting rather than a trip with the soundest academic rationale (Maguire 1998: 209). Sarah Maguire, who conducted a survey of optional fieldwork, found that students thought carefully about the financial implications of fieldwork but were not primarily interested in minimising costs. Many opted for longer distance fieldtrips that seemed to represent value for money, providing what one English student – who chose the Alps over a more local trip to Wales – described as 'a cheap opportunity to go abroad' (Maguire 1998: 210). Still, even if your real reasons for choosing a trip are really about glamour and wanderlust, you can still benefit from understanding a more sober rationale for fieldwork. This may come in handy when trying to persuade your relatives to help pay for this! It will also help you to profit from the trip, both academically and, when the time comes, within the world of work.

The first of these issues is explained in the next section, which examines the potential academic benefits of fieldwork. Some geographical topics are more easily and effectively researched in particular locations: studies of indigenous peoples are very difficult in the UK, for example, and global financial power is most easily 'brought to life' in locations such as New York, Hong Kong or Singapore. Non-local fieldwork also brings with it opportunities to develop more generic skills and to 'stimulate critical reflection on geographical practice' (Nairn et al. 2000: 242). In this chapter we unpack this claim, explaining specifically the skills you can gain through fieldwork and how you can become conscious of these. We then go on, in the next section, to relate these academic considerations to the skills and experiences that employers may be looking for when you graduate and which you can use to sell yourself and enhance your employability.

WHY SHOULD YOUR GEOGRAPHY DEGREE INCLUDE FIELDWORK?

Geographers have traditionally viewed fieldwork as an integral and essential part of teaching and also as an extremely effective and enjoyable learning and teaching method. As explained in the Introduction and Chapter 1, fieldwork is frequently perceived as being fundamental to, and definitive of, geography. However, fieldwork practices vary between institutions and countries and they have changed over time. Karen Nairn (2003: 68) explains that 'notions of fieldwork might have broad applicability across the discipline internationally' yet 'the practice of teaching fieldwork varies depending on the geographical context'. In some countries, including Australia and the UK, fieldwork tends to be residential and non-local and increasingly includes long-haul travel, whereas for others such as the United States and New Zealand it is more common for students to conduct fieldwork locally and for shorter periods of time. So this chapter does not speak to you about just one type of fieldwork. All the skills that will be outlined and discussed are generic to fieldwork and are applicable to you, whichever form your fieldwork experience takes.

What academic skills should a geography graduate possess?

In order to monitor and appraise the standards of education offered by higher education institutions, many countries have organisations that review degree programmes including geography. This setting of standards may be referred to as 'benchmarking'. Such 'benchmarks' aim to provide a generic minimum level of attainment that graduates of disciplines should achieve upon completion of their degree. Why is it important for you, the student, to know about this? First, this process of standard-setting is also used to make sure that higher education institutions are accountable and give 'value'. Second, you can use these standards to place your education in context. This section uses the UK benchmarking statement for geography to illustrate how a particular country sets the standards for geography departments and students and then explains how fieldwork can help meet these goals. How academic and associated learning can be communicated in skills-based terms is discussed later in the chapter.

While this chapter uses benchmarking as a framework to discuss the skills a geography graduate should possess, it should be noted that these standards are not universally accepted. In Australia the Institute of Australian Geographers (IAG) has decided not to implement benchmarking standards for geography as an acknowledgement of the fact that 'many of (geography's) core components can be approached through a number of routes, and so any attempts at prescription can be discarded' (Jones, 2000: 421). Internationally there has been a shift in focus towards skills development, resulting in an increase in the amount of discussion regarding skills and subsequent curriculum revisions over the last decade. In North America, the impetus for this focus comes in part from the Boyer Report (US) and the Smith Commission (Canada). We would therefore encourage you to interpret the guidance offered in this chapter and – if necessary – adapt it to suit your own university learning experience. Not all countries have organisations that 'benchmark' geography, or even make explicit links between a geographical education and the workplace.

This section suggests that it can be helpful for you to understand what benchmarks are, consider which benchmarked skills and knowledge you can gain through your degree, and be clear about which of these you can acquire through fieldwork. It can also allow you to identify your learning experiences, objectives and potential outcomes. The core skills contained in the benchmarking statement do not necessarily only relate to single-honours geography students, nor students in any particular geographical context. Indeed, the generic skills can be applied to a wide range of undergraduate degree disciplines. Figure 2.1 identifies the fieldwork-related skills that one academic regulator – the UK's Quality Assurance Agency (QAA) – says a 'typical' geography graduate should possess. This figure is drawn from more detailed material provided by the QAA that includes other generic skills. Figure 2.1 shows those skills that particularly relate to fieldwork. We elaborate upon these later in this chapter.

To understand how fieldwork can help your skills development, it helps to make connections between the generic geographical skills and knowledge identified in Figure 2.1 and those that might be gained and developed in the course of fieldwork. These are explained in more detail in Figure 2.2.

KNOWLEDGE AND UNDERSTANDING	INTELLECTUAL (THINKING) SKILLS
• Comprehension of the nature of change within human environments. • Comprehension of the significance of spatial relationships as influences upon physical and human environments. • Apply understanding of geographical concepts in different situations. • Have a systematic approach to accuracy, precision, and uncertainty.	• Identify/formulate and evaluate questions or problems. • Identify and evaluate approaches to problem solving. • Synthesise information and recognise relevance. • Develop a sustained and reasoned argument. • Evaluate and articulate weaknesses in the arguments of others.
DISCIPLINE-SPECIFIC SKILLS	GENERIC SKILLS
• Evaluate the issues involved in applying research design and execution skills within the specific context of field-based research. • Evaluate the diversity of specialised techniques and approaches involved in collecting, analysing and presenting geographical information. • Articulate and communicate personal views about geographical issues. • Apply ideas to new situations.	• Communicate geographical ideas, principles, and theories effectively and fluently using written, oral, and visual means. • Relate material appropriately to the intended audience. • Undertake independent/self-directed study/ learning (including time management) to achieve consistent, proficient, and sustained attainment. • Work as a participant or leader of a group and contribute effectively to the achievement of objectives. • Reflect on the process of learning and evaluate personal strengths and weaknesses.

Figure 2.1 **On completion of a degree course in geography, a typical student should be able to do the following, according to one academic regulator, the UK's QAA (2007). Adapted from: www.qaa.ac.uk**

Figure 2.2 demonstrates a range of different skills related to 'thinking' (about theoretical ideas, planning research) and 'doing' (communicating with peers, collecting data, presenting findings) and the broader 'societal' skills that encourage ownership of your own learning and a responsibility towards others. These skills are not exclusively acquired through fieldwork. Rather, their development is facilitated by being in the field: the unique experience of applying 'general' ideas to 'specific' places, experiencing 'real' research and working closely with peers and staff.

While fieldwork can be an important route to gaining the specific skills and knowledge expected of geographers, as illustrated in the benchmarks defined by the QAA and shown in Figure 2.1, these can appear rather prescriptive and utilitarian, lacking adventure and stifling curiosity. Indeed, learning involves something more fundamental and exciting than might be implied in some of the checklists and tables published by organisations such as the QAA. But

1   *Awareness of geographical issues* (cultural, political, economic, environmental): being able to identify different geographical processes occurring in a specific location; able to make connections between processes and understand how they are related; being in the field should also create a respect for the environment and for others.

2   *Analysis*: being able to critically review and evaluate data collected and observations made; going beyond describing ideas to examining the relationship between ideas; understanding not just 'what' but 'how' and 'why'.

3   *Communication*: being able to think through, discuss with others, and present academic ideas clearly; developing oral communication skills in addition to expressing ideas in written forms.

4   *Acting ethically*: being able to plan and execute research that makes a serious consideration of others and the impact of your research (see Chapter 4 for more discussion of research ethics).

5   *Flexibility and adaptability*: developing the skills that will enable you to respond to changes in your research plans; planning data collection that allows research to evolve; problem solving.

6   *Identifying a research idea*: reviewing the existing literature, identifying an idea that is applicable to the location you are visiting, and making sure the research is valid and achievable (see Chapter 3).

7   *Literacy, numeracy and graphicacy*: being able to effectively communicate ideas in written, numerical, and graphical forms and evaluating the most appropriate way(s) of presenting data.

8   *Observation*: being able to view and critically interpret landscapes and apply what you see to what you have learnt; going beyond 'looking' to interpreting what you observe (see Chapter 6).

9   *Project management*: being able to see a project through from start to finish; incorporating the practical elements of conducting research (planning, execution, working with others, time management) and the practical application of theoretical ideas (see Chapter 5).

10 *Responsibility*: being able to take ownership of your own learning and strategically guiding your field experience to achieve your aims.

Figure 2.2   Skills and knowledge development in fieldwork

this body has also stated explicitly that 'Geographers develop their geographical understanding through fieldwork and other forms of experiential learning, which helps to promote curiosity about the social and physical environments, discerning observation and an understanding of scale' (www.qaa.ac.uk). In other words, fieldwork can not only be an important means of gaining specific skills, it can also open your ideas to the world in a broader sense and be a form of what pedagogical experts call 'deep learning'.

Deep learning involves engaging deeply with ideas and learning independently and critically, as well as moving beyond a passive acceptance of ideas and information. Since deep learning is challenging it is often conducted after the first year of undergraduate study when students move beyond passive forms of study, such as sitting in lectures and simply taking notes. Fieldwork is specifically suited to deep learning since this form of study can demystify the knowledge derived from textbooks; provide coherence for fragmented or compartmentalised knowledge (making links between individual courses and broader theoretical ideas); and give an opportunity to acquire tacit or intuitive knowledge (Lonergan and Andresen 1988). For these reasons many progressive educators would champion deep learning, though it should be noted that more passive 'observation-based' fieldwork is still valued by others also, including academic staff and students, and particularly in South-East Asia (Fuller et al. 2006).

In summary, though it is important to be aware of the skills you may cultivate during fieldwork, we should add that fieldwork also provides you with the opportunity and necessity to cultivate some other life skills which may be equally valuable if perhaps less utilitarian. In particular, the social aspects of fieldwork are important and form part of our lifelong challenge to engage with others in friendly and mutually respectful ways. It is unlikely that your fieldtrip cohort will be homogeneous (in either age or background) so fieldwork can be a chance to meaningfully engage with people from other walks of life. Although important on all fieldtrips, the social dynamics of residential fieldwork are especially intense. You will study together, of course, but in most cases you will also eat, sleep and travel together, and as we explain in Chapter 5 this can be the most challenging and potentially rewarding aspect of fieldwork (see Maskall and Stokes 2008). Like other aspects of fieldwork, these social experiences will enable you to develop fundamental life skills, including specific skills that you may draw upon when deciding what kind of work you would like to do after graduation, and then applying for jobs and giving interviews. These issues are discussed in the next section of this chapter.

HOW WILL FIELDWORK HELP YOU GET A JOB?

A degree is an important investment in your future. As universities come under growing pressure to produce 'employment-ready' graduates, departments and institutions are increasingly recognising the importance of employment-related skills and equipping you for the workplace. Fieldwork can play an important part in this and this section explains how it can enhance your job prospects.

Many different terms have been used to describe the 'non-academic' skills that students gain in the course of a degree. These include 'employability', 'transferable skills', and 'lifelong learning'. This book adopts current thinking that emphasises the long-term nature of skills development and the necessity for individuals (at whatever career stage) to review, reassess and reflect upon their skills and how these can be maintained and developed. It could also be argued that to separate 'academic' and 'non-academic' skills assumes that there is no relationship between the two, which of course is not the case. As this section demonstrates, through striving to develop the skills detailed in the previous section, a range of long-term skills can be developed that students can take with them after graduation. This has always occurred, but as part of broader debates questioning the relevance and contribution of higher education to national and regional labour markets, institutions globally are seeking to articulate more clearly how the education their students receive prepares them as graduates. This has involved some intervention in degree curricula, but it has been (as with benchmarking) geographically uneven. While there is international concern that higher education should enhance the employment prospects of graduates, there is scant evidence of systematic thinking about how best to do it, let alone any model that can be badged as 'best practice' and adopted wholesale (Little 2003).

The idea of employability provides some insights that can be helpful in making connections between academic education and job prospects. Employability has been defined as 'a set of achievements, understanding and personal attributes than make individuals more likely to gain employment and be successful in their chosen occupations' (Little 2003: 1). A related term – 'sustainable employability' – focuses on how to remain employable throughout life. Employability 'does not rest when the first graduate job is achieved' but needs 'to be constantly renewed to be sustainable' (Knight and Yorke 2004: 46). In other words, you need to be reviewing and updating your skill sets and knowledges constantly and managing your career development in ways that will sustain your employability.

What employment skills do geographers have?

Given the broad nature of geography as a discipline, geography graduates often feel that they have a lot to offer employers but may struggle to express exactly what skills they have developed. Writing in New Zealand, Richard Le Heron and James Hathaway (2000) cite the following employment skills that geography graduates should have: thinking; analysis; research; computer literacy; writing; presentations; organisation and planning; teamwork and peer evaluation. These are indeed valuable skills but we would argue that the list is rather general and could refer to any social science graduate. The question surrounding how geographers differentiate themselves in the competitive labour market still remains. Others identify skills that are associated more specifically with geography graduates (Kubler and Forbes 2006):

- Knowledge of cultural, political, economic and environmental issues.

- Knowledge of moral and ethical judgements based on an understanding of diversity in people and places.

- Expertise in integrating, analysing and processing information from a range of sources, gained by working in complex environments and with complicated issues.

- Project management skills including time management, risk assessment and problem solving, resulting from laboratory, desk and field-based research.

- Well-developed literacy, numeracy and graphicacy skills.

- Flexibility and adapatability, including the ability to deal with the unexpected.

These skills can be 'translated' from abstract to concrete terms and expressed in a language that employers will more easily recognise and relate to.

What do employers want?

Andrew Bottomley, former Head of Recruitment at PricewaterhouseCoopers (one of the world's largest providers of assurance, tax and business consulting services), has stated that 'It is not what graduates study, but how they benefit from their studies that interests major recruiters' (2001: 25). As a geography student, you may be aware of some of the challenges and opportunities presented by the global economy. Globalisation and industrial restructuring continue to transform national economies and the world of work. In many advanced economies most new job creation is within the service economy. As all national economies seek growth, policy makers are emphasising the shift towards 'knowledge economies' and as such the jobs available (and employers' demands) have transformed over the past three decades. Reich (2002) argues that advanced economies need two main types of high-level expertise: one emphasising discovery and the other focusing on exploiting the discoveries of others through market-related intelligence and the application of interpersonal skills. As higher education in most countries does not explicitly respond to this suggestion in its curriculum planning, the emphasis still falls upon individual students to consider how their skills will respond to the demands of the labour market. This process is two-fold: each student should firstly develop an awareness of their academic skills, and secondly they should learn how to articulate these skills.

It is important for you to learn to translate your academic skills and knowledge into terms that will be understandable and attractive to potential employers. In the previous section, we began by identifying generic geographical skills and then went on to show how these can be gained through fieldwork; we also identified ten ways in which this can take place. We will now present another list of skills, but these have been translated into terms that will be relevant to employers. Understanding such 'buzz' words and being able to relate these is crucial during the transition from communicating in 'academic' language to using 'business-speak'.

Surveys of large graduate employers show that a number of skills are frequently cited. Reading through these, you will notice the importance of these 'buzz' words that tend to be used by employers and which it will be helpful for you to use when applying for jobs or attending interviews. The most frequently cited terms, identified in a recent survey (http://ww2.prospects.ac.uk), are identified in Figure 2.3.

Understanding and responding to the demands of employers and the skills they seek is not simply a case of changing the language used. In order to communicate the skills you possess effectively, you will need to understand the workplace in which you would like to work and then reflect both on the skills that you may already have and the ones you will need to acquire and develop in your transition to employment. For example, the majority of the assessed work that will have formed part of your degree will have been conducted individually. In contrast, it is likely that the majority of your daily activities in the workplace will involve you collaborating with others. Potential employers require evidence that you can work collaboratively (and effectively) and that you are keen and able to

1 *Self-reliance skills*

   a Self-awareness: being purposeful, focused, self-belief, realistic

   b Pro-activity: resourceful, drive, self-reliant

   c Willingness to learn: inquisitive, motivated, enthusiastic

   d Self-promotion: positive, persistent, ambitious

   e Networking: initiator, relationship-builder, resourceful

   f Planning action: decision maker, planner, able to prioritise

2 *People skills*

   a Team working: supportive, organised, co-ordinator, deliverer

   b Interpersonal skills: listener, adviser, co-operative, assertive

   c Oral communication: communicator, presenter, influencer

   d Leadership: motivator, energetic, visionary

   e Customer orientation: friendly, caring, diplomatic

   f Foreign language: specific language skills

3 *General employment skills*

   a Problem solving: practical, logical, results orientated

   b Flexibility: versatile, willing, multi-skilled

   c Business acumen: entrepreneurial, competitive, risk taker

   d IT/computer literacy: office skills, keyboard skills, software packages

   e Numeracy: accurate, quick-thinker, methodical

   f Commitment: dedicated, trustworthy, conscientious

4 *Specialist skills*

   a Specific occupational skills: e.g. languages, IT

   b Technical skills: e.g. journalism, engineering, accounting, sales

Figure 2.3 'Buzz' words and terms used by employers to describe skills

continue learning. In order to best achieve this, you will need to learn to reflect upon your own learning process and skills development. The final section of this chapter says more about how to do this.

Having identified the skills and knowledge that are expected of geography graduates (in the previous section), and identified the skills sought by employers (above), we are now ready to explore the ways in which fieldwork can help you not only to do better in your studies, but also to prepare for employment and effectively present yourself to employers. We surveyed the top ten global employers and identified the sought-after skills and knowledge that can be gained specifically through fieldwork and evidenced with reference to fieldwork. Different employment advice, terminology and 'buzz' words were collated and applied to the fieldwork learning experience. Skills sought by employers, include:

- Group work: communicating clearly; demonstrating leadership; conflict resolution; empathy (listening to others' opinions); building relationships;

- Practicalities of fieldwork: organisation and planning; time keeping; working under pressure; working in a new environment; trying new things outside one's comfort zone; understanding different cultures.

- Project work in the field: strategic decision making; taking ownership of particular tasks; planning and executing a project from start to finish; responding to feedback; changing one's approach after feedback.

- Conducting research: awareness of real-world and global issues; defining the aims of a project; selecting the best approach to achieve these aims; prioritising tasks; being flexible enough to meet these aims; adapting positively to change; meeting deadlines; identifying and approaching interviewees; contacting and engaging with interviewees; networking (snowballing, focus groups, etc.); listening to others' opinions; utilising technology to find information (e.g. the internet); collecting and analysing different types of data.

Though a fieldtrip will not necessarily enable you to master all of these skills it will help with some of them: it can also provide new material for your cv/résumé and evidence to back up the claims you may make about yourself in applications, interviews and assessments. An important factor in 'standing out' to employers is the ability to differentiate yourself from others – being able to draw on learning experiences gained outside the classroom may be able to partially provide this.

How do you communicate your fieldwork skills and experiences?

When you successfully complete fieldwork, you will have added to the experiences you can draw upon. This can be done in a number of ways – through inclusion on your cv/resumé, detailed in a covering letter (if this is appropriate to the job for which you are applying; see Postcard 2.1), and/or used during a job interview (see Postcard 2.2). This sub-section draws upon a selection of experiences and views that have been expressed to us by some previous students we have taught on fieldtrips over the last decade.

Anthony, who participated in fieldwork during his degree, explains some of the ways that this has been useful in his applications for employment:

> I have mentioned it [fieldwork] in a job interviews for my post-university career. I spoke of how I worked in a team towards a common goal and the different types of skill I gained. Being able to highlight specific experiences gives the employer an indication that I know the types of skills that I have gained and I know when and how to use them in a real-life situation. I think that this was one of the main reasons that I have gained a job so quickly.

Other students have made similar comments. Hannah told us that she 'gained more confidence in [her] ability to conduct interviews and to talk openly and passionately about the area that [she] studied'. Jennifer, a British student who participated in a fieldtrip to Vancouver, illustrates some of the ways in which this proved useful in her applications for employment and training (see Postcard 2.1). In her covering letter Jennifer used her fieldwork experiences extensively to illustrate her skills.

Postcard 2.1: Using Fieldwork in a Job Application, by Jennifer Grehan (excerpts from a letter of application to a law firm, citing various skills and experience gained during fieldwork)

I dealt with different types of cultures which meant that in most situations I needed to be socially sensitive as I was being seen as an 'outsider'. Diplomacy had to be applied here – a skill that I feel will benefit me greatly in law.

During fieldwork I switched from my own project to compulsory projects, which all students were required to complete. This displayed adaptability and flexibility, including the ability to prioritise and move between different projects.

I developed my ability to work within time constraints while staying focused on targets. My organisational ability was key to this situation in successfully completing interviews and paperwork to the highest standard within a set time limit.

My project – working with Native North Americans – prompted me to try to understand the perspectives of people with different backgrounds. This built on my ability to stay clear-headed and focused in any situation involving conflicting views.

What I was studying in Vancouver aroused so much curiosity and genuine interest in me that I went further than just completing my fieldwork and made valuable friends among the people I am still in regular contact with. I displayed commitment to the people I studied and a determination to learn about their full background and reciprocate some of their kindness: my colleagues and I were invited to a 'naming ceremony', a play, to dinner, and to a cultural music and dance event.

The field course also required me to make a series of presentations, both before and during the fieldwork itself. This improved my presentation skills, vocalisation and confidence, to the extent that I no longer feel daunted by the prospect of standing up in a room full of people, presenting my argument, and taking questions and criticisms.

Fieldwork can also be effectively used in interview and job assessments. Postcard 2.2 provides an example of how a geography graduate has used his fieldwork experience to gain employment with one of the world's largest management consultancy firms.

Postcard 2.2: Using Fieldwork in a Job Assessment, by Andrew Gregory (a British student who participated in a field course in France, successfully completed an assessment at Accenture – a global management consulting, technology services and outsourcing company – which employed him as a management consultant)

In my interview and assessments for Accenture I drew on both academic and practical aspects of the fieldwork. In my first assessment I had to review some company data and provide a synopsis of the key issues. Fieldwork helped with this as it had taught me how to analyse a lot of data, including how to interpret graphs and charts and identify trends. The ability to critically analyse information was very important in this task.

My second assessment task involved discussing a business scenario with a senior manager from Accenture. In the task you are presented with some quite complex information (which you are not really meant to fully understand) and you need to decipher what is relevant to the questions you are being asked. Here, critical thinking – and thinking quickly 'on your feet' – was really important and I had to be able to assimilate the information and use it constructively. This task involved problem solving. My fieldtrip experience had used a problem-based learning approach so I was familiar with the process of analysing numerous problems and then forming and communicating an effective solution with confidence. After this assessment I was told that Accenture were looking for individuals who could present a logical and structured argument.

The third assessment was a group project in which we had to produce an advertising campaign and plan. One of the main objectives of the task was to simulate a working environment where a series of team objectives are provided. Communication skills were really important and something I suggested – that I remembered done frequently whilst out on a field visit – was to include everyone up front. This seems like a very logical and obvious thing to do but something as simple as reading out and discussing the objectives together builds trust and assurance within the team and everyone

(Continued)

(Continued)

knows they are aiming for the same goal. Something that I really felt I learnt from fieldwork was a 'sense of self' (if that's even a term!). What I mean here is an awareness of what my own strengths are and how I can best apply these within the team.

On my fieldtrip the group work we conducted always consisted of more work than one person alone could complete. This meant I developed skills that allowed me to delegate tasks and work to my team's strengths by identifying who was good at what. As a result of having to delegate and work independently (or in small groups) I developed techniques that helped me to present back to the group while effectively positioning my arguments with justifications and sound reasoning. My fieldwork experience, and the degree programme as a whole, increased my presentation abilities which in turn helped me in the Accenture interview and assessments.

Andrew has used his field experiences in both practical and academic ways. He has gained the communication skills needed to present analyses and to work effectively in a team. Andrew has also reflected on his own abilities and is able to contribute to teamwork based on an understanding of what his most valuable role is. He refers to this as 'a sense of self', which in this chapter is described as 'reflection'. It is also interesting to note that the fieldtrip Andrew attended was cut short due to a severe outbreak of gastroenteritis. Despite this, he was still able to identify many of the skills derived/developed through fieldwork to draw upon during his assessment.

It is important to highlight that while most graduates focus on the positive aspects of fieldwork and the numerous ways in which the learning experience has enhanced their employability, the challenging nature of conducting research in the field can also present negative experiences. These can include problematic group working (group work is discussed in more detail in Chapter 5), ill-conceived research methodologies, or practical problems such as flight disruptions, outbreaks of illness and conflicts within the group. Rather than just becoming frustrated or disappointed by negative experiences, these can be 'turned around' to provide exemplars for potential employees. One classic (and dreaded) interview question asks the candidate to detail their weaknesses: 'I don't have any' is not considered an appropriate response here. However, it may be possible to reflect upon a negative fieldwork experience (while also crucially emphasising that this challenge has been met). A new generation of tricky interview questions is, however, emerging. PricewaterhouseCoopers ask 'Have you ever completed a tedious task with enthusiasm?' The company essentially wants to know if you can do routine work without complaining. A fieldtrip-based response might be 'Yes,

I had to transcribe our research interviews. It is very laborious but I realised the value of having completed the task as by the time I had finished I had an overview of all the material. This made analysis much easier and I had a much better handle on the data than my other group members'.

HOW CAN YOU BUILD ON PREVIOUS EXPERIENCES AND LEARN TO REFLECT?

We have repeatedly asserted the importance of 'reflecting' on fieldwork in order to identify your academic and employment skills and understand what you are learning from the trip, thereby changing your understanding of a situation, concept or place. But how do you do this and what does it mean to reflect? In this section we suggest various ways in which you can learn to reflect, providing some practical exercises that might help you to do this and thereby get the most out of your fieldwork.

Reflection is an active process, addressing a number of different themes in the context of fieldwork. These should include thoughts about your observations and also on:

- The research process i.e. how your plans have had to adapt in the field.

- How you are conducting your research i.e. your positionality, ethical considerations, and how you might improve upon your data collection.

- How you are learning and how you might improve the ways in which you learn and interpret information.

- Academic and transferrable skills you have gained or developed.

A 'reflective diary' can be a useful vehicle for making critical observations in the field and for identifying academic and employment skills as well as tracking your own learning. Reflective diaries invite students to capture - in their own words – their changing experiences and abilities. They enable students to evaluate their progress in their own terms. You may be required to keep a reflective diary. But even if a reflective diary is not a required part of your fieldtrip we would suggest that you do keep one for reasons that will become clear below. But what is a reflective diary and what should you put in it?

First, a reflective diary can be distinguished from a descriptive field notebook. These differ in significant ways and if your assessment includes one of these it is important that you understand which type you are being required to produce. A field notebook is a more descriptive method of recording the people, places, and events you observe in the field. These notes form the first stage in the process of observation, interpretation and presentation, and may need to be followed by the production of a written piece of work. If the notebook is to be assessed it would be wise to find out in advance how 'polished' it needs to be and whether, for example, you are expected to go beyond the recording of data and include interpretation. In contrast, a reflective diary asks questions not just about what you have observed but also how you observed it, what you were able to learn through doing so, and what your observations and reflections will mean in a wider theoretical context (McGuiness and Simm 2005).

Reflection can help you to take stock of whereabouts you stand in your studies and skills development and what you have to gain from doing fieldwork. Your field course may have prescribed 'learning outcomes' in which specific skills are developed and knowledge is gained, but it is worthwhile remembering that each student will come to the course with their own personal history that will include distinctive strengths, weaknesses and experiences, so the real learning outcomes will be different for each person. For some the challenge will be how to cope with living and working as part of a group every day for a week, whereas for others it will be working and producing assignments within concentrated periods of time. For some people being away from home will present them with real difficulties (emotionally or financially) while others will face the hurdle of overcoming their shyness in order to contact organisations and request a research interview. This is particularly evident in field classes composed of students with different interests – for instance, some students will be geography majors or single honours geography students while others will have different backgrounds. Each person, in their own way, will bring a distinctive set of experiences to the field. Fieldwork can also be conducted at various points in an undergraduate degree, so each time you take a fieldtrip you will have different things to gain and learn.

You should begin your diary before you go into the field. One way to structure a reflective diary is by attempting the following practical tasks:

- Reading through the lists and descriptions of abilities that it has been suggested geography students should have on completion of their degree, how would you place yourself at your current stage of your degree? Note that some of these skills – such as 'applying research design and execution within field-based research' and 'applying ideas to new situations' – are difficult to achieve without completing a field course. Remember that you can build on your wider life experiences and the skills you have learned, for example, in previous employment.

- The 'benchmarking statements' discussed earlier in this chapter describe the 'typical' student, but are you striving to be more than ordinary, in a highly competitive world? How can you set yourself apart from your peers? Will a field course help you do this?

- Are you aware of how you learn best? What are your strengths and weaknesses? Would conducting fieldwork enable you to improve upon some of your weaker areas (be it working in groups or linking theoretical ideas and empirical findings)?

- What are you really trying to achieve in your degree? Many graduates find that the details of courses fade but practical and skills-based learning will be reinforced over time. Fieldwork can supply a helpful mechanism for remembering theoretical ideas as they are observed in 'real world' settings. So can fieldwork help you not only to get good grades and find employment, but also to cultivate a geographical imagination and curiosity that will remain with you for life?

If you begin reflecting before you go into the field this will also involve you looking back on your past experiences, whether in the field or elsewhere. Everyone brings distinctive skills to the field whatever their background, and whether they are in the field or in the world of employment for example, as Figure 2.4 illustrates. Reflection will continue in the field, of course, because you will benefit from your engagement with and feedback from field leaders and other students. Indeed, fieldwork gives you a rare opportunity to gain continuous and rapid feedback, including 'formative' (not-for-credit) assessment. In other words, you will rarely have this much access to your lecturers and professors at other times, so do take advantage of this and engage them in discussions about what you are learning and how.

While you are taking stock of and building up your skills and knowledge, you may also want to consider how you could present all of this to a potential employer. Reflective skills, identified above in relation to academic learning, can also be framed in terms of employability, using the 'buzz words' favoured by employers, which have been described above. You may want to structure this part of your reflective diary in a way that specifically anticipates the demands of employers, and the following format has been suggested with US employers in mind (Duttro 1999):

- *Learning profile*: what you have learnt in each project/fieldtrip.

- *Professional career profile*: the roles/occupations you have performed.

- *Interview profile*: material that is relevant to the post or project you wish to apply for.

These suggestions are responding in part to the growing importance of work-based placements or internships in North America, a trend that is being echoed in other parts of the world where students will compete for (generally unpaid) work experience with employers which will enhance their employability. In the course of your studies and also your employment, you will be advised to continually monitor your experiences, strengths and weaknesses and to find ways to enhance your profile as you go. Andrew Bottomley (the former Head of Recruitment at PricewaterhouseCoopers) advises that 'while reflective learning is important in academic studies, it is no less important in the workplace' so each 'student would do well to routinely assess their own abilities' (2001: 25). This serves to highlight, once again, the benefits from conducting fieldwork as you will become more proficient in reflective learning – a skill that you will then be able to apply to your future career development for decades to come.

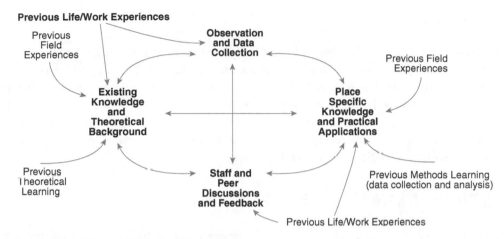

Figure 2.4   Reflection and learning in the field

So reflection – on first glance a rather woolly term – is in fact a practical process, in which you will keep track of and actively direct your own learning while always remembering your reasons for learning, whatever these may be.

SUMMARY

This chapter has discussed the potential benefits of doing fieldwork. As with most things in life, the more you invest in fieldwork (in terms of time, enthusiasm and simple hard work) the greater the benefits will be. The key points of the chapter were:

- Fieldwork provides a unique learning experience in which academic skills can be developed and existing skills can evolve. In particular, being 'in the field' can aid the transition from 'shallow' to 'deep' learning in which you are able to make connections between theory and real world examples and critically analyse your own data. In this chapter we have distinguished between academic and employment-related skills.

- As learning is a life-long process, this chapter has emphasised the longer-term 'employability' that you may be able to derive from fieldwork.

- The process of reviewing your own set of skills, and understanding how fieldwork may enhance them, involves a degree of self-reflection. This chapter has offered some guidance on how to develop the ability to reflect.

CONCLUSION

If you have been able to rationalise and justify your own participation in fieldwork, you will now need to address the issue of what you will do when in the field. You may wish to continue reading the chapters in this section before your course begins to gain an idea of what the research process involves. It will be necessary to return to Chapters 3–5 once you have decided on the structure and objectives of your fieldwork. This will enable you to tailor the guidance provided on developing a research idea, considering the relevant ethical issues and working in groups to your own specific field class and situation.

FURTHER READING/KEY TEXT(S)

Despite an increase in employability and skills development in higher education, there are relatively few accessible texts that are aimed at students. As a result, the most appropriate sources of further reading are those provided by national institutions.

- Your own national government should publish information on the standards expected from graduates in all disciplines. Associations of geographers periodically review 'what a geography graduate should look like'. For example, you may wish to visit the American Association of Geographers at www.aag.org

- Information about skills development for graduates is available on the internet, on sites such as www.prospects.ac.uk. Also visit your university career centre and visit the websites of employers that interest you.

For a useful insight into a large graduate employer's perspective on student skills development, see Bottomley (2001).

3

BEFORE YOU GO: RESEARCH DESIGN AND PREPARATION

OVERVIEW

This chapter addresses the following questions:

- How can you develop your own feasible research idea?
- What kind of challenges might you face and how can you overcome these?
- Which research methods could you use in your fieldwork and how should you select the most appropriate ones?
- How can you consider, and plan for, the practicalities and potential risks of fieldwork?

The chapter offers guidance on how to identify a research topic and focus an idea into achievable research questions that you will then seek to answer via your fieldwork. It discusses the development of a methodology, including choosing your research methods, and suggests some sources of data that you can access before entering the field. Finally, a consideration of the practicalities of conducting fieldwork and risk assessment is made.

Good research is dependent upon careful thought and planning. Fieldwork, in particular, demands that researchers take the time to prepare for their visit to the field. This chapter outlines the key stages of the preparation required for fieldwork, beginning with the challenging process of coming up with a research idea. Although fieldtrips will vary in the degree to which students will be asked to find their own topics – ranging from total freedom of choice to more prescribed and specified themes or foci – the process of forming a research idea and planning its execution involves a level of engagement and critical insight that all students should be encouraged to develop. The first section will provide guidance on how to develop and focus a research idea as well as form research questions. The second section addresses the issues of choosing research methods and planning the execution of the research. Finally, two other considerations have to be addressed within your fieldwork plan: health and safety, which is addressed in this chapter; and ethical issues, which are explained in Chapter 4.

RESEARCH DESIGN: FORMULATING A RESEARCH IDEA

Fieldwork begins not when you arrive in the field but much earlier, when you plan and design your research. Gary Bouma (1993: 9) states that 'although many have the impression that data collection is the major enterprise in research, this is not strictly correct. Preparation, Phase 1, takes the most time, and drawing conclusions and writing the report takes more time than data collection in most cases. Data collection itself takes the least time'. Successful data collection depends upon rigorous planning and research design – without it you will waste much of your time in the field trying to find your feet and focus. Your fieldcourse may include preparatory lectures covering background information on the field location, methodological advice, and/or addressing practical issues. However, not all students will receive pre-field lectures and many will be left to fend for themselves during the planning stage, so in this chapter we will not assume that you have any prior knowledge of how to set about planning fieldwork. If you are lucky enough to have some structured time with staff before the trip make the most of this opportunity by working through the research design process independently: try to 'check in' with staff if you have any concerns or require reassurance. As explained in Chapter 2, ownership of a project is an important part of the learning process and contributes significantly to skills development and the ability to reflect.

Begin the research design with a positive outlook, confident in the knowledge that you have the skills that will guide you in completing the project. The journey may seem a long and daunting one but this chapter seeks to make it a little less arduous, and if you follow the guidance offered your time in the field will be much more enjoyable and effective.

How do you come up with a research idea?

Your fieldcourse may require you to formulate your own research idea. This could seem somewhat scary, especially if you have not already been through the process of writing a dissertation, and you may initially feel confused and at a loss regarding where to start. This section gives you some advice on how to approach the process of developing a sound research idea. We suggest that the process is a positive one and you have an opportunity to conduct research on a topic that really interests you. If your fieldcourse has more clearly defined links to a particular research subject or area of geography, you may be provided with a topic or 'problem' to investigate. This chapter will still assist you in developing those themes and devising your research methods.

So, where do you start? Geography is an eclectic discipline that offers a wide range of potential research topics. As Matthew Miles and A. Michael Huberman state, 'any researcher, no matter how unstructured or inductive, comes to fieldwork with *some* orienting ideas, foci and tools' (1984: 27, author emphasis). To begin, you (and your group) should decide if you wish to build on your knowledge of a particular research theme that you have covered in previous courses. For example, you may have already completed course(s) on agglomeration and clustering and decide to use this as a starting point to examine the geography of economic activities in your field location. As you already have a foundation for your knowledge, particularly in the key literatures, you may find it easier to focus in on a particular issue to research. Conversely, you (and your group) may decide to take the opportunity to research a new area of investigation. Are there any specific subject areas that are of particular interest to you that you now have the chance to investigate? An example may be that you are personally interested in environmental issues and chose to focus on the environmental impact of an activity in your field location. This approach has the benefit of being novel and engaging so you may find yourself feeling more enthusiastic and prepared to invest more time in the research. If you are working in a group it is of paramount importance that you find a topic every member is interested in covering.

How do you find out if your idea is suitable for your field location? Our experiences of supervising field research suggest that students can find the formulation of research ideas difficult, especially if they are not familiar with the place they will be conducting the research in. This is a natural response to the unknown, but there are a variety of sources of information that can inform you about your fieldsite. These can be accessed either before you begin to develop an idea or after you have had an initial idea to confirm that the phenomenon you wish to examine does actually occur in the field location (see Figure 3.1).

---

1 *Use the internet to access the popular press in your field location* – this is a quick and easily accessible source that will give you an initial grounding in issues that are of current relevance. Sources include: national newspapers – what are the important issues of the day? Many of these will be of geographical significance; and/or regional or country reports in magazines/journals such as *The Economist or Newsweek.* The detail of this content may not be crucial at this stage, so language issues may not be a barrier – if you do not speak the national language use one of a number of translation sites on the internet.

2 *Refer to previous lectures* – was your field location referred to as a case study related to a particular topic? There are many 'famous' examples in literature which may lead you to make an association between the place and geographical theory. For example, Manchester is associated with the Industrial Revolution and post-industrial development; Singapore is a widely cited example of post-World War II economic development and as a financial services hub; Vancouver is termed 'Hollywood North' due to its strong connections with film productions funded from Hollywood. A quick but thoughtful review of your existing knowledge-base may reveal some initially hidden associations.

3 *Have any significant events taken place in the field location?* – these could include large sporting events such as the Olympics, the Commonwealth Games or the World Cup. These have significant geographical impacts and can be examined in the planning, event, or post-event stages. Other events could include World Expos, large industry trade meetings, or political meetings such as the G8.

Figure 3.1 Sources of information on your field location: developing a research idea

Why not just ask someone? Your first instinct might be to seek guidance from the teaching staff in your geography department. Tony Parsons and Peter Knight (1995: 32) suggest this is 'a bit wimpish' and offer a word of warning here: 'Don't go into your tutor's office and start with some whining "What can I do my research on?". This will not go down well'. You will rarely find a member of the academic staff who is prepared to give you a research idea on a plate. This is counter-productive to current teaching and learning strategies which are increasingly being oriented towards equipping students to learn for themselves. Instead, undertake your own investigations first and by all means go into the department armed with a list of possible topics and discuss them logically with a staff member. This will be far more productive and you will achieve much better engagement and guidance.

You have a topic, but how can you start to focus your idea?

Colin Robson (1993) likens research design to crossing a river, whereby with each step you move between stepping stones which represent your focus, questions, strategy, methods. Before questions or hypotheses can be set up, it is necessary for you to step on the first stone and come up with a focus for the study. This period can be both stressful and enjoyable, involving you in a fair amount of exploration of the literature. Having found an idea, the process of research design should now proceed to your identification of a tightly focused and practical research agenda. Your aim here should be to specify two or three research questions and then devise a methodology to answer these. Alternatively, you may have been asked to adhere to a 'Problem-Based Learning' approach. In either case, using a research 'problem' can be an effective method for identifying a focused research area.

In order to contextualise your research idea, and find your focus, a trip to the library is vital in order to see what other researchers have undertaken. This will serve a number of purposes; first, you can establish the previous research has been done on your topic; second, you can see if any issues/problems remain under-researched; third, you can review and critique the existing literature and identify the research methods used to research your topic; and fourth, you are beginning the process of forming a literature review (which should always be started before entering the field). There are a number of sources of information that you can use to find existing literature including course reading lists; 'snowballing' using the bibliographies of those sources you have already found; searching the library catalogue: using internet sources such as www.ingentaconnect.com; and reviewing the key journals related to your topic (for example, *Progress in Human Geography*). Figure 3.2 below offers a framework on which to structure your literature search.

While you should aim to read as widely as possible, it is crucial that you identify about 15 articles that are of key relevance to your research. It is valuable to have a general overview of the important issues, but making the jump from the general to the specific is often challenging. As you become more familiar with the literature you should be able to start to identify gaps in

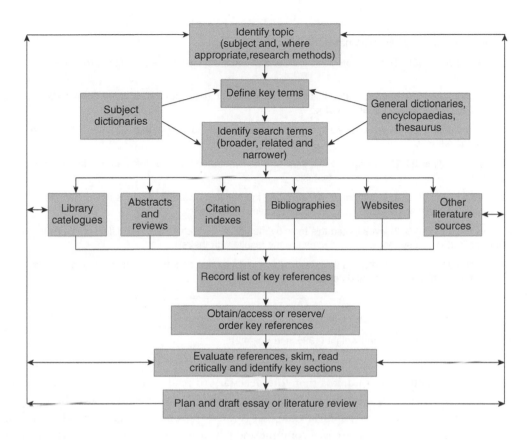

Figure 3.2   A framework for undertaking a literature search

Source: Healey and Healey (2010: see Figure 2.1)

what is known and be able to formulate questions to which you would like to know the answers. Figure 3.3 offers some guidance on how to narrow the focus of your study.

The guidance offered in this section takes on particular significance when it is specifically related to fieldwork. Reading the literature on research conducted in your field location should provide you with contextual information and enable you to build up a picture of the important issues. However, you must be careful not to focus solely on research that is specific to the field site for a number of reasons. First, there may be scant research on your topic in your field location (which makes justifying the originality of your research easier, but building up a body of literature more difficult), or there may be valuable contributions (e.g. seminal articles) that are purely theoretical in nature or based on research that has been conducted in different locations. In either case, your review of the literature would be partial at best if you only focus on one

It appears that nobody has investigated this topic – I'll have a go.

Phillips and Johns (2012) investigated this topic and raised the questions regarding the role of x. I'll investigate x.

Phillips and Johns (2012) investigated this topic and found out that ... but they ignored the possible effects of x. I'll investigate the effects of x.

Phillips and Johns (2012) investigated this topic at location x and found out that ... I'll see if the same is true for location y.

Phillips and Johns (2012) investigated this topic and demonstrated that the dominant controls on x were y and z. This may be wrong. I'll test this.

Phillips and Johns (2012) investigated this topic and found that ... I wonder if things have changed since them. I'll repeat their study and compare my results with theirs.

Phillips and Johns (2012) investigated this topic by method A. I wonder if you get different results by using method B. I'll use method B and compare my results with theirs.

Since Phillips and Johns (2012) did their study a new data set has become available. I wonder if the new data set supports Phillips and Johns' conclusions.

Figure 3.3 Reaching a research focus

Source: Adapted from Parsons and Knight (1995: see Box 4.2)

site (your field location). Second, it is therefore necessary to read around your topic including a range of different geographical scales. Fundamentally, it is up to you to select the focus of your research and find the geographical scale that is most appropriate (and practical). Third, as geographers we understand that social, economic and political processes operate along a variety of geographical scales and that local and global processes intersect and interact differently across space. Therefore, an understanding of these processes is important when researching – too narrow a focus on a small geographical site would be myopic (short-sighted) if it has been researched as if it were isolated from other people and places.

The dual demands of achieving a research focus while taking into consideration the broader issues and processes will often lead to confusion for students and understandably so. We would therefore suggest that you use the literature review to inform you in three stages:

- *Soak up the context*: Read the literature to gain an understanding of the key issues related to your research. Do not constrain yourself geographically; instead, include sources that discuss your topic in places other than your field site.

- *Zoom in to define your research question(s):* Review your sources in line with Figure 3.4 (p. 52) to narrow down the topic to one to three research questions. These should be clear, specifying exactly what questions you are asking, and also practical. Asking relevant questions is what 'good' research is all about and you should keep these simple.

- *Return to the wider focus:* Decide which literatures you will use to illustrate the broader context in which your research is situated. These observations should be included in your literature review.

Where might you go wrong?

Although all individuals learn differently there are some common 'traps' that students (and academics!) can fall into. These are often a result of pattern-forming behaviour based on privileging some parts of the research design process over others. It is easy to spend more time on tasks we find easier and/or more interesting than others! If you have begun to reflect on your own learning (as suggested in Chapter 2), you may already be aware of some your strengths and weakness. This section introduces a few of the potential pitfalls you may face, based on the work of David Silverman (2000) but applied specifically to fieldwork. There are three main 'traps' which you may identify with if you have previously received the following comments on your academic work. These are outlined, with their possible solutions, below.

First, simplistic inductivism or 'let's just get there and go with the flow'. Yi Fu Tuan (2001) has argued that just being in a place without thinking through what you want to learn may lead to confused, unfocused work. There can be good reasons for exploratory research, and these are discussed in Chapter 9, but it is also vital to avoid the pitfall of simple inductivism, which means making lazy observations and failing to think carefully and rigorously about what you have observed. You may have been told your work is 'too descriptive' or 'lacks clear links between theory and empirics'. A lack of planning may result in poorly structured written work. In order to develop a research problem that avoids simplistic inductivism you will need to contextualise your observations in relation to broader processes and link these to various concepts and theories.

Second, we have the 'kitchen sink' gambit or 'everything is important so I'll throw it in'. You may have received comments on your work such as 'lacks focus', 'lacks depth', or 'more critical insight needed'. It is very difficult to achieve depth (in focus and analysis) if you are unable to prioritise what is significant. Visiting a place for the first time will often raise a range of questions that may or may not be relevant to the research topic. To avoid 'kitchen sink' fieldwork you should seek to 'do less, more thoroughly' (Wolcott 1990: 62). This means deciding which ideas/theories are more important than others and asking yourself what it is you are trying to find out and therefore what your priorities are. It may be useful here to visualise your ideas by drawing a flow chart or 'mind map' showing the key concepts and observations and any connections between them.

Third, there is grand theory or 'I'm happiest using existing research to form an argument, not collecting the data myself'. This may be harder to identify if you have not previously been asked to do empirical data collection. It may be that you have received comments on written work such as 'lacks case study examples' or 'poor integration of different theoretical approaches'. In the context of fieldwork this is not a common problem but it can be observed in students who do not acknowledge, or put any effort into, making observations or collecting mere 'facts'. This can manifest itself in group situations where grand theorists will leave other members to 'do the dirty work' of collecting data. To avoid this you need to acknowledge that in order to make the most of your field experience a closer engagement with the environment and the people in it will make for a more rewarding experience – and a better piece of research.

If you can identify any of the elements of these potential 'traps' in how you learn and produce work, you are well on the way to being able to overcome them – forewarned is forearmed!

RESEARCH DESIGN: CHOOSING METHODS

The next step in creating a successful research design is careful consideration of how you can find answers to your research questions. Again, the particularities of fieldwork place unique demands on planning research for a number of reasons. First, you are distanced from the field location, so 'imagining' what is possible may be initially problematic. This section offers you some guidance on how to overcome this perceived hurdle. Second, conducting a pilot project (to refine your methodology) in the field location is likely to be impossible. There is, however, nothing to stop you from 'practising' methods at home; for example, testing questionnaires or interview schedules. Finally, you will have a defined period of time in the field which will place practical limitations on your research methodology. Also bear in mind that you may wish to adapt your research questions in light of considering the exact methods you will need to use. This is not problematic as an important part of good research design is the ability to reflect and adapt in order to overcome the practical challenges (and this will continue when you are in the field).

You should begin this stage by considering your broad approach to research. Fieldwork in human geography tends to adopt an intensive approach – which is due in part to the practical limitations on time and resources and also because the aim of 'thick description' results from a greater engagement and 'embeddedness' in the field (see the Introduction). This is not to say that extensive methods are not possible, but they do require access to large amounts of already published data and/or data generated from secondary sources which may not help you to achieve your aim of collecting primary data in the field.

Which methods should you choose?

'Field researchers always live, to some extent, with the disquieting notion that they are gathering the wrong data ... that they should be observing or asking questions about another event or practice instead of the present one' (Shaffir and Stebbins 1991: 18). This makes it necessary to develop an overall research strategy as your methodology will shape the methods you must use and how each of these is used. You can then refer to this strategy during moments of uncertainty and use it to refocus on your research aims and data collection.

As a discipline, geography has always spanned a wide range of methodological and interpretative approaches and recent decades have witnessed the adoption of a range of alternative research methods. The commonly cited dichotomy of quantitative and qualitative methods is gradually being reconsidered and more appropriately thought of as a continuum. Extensive and intensive approaches can adopt both qualitative and quantitative methods. While conducting fieldwork research you may well find yourself collecting and analysing secondary data (some of which may be numerical) before adopting qualitative methods such as interviewing to collect data in the field. Chapters 6 to 9 are designed to help you make informed decisions about why particular methods are utilised in the field, how these can be used and collected, and their advantages and disadvantages.

It is essential that you are very clear about why you have chosen a particular method (or methods) in relation to how this will help you to answer your research questions. All too often undergraduate students do not make explicit the links between their research objectives, the theories they are trying to access, and the research methods they have chosen. A good starting point for this would be to assess each research method (with your research questions in front of you) and to make a note of why (or why not) each method is suitable and practical for your fieldwork. Figure 3.4 shows the links between data sources, methods of data collection and analysis and research topics for a study of the film and television industry in Manchester. It is a simple method by which the researcher can show that various methods were required to investigate different aspects of the research.

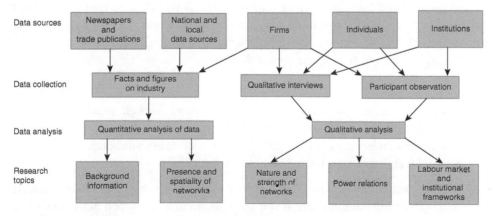

Figure 3.4 Relating data sources, collection, analysis and research topics

Source: Johns (2004: see Figure 4.4)

How do you know your data will be valid and reliable?

The validity of research concerns the soundness, legitimacy, and relevance of a research theory or its investigation and issues of research validity and reliability are in many respects related. David Silverman (2000) argues that these apply just as much to qualitative-based studies as they do to quantitative-based ones. You therefore need to be ready to defend your research strategy and, as Henry Yeung reminds us, also remain aware of the 'relative advantages of different methods and how to use them discriminately and flexibly under different research contexts' (1995: 320).

Good research design is partly achieved by attempting to anticipate and minimise various types of error which may ruin the reliability or validity of research data. Such errors include those associated with sampling and response (both of which are discussed in more detail in Chapter 7, which covers interviewing in the field) but also need to be considered when designing your research. Sampling errors occur when a sample population is not representative, either through skewed response rates or ill-informed decision making. This can only be overcome by collecting sufficient data on the whole population before making a sampling decision. For example, if you wished to study and interview Chinese-owned firms in a city you would need to establish how many such firms are present and then select a sample from the total (and justify those selected by using a sampling strategy). Response errors occur because the process whereby ideas are exchanged and recorded during interviewing is subject to misunderstandings, leading questions, and other biases. These can only be reduced by adopting a careful questionnaire and research design.

The disadvantages of particular methods (and there will always be some) can also be overcome by combining various methods and thus using a multi-method approach. This relies on the argument that it is not the method itself that is weak or strong but the relationship between theory and method and how the research attends to the potential weaknesses of the methods. One of the key benefits of using more than one method is that the different methods will generate different types of data which can be 'triangulated'. Triangulation can take four forms, all of which are relevant to fieldcourse data collection:

- *Data triangulation* – which entails gathering data through several sampling strategies so that slices of the data at different times and situations, as well as from a variety of people, are gathered. In terms of fieldwork this means thinking carefully about when and where to collect data (e.g. in different streets or neighbourhoods and at various times of the day) and who you will include in your study.

- *Investigator triangulation* – which refers to the use of more than one researcher in the field to gather and interpret data. If you are working in a group you don't have to collect all your data together; you can split up, conduct some research, and then discuss your findings together. This is an effective form of early analysis and also has the benefit of maximising your time in the field.

- *Theoretical triangulation* – which refers to the use of more than one theoretical position in interpreting data.

- *Methodological triangulation* – which involves the use of more than one method for gathering data. The researcher can use triangulation as a methodological tool to combine specific research methods and find connections between research findings.

You will probably be using multiple methods in your fieldwork. Many projects will require the collection of background data (not least as a result of developing a topic and research questions), so you are likely to combine secondary and primary data collection. You may also wish to 'triangulate' methods and data collection, so that you do not rely too heavily upon any one source. But do be wary of falling into the 'kitchen sink' trap methodologically. More methods do not necessarily make for better data since they could lead you to spread your time and efforts too thinly.

Time is a highly necessary consideration as you plan your fieldwork. As the length of time you will spend in the field and the nature of the field environment will vary from trip to trip, we cannot offer specific advice on the volumes of data collection you should collect. We can, however, advise you to make sure your field research plans correspond to the time you have available. This can sometimes mean recognising the limits to what can be achieved in a short period of time and deciding to do less but to also do it better. In Postcard 3.1, Nick Clarke discusses a fieldcourse that acknowledged the limits to what could be achieved in a week or so and set a realistic task: to produce a pilot study which explored an issue, thereby providing the basis for a more detailed research, but made limited claims about substantive findings.

Postcard 3.1: Fieldwork as a Pilot Study, by Nick Clarke

Fieldtrips tend to be short, usually lasting for between a couple of days and two weeks. This poses problems for what can realistically be done in terms of research. Sometimes students will be asked to complete small pieces of research, and numerous bad habits will be picked up as a result (e.g. drawing conclusions from a few hours' observation or a poorly sampled survey). One way in which students can use this problem to engage more thoughtfully with the research process as a whole – instead of simplifying that process by cramming all of it into just one or two days – is to approach research projects as pilot studies.

(Continued)

(Continued)

Every year another member of staff and I will take 30 students to Berlin for a week (see Figure 3.5). My approach has been to use the city as a laboratory in which to study the production of urban space in twentieth-century Europe. Students are given reading packs to study over their summer break. They are required to prepare beforehand and should therefore arrive in Berlin having read a general history of the city and a set of theoretical and empirical papers on its urban geography. Each day begins with a lecture and discussion of a particular theme. Students then go off around the city in work-groups of five or six. In the evening, they return to the hostel and two members from each group will present a brief report of a pilot study, followed by a research proposal detailing how research at this site could be done properly with adequate time and other resources.

During the course of each day, students need to isolate one or two answerable research questions, find the most appropriate research methods for answering these (e.g. observation based on a rigorous sample frame), have a go at completing some research (for a couple of hours), and then record the findings. They also need to think about what they would do if they were in Berlin for a year instead of a week, if they spoke German, and if they had the financial and other resources necessary to do rigorous research in the field. Students present their ideas that evening in the form of a brief report of their pilot study and then a more substantial research proposal which usually includes: a short introduction to the research area; a statement of the questions to be answered; a description of the methods to be used; a timetable for the research; and a wish-list of necessary resources.

In this way, the problem of short timeframes on undergraduate fieldtrips is turned into an opportunity. Students do bits and pieces of research but they are also encouraged to think of them as just that – bits and pieces which should not be thought of as constituting high quality research that will lead to new knowledge. They are asked to think in terms of pilot projects (which should not be overstated or pushed too far) leading to research proposals (in which advanced knowledge can be demonstrated). The objective is for students to understand more about the research process as a whole. It also requires them to engage with fieldwork sites in a more self-reflexive and critical way. Few of them leave Berlin thinking they know the city, but many of them depart with a clear idea of how elements of it could be known. This is what can be hoped for on a short fieldtrip and it is more than enough.

Figure 3.5 Students conducting fieldwork in Berlin. Photograph by Nick Clarke

HOW DO YOU WRITE A GOOD RESEARCH PROPOSAL?

Once you have found a research focus, identified one to three specific research questions and selected appropriate research methods, the next stage (and note that this still isn't the final stage!) is to produce a research proposal. You may be required to submit this to your tutor/fieldwork supervisor for feedback and/or assessment. Even if this is not necessary we would strongly suggest that you complete your own proposal as part of research planning. A clear plan will be invaluable in the field as you can refer back to it when writing up, and anyone reading your work will be able to see that you have been thorough and rigorous.

A typical research proposal would ask that the following be completed:

- *Title of the research*: this should be a sentence that places your research in context (i.e. a general description of what your research covers).

- *Aim of the research*: here you should list your research questions or provide a paragraph on the research followed by the research questions.

- *Background and justification*: why is this research of interest? Refer to the key pieces of literature that you are using. Also identify the research 'gap' that you are going to fill.

- *Methodology*: produce a justification of the methods that you have chosen, remembering to link these clearly to your research questions. Why these methods? If using more than one method, how will you combine them? What kinds of data are you seeking to collect and analyse?

- *Research timetable*: be as specific as possible and realistic about how long your data collection will take. Refer to the fieldcourse timetable while also remembering to block out any days and times that may already be filled with staff-led activities (such as tours). Remember to incorporate practical considerations and don't just focus on time in the field. You should include information on when you will start to approach potential research participants (for example, interviewees or 'gatekeepers' whose permission you may need). Also include your writing-up schedule.

The greater the level of detail included in your research proposal, the more feedback you will receive. Pay close attention to this feedback and try to address it as comprehensively as possible. This will boost your confidence before entering the field and will save you time once you are there. Finally, remember that the research design process will only finish once you have left the field location. It is extremely unlikely that your research plan will proceed exactly as you intended so you need to be prepared to modify your research timetable. As Chapters 6 to 9 explain, every method will produce certain challenges that will need to be overcome in the field. If you already know exactly what it is you will find, the research would be pointless and more than a little boring.

BEGINNING THE RESEARCH PROCESS BEFORE LEAVING FOR THE FIELD

You can, and indeed should, begin the process of research before entering the field. There are several sources of data that you can use here to help inform your research methodology and plans and these can help form the beginning of your data collection. This section will review some of the key sources of data available to you via the internet (a comprehensive list is impossible!), with guidance on how to interpret this data in meaningful ways that will contribute to your research. It concludes with a postcard (3.2) that provides a case study example of students using local contacts in the field.

Government and organisation sources

Given the inherently place-based nature of fieldwork, questions about access to data will tend to be specific to the country in which the field site is located. A natural place to start will be the website of the national statistical office of the country for which information is required. These offices produce the 'official' statistics for their nation and present the data as neutral. However, do be cautious about how you select and use such data and remember that various countries use different methodologies and definitions to collect their data. A classic example here relates to the collection and dissemination of unemployment data which are difficult to trace over time − even using national statistical data − as definitions of what 'unemployment' is and how it is measured can change over time for political reasons. Just as with qualitative data, we should always question the origins and purposes of quantitative data.

A second national source of data and documentation is national governments. However, you should bear in mind that government departments are organised differently in each country so you may have to spend some time getting to grips with the right departments and agencies to access (and making sure these are also the most appropriate for your research topic). The internet has made accessing governmental data and policy documents a great deal easier, but a language barrier will still exist if the researcher does not speak the language used (although many governments do produce some information in other languages such as English). Be aware also that accessing governmental data is a time-specific enterprise due to the political nature of its content and the duration of its posting on the internet. Often only the most up-to-date documents will be available and websites will change (and texts will be removed) if there is a change of government. You do not have to be an expert in textual analysis to realise that political texts are attempting to persuade the reader and should be interpreted carefully. This is particularly difficult when you are researching in a country and you are less familiar with the historical background and contemporary workings of its political situation.

International sources such as the United Nations and its various divisions offer statistical databases, policy documents and publications on their websites. These include, for example, the Organisation for Economic Cooperation and Development (OECD) www.oecd.org, UNICEF www.unicef.org, International Labour Organisation www.ilo.org, etc., and Eurostat which provides data on the EU and candidate countries (http://epp.eurostat.ec. europa.eu/portal/page/portal/eurostat/home) will have often waded through the methodological minefields of combining and comparing data that have been collected differently from each country and already made the necessary adjustments. This information can therefore be used to place national data within a broader context. As with national governments these organisations are not politically neutral − each will have their own agenda so their policy documents and publications can be analysed. International non-governmental organisations (NGOs) and charities such as Oxfam are also increasingly collecting and publishing their own research findings, many of which are available via the internet.

Where available, a potentially valuable 'official' source of data is national censuses. Many 'developed' countries conduct a census – not to produce data for researchers but as a monitoring and policy development tool. In Britain a census has been conducted every ten years since 1801 and it has collected data on all those individuals who completed the survey, but the published data are aggregated. It is important to remember that all statistical data are socially constructed and the researcher should therefore ask some hard questions about the data they are about to use. Paul Cloke et al. (2004: 54) suggest the following:

- Why was the information constructed?

- To which government policies does it relate?

- Have policy concerns influenced which data were constructed and in what ways?

Depending upon the nature of your research topic, a final set of organisations that can provide relevant data would be companies. The internet has revolutionised researchers' ability to access data on many companies through their own websites, the publication of their annual reports (via company websites and through regulatory bodies such as the Security and Exchanges Commission in the USA, www.sec.gov), and through online industry analyst reports. In the not too distant past, information on the financial and operational status of firms was available only by requesting hard copies that had to come by post. Now the websites of many large companies will hold electronic copies of their annual reports and press releases, with some going back as far as 1999. Rather than just providing simplistic data such as their turnover in 2009, for example, it is now possible to conduct more sophisticated analyses of the quantitative data and qualitative discourses contained in company annual reports and associated documents. Just as in the case of governmental sources, these reports present the company and its financial position in a carefully crafted manner that is designed to encourage confidence in the management of the company, its strategies and its future for investment.

Online archives

While it is possible to find documentation on the internet, it is also possible to find out about archival collections online and, increasingly, to access the archives themselves over the internet. For example, the UK censuses from 1841 to 1901 are now all available online. Miles Ogborn (2010: 97–8) provides details of some UK-specific online archives which demonstrates that quite a broad range of sources are now accessible, including a digital library of primary and secondary sources for the history of Britain (www.british-history.ac.uk); the Great British Historical GIS project, which makes available geographically located social, economic and demographic data (from 1801 to 2001) and the GIS through which they can be mapped (www.visionofbritain.org.uk); and the National Maritime Museum's many collections (www.nmm.ac.uk/collections). The availability of such resources to a wider community of researchers (or rather, those with access to the internet) is a positive development and the electronic online archives also enable the resources to be searched in different and often more comprehensive ways.

As virtual archives are being established we are also witnessing the development of more exciting and innovative ways of collecting, storing, and presenting documentary evidence that can further inspire researchers. Gary McCulloch (2004: 35) discusses two such projects that, for him, undermine existing assumptions about documentary research. The first is the Centropa project (www.centropa.org) which seeks to combine oral histories with family photographs to produce a 'cyber-museum giving a voice to the last generation of east European Jews who survived the Holocaust' (*Guardian* 2003a: 17). It puts together 1,300+ interviews with elderly Jews with over 25,000 digitised images, converting life history interviews and family snapshots into documentary records. For McCulloch this is a radical step as it establishes a close connection between the private suffering of so many Jewish families and the public tragedy of the Holocaust.

The second project is the website www.movinghere.org.uk which documents two hundred years of Caribbean, Irish, Jewish and South Asian migration to Britain. The site consists of more than 200,000 digitised sources including film, photographs and texts from 30 archives, libraries, and museums. The project also has a broader significance according to the lead coordinator of the project Sarah Tyacke, who stated that 'archives are moving away from their "dusty and musty" image by making these documents available at the click of a mouse' (*Guardian* 2003b: 7). For a more detailed discussion of how you can use archives for fieldwork, both in preparation and in the field itself, see Chapter 6.

As you begin to learn more about your field site, particularly through the methods we have suggested here – identifying and contacting relevant individuals and organisations, and using online archives – your research plans will develop and become more realistic. It may be that your topic or focus changes as you become more aware of data sources and of the relative viability of different research methods, some of which will depend upon assistance from locals. Thus, with thorough and imaginative pre-field research, your plans and proposals will become sharper. Joseph Assan describes how some students, when planning research in a rural district of Rwanda, were able to identify and focus their projects. Though conducting research in an unusually challenging environment, their experiences provided lessons for other students who were planning fieldwork in other parts of the world.

Postcard 3.2: Developing a Field Research Project in Rwanda, by Joseph Assan

The idea of devising and undertaking field research projects in developing countries has been an exciting but a daunting process/experience for my students. This postcard discusses the process in the context of Rwanda. Two students – Niamh and Melaine – were keen to develop projects focusing on ecosystem services and sustainable livelihoods around conservation parks. A third student – Andy – was interested in the impact of international organised crime and illicit activities (including trafficking, drugs and money laundering) on the political economy and societies of developing countries. This raised various challenges: Niamh and Melaine wanted to stay together for security and logistical reasons so they needed to find a conservation park that was able to host both of them; Andy needed to find individuals and/or organisations that were prepared to discuss his (sensitive) topic.

Each student defined three associated research questions and tried to develop a proposal. This proved a challenge because they had little local knowledge. They started by reviewing national and regional development reports and studies on the environment, development and economy, which were produced by government agencies in Rwanda and neighbouring countries. Most of this information was obtained at the university library and via the internet.

This process allowed all three students to establish potential challenges, issues of research concern, and gaps for further research, as well as ethical implications for the proposed projects. The students also wrote to various agencies and international organisations located in Africa and in Europe for current reports on their respective topics. Andy, for example, contacted Interpol and the CIA for various suggestions and documents that turned out to be very helpful.

The students also used their contacts to get in touch with a visiting professor at the National University of Rwanda. Their initial emails to this professor had gone unanswered, but he proved more responsive when contacted through a mutual acquaintance, an Ethiopian postgraduate student. The professor then put Niamh, Melaine and Andy in touch with the park management team and also with staff at the Rwanda Development Board who oversaw conservation programmes in the nearby Nyungwe National Park (the only Black Mountain Forest left in Africa).

(Continued)

(Continued)

Given the sensitive nature of the research there it was necessary to go through a series of bureaucratic research clearances to secure permission for the students to undertake their research on their proposed topics. This involved submitting draft research proposals in advance; these were forwarded to the Rwandan Development Board for approval, which was subsequently granted.

This postcard from Rwanda illustrates the importance of making contacts in your proposed fieldsite, well before you plan to go there, and it also shows how the imaginative use of contacts can help open doors for your fieldwork.

Figure 3.6 Students from Trinity College Dublin conduct a 'key informants interview' in Bisate, a rural community in Northern Rwanda, while members of the community look on. Photograph by Joseph Assan

RISK ASSESSMENT AND FIELDWORK PRACTICALITIES

Whilst exciting and rewarding, being in the field can also be dangerous and uncomfortable. Imagine the following scenarios, all of which have taken place:

- You are with a group of students in Botswana, driving in a rural area. Your vehicle turns over on a dusty road, six hours' drive from the nearest hospital.

- Your entire field class – including staff – are struck down with a severe bout of gastro-enteritis. You are in a foreign country and do not have the language skills to explain this to a doctor.

- You arrive in a country in which, for religious reasons, all the shops and banks are closed the day you arrive. You have no cash and are hungry!

Each of these situations will make you wish that you had planned properly. This section explains the preparations and considerations you would have been wise to make.

It is therefore of paramount importance that institutions and individual students work together to minimise the risks and hazards involved in fieldwork. It is sometimes easy for human geographers to associate hazards in research with physical geographers climbing mountains or working in extreme weather conditions. However, working in urban environments also presents risks as the potential dangers of working or travelling alone or conducting interviews in unfamiliar residential areas may be just as great (Lee, 1995). This section will offer some guidance on how to achieve this, not only for your safety, but also in order to aid the research process. Rest assured that, while fieldwork can be a risky business, considering the variety of locations in which geographers undertake fieldwork and the amount of time they spend in the field, only a few incidents and accidents do actually take place.

Who is responsible for your safety in the field?

Given the diversity of different types of fieldwork (and associated levels of staff supervision) and range of contexts (i.e. different environments and in groups or individually) each presents a range of health and safety considerations. As a result the roles and responsibilities of both students and staff may change accordingly (Bullard 2010). Levels of responsibility for your safety are multi-scalar, ranging from national government to yourself as an individual. National legislation exists in many countries that provides a legal framework for health and safety – both in general, and often with specific guidance for fieldwork. These forms of regulation will be addressed by your institution which must assume full responsibility for risk management as well as a duty of care and ensure that fieldtrips are health and safety compliant (Herrick 2010). However, your safety in the field is not solely the responsibility of your institution and its staff members! Your institution will expect you to take seriously the process of risk assessment for your proposed project and will probably provide a standard template for this (Flowerdew and Martin 2005). In addition, participants in fieldwork must give 'informed consent' to any potential risks as well as committing to 'reasonable behaviour' in the face of these anticipated risks. As Robin Flowerdew and David Martin state 'the purpose of risk assessment is to ensure that potential hazards are fully recognized and that appropriate actions are taken to mitigate them: in completing the risk assessment you commit yourself to taking these appropriate actions!' (2005: 3). Risk in fieldwork incorporates adherence to institutional frameworks and a consideration of your actions whilst in the field: note also that it should be an important factor when planning your research. In addition to the physical hazards, research involving personal interactions with others may present emotional and psychological hazards and Flowerdew and Martin advise that no one should 'be a hero for the sake of their research project' (2005: 3). All research methods will have some aspects that are risky – for example, conducting an interview may involve meeting a stranger in an unfamiliar place – so completing a risk assessment enables you to be aware of, and to minimise, the potential risks of your research.

How do you conduct a risk assessment?

As stated above, your institution will have procedures in place for completing any required risk assessments. These will probably require you to have a discussion with your supervisor/fieldtrip coordinator prior to completing and signing these.

- *Identify the hazards*: what can reasonably be foreseen as having the potential to cause harm?

- *Identify who might be harmed*: is the fieldworker exposed to a hazard or is his/her fieldwork activity causing a hazard to other people? How might people be harmed?

- *Evaluate the risks*: consider the likelihood and severity of any hazards occurring. Are existing controls sufficient to reduce the hazard?

- *Record the findings.*

- *Review the assessment periodically.*

In practical terms, stages 1–3 are the most significant aspects to consider while preparing for, and conducting, research in the field. As with coming up with a research idea, this process of risk assessment may seem difficult if you have not previously visited your field location. This may also be true if you are familiar with the site as you might not have considered the risks in relation to conducting research there. Regardless of whether a formal written risk assessment is required by your institution, it is your responsibility as a researcher to complete this process. Upon arrival at the field site, you should review your risk assessment to include any risks that you did not foresee (stage 5). These should be noted down and you must then think about how you will minimise these. This is of particular importance when you are conducting unsupervised research and you should report any changes to your assessment to the fieldtrip staff.

What equipment do you need to bring?

It is a common misconception that human geographers, unlike our physical geography counterparts who seem to require vehicles loaded with measuring equipment and even inflatable boats, can enter the field armed only with a clipboard. There are some core pieces of equipment which you should bring along with you:

- *Appropriate clothing*: fieldtrips often involve a lot of walking, so make sure you have suitable walking shoes or the trip will be very uncomfortable. Even urban-based fieldtrips may include visits to more rural areas. Bring clothing that is suitable for the climate (i.e. a waterproof coat) and your research environment (i.e. you will need some smart clothes if you are conducting corporate interviews). This may seem rather obvious, but on every trip there will be students who have not brought suitable clothing!

- *Writing tools*: clearly you will need a method of recording your observations and research findings. A notebook and pen are the minimum requirements.

- *Maps of the fieldsite*: it may be more convenient to buy this once you arrive, but if you source a map before entering the field you will be more easily able to plan your research (and mark sites on it).

- *Printed copies of your fieldtrip handbook/handouts.*

- *Details of your travel itinerary, accommodation and emergency contacts.*

Additional practical considerations will vary depending upon the location of your fieldtrip and the methods of data collection you have chosen. Table 3.1 provides a checklist of possible considerations. You should think through which of these apply to you and act accordingly.

Table 3.1 Quick checklist for fieldwork preparation and equipment

Fieldtrip requirements	Notes	Tick if this applies to you
Health issues		
Vaccinations	Find out if you will require vaccinations. This is highly likely if you are travelling to a developing country and/or tropical areas. Check your national government advisory services (available on the internet).	
Prescribed Medication	Make sure you have sufficient supplies of any medications you take. Allow extra in case of travel delays. Replenishments may not be readily available in the field. It is also advisable to bring a letter from your doctor explaining your medical condition.	
First Aid Kit	You should invest in a small first aid kit that you can carry with you, even if you are researching in an urban area with access to hospital facilities	
Health Insurance	Check the circumstances in your field location. Travel outside home countries will normally require health insurance.	
Food and Drink	Be careful regarding sudden changes in your diet. Avoid drinking alcohol in excess. Check if you can drink the local water, and if not, make sure you have sufficient supplies of safe drinking water.	
Environmental Conditions	Research the local conditions in your field location. What will the weather be like?	
Safety and Insurance		
Travel Insurance	Check if travel insurance is included in the cost of your fieldtrip (i.e. taken out by your university). If not, take out your own insurance. In either case, bring copies of your policy and emergency contact numbers.	
Local safety and personal security	Make yourself aware of the safety issues that are particular to your field location (for example, high rates of pick-pocketing, dangerous road travel, etc.). Investigate how to access help if necessary (such as police).	

(Continued)

Table 3.1 (Continued)

Fieldtrip requirements	Notes	Tick if this applies to you
Valuables	Do not bring any unnecessary high-value items with you. Find out if you will have access to a secure place to store other valuables such as your passport (for example, a hotel safe or hostel locker).	
Baggage		
Size!	Travel light. Be aware that you may have to carry your luggage for some distance.	
Appropriate Clothing	Make sure that you have clothing appropriate to the climate and local customs of the field location. Be sensitive to local modesty (i.e. covering shoulders; not having bare legs). Also make sure that you have clothes that are appropriate for your research, for example smart clothes for formal interviews.	
Toiletries	If you are travelling to less developed countries you should be aware that some toiletries (such as contact lens solution, tampons, sun cream) are much more difficult (or expensive) to obtain.	
Computing Equipment	Investigate the availability of computing facilities in the field location. Are internet connections and/or internet cafes widely available? If so what is the cost? Does your accommodation offer these facilities? Will you bring your laptop and, if so, do you have the necessary adaptors to charge it?	
Cameras/Mobile Phones	Cameras and mobile phones have made some aspects of doing research much easier – it is easier to contact staff, other group members, and research participants by phone and to record field observations using photography (see Chapter 6). Find out if your model of phone will work in the field location, and if so, what the rates of use are. In many countries it is possible to buy/rent a local mobile cheaply.	
Tape Recorder/ Dictaphone	Once you have planned your research and chosen your methods, you will have to decide what equipment is required. For example, if you are interviewing you will need a tape recorder to record the interview, if your mobile phone does not have this facility. Make sure that you have tapes/memory sticks and spare batteries.	
Presents	You may consider bringing small mementos/souvenirs from your home country to give to research participants as a thank you for their assistance. These should be an inexpensive (but thoughtful and appropriate) token, such as a postcard showing a famous landscape in your university town/city.	

Source: Adapted from Robson et al. (1997)

SUMMARY

This chapter has discussed the stages of preparation required for fieldwork, from developing a research idea to forming a concrete research strategy and subsequent consideration of the practical dimensions of fieldwork planning including equipment needs and risk assessments. The key points of the chapter were:

- It is extremely important that you invest some time in planning your fieldtrip.

- If you have been asked to come up with your own research idea this may seem daunting. The chapter suggested that there are many sources of inspiration and/or information that can help you form a research focus. Reading around your topic is a crucial part of this process.

- There are some typical traps that we can fall into when planning and executing a research strategy. By reflecting on your own learning and planning processes you may be able to identify with one or more of the potential pitfalls and thereby begin to overcome these.

- In many universities there are some institutional checks that have been designed to ensure your safety and impact on your research site. These include a risk assessment, which was discussed in this chapter alongside issues of practical fieldwork planning and ethics approval which is addressed in detail in Chapter 4.

CONCLUSION

The key message of this chapter is that preparation is everything. The amount of time and thought that needs to go into preparing to conduct fieldwork is substantial and there is a positive relationship between length of time invested and rewards gained.

FURTHER READING/KEY TEXT(S)

- Silverman, D. (2000) *Doing Qualitative Research: A Practical Handbook*. London: SAGE. This includes case studies and examples of students' experiences in the field as well as offering practical advice on planning qualitative research. Chapter 4 offers guidance on how to identify an original topic and Chapter 5 provides details on how to select a topic together with a further discussion of Silverman's advice on avoiding pitfalls.

- It can also be a good idea to buy a travel guide for your fieldwork destination such as a *Rough Guide*, *Lonely Planet* or another student-friendly travel guide. Travel guides are also increasingly available on the web.

4

ETHICS: POSITIONING YOURSELF AND ENCOUNTERING OTHERS

OVERVIEW

This chapter addresses the following questions:

- What ethical questions should you ask yourself and how can you formulate answers to these?
- Will you be required to complete a formal ethics form? How and why should you do this?
- How do you communicate with research participants about your research?
- How can you think about, and begin to formulate, your approach to the field and how you will interact with others?

The chapter offers a range of different perspectives on how others have engaged with the field, raising challenging questions about what it means to do research and how our actions can impact on others. Your role is to apply this to your own research context.

Fieldwork has been described as a 'brash, awkward, hit-and-run encounter of one sensibility with others' (Kumar 1992: 1). Your job is to see that your own fieldwork is none of these things! You can do this by interrogating the ethics of proposed research before you begin. To start to understand the ethical issues associated with fieldwork, consider the following scenarios:

- You are visiting Australia and are interested in urban Aboriginal communities. You have read about the high levels of deprivation in these 'settlements' and the histories of tense relationships between Aborigines and researchers from outside their communities. You are wondering about whether it would be right to try to contact and seek interviews with residents of a particular Aboriginal Settlement.

- You are conducting research in Central America and have found that some local people find you attractive. You find this flattering and exciting, and also sense that responding to their advances may pay off in your research, gaining access to individuals and communities. What should you do?

- You would like to interview the owners of small businesses in Europe but you know they are busy and you are worried about taking up their time with little to offer in return. You are also concerned about how to ask for information that they may feel is commercially sensitive. How should you approach these business owners? And how should you treat the data you collect?

- You are on a fieldtrip in West Africa. You have justified this to yourself on academic and professional grounds, but as you encounter people much less privileged than yourself you begin to feel uneasy. As a team of physical geographers in similar circumstances asked themselves, 'Why were we doing this research anyway? Whom were we really trying to help? Were we just research tourists on a "tropical jolly"?' (Mistry et al. 2009: 86)

In order to work your way through dilemmas such as these, you will need to understand some of the broader ethical issues associated with fieldwork and anticipate the specific ethical dimensions of your own research in the field. Increasingly you will be formally required to do this, since university ethics committees will routinely scrutinise projects before students are allowed to begin their research. This scrutiny revolves around the potential impacts of projects on people who are 'researched' and are referred to as research participants or informants. It is vital for you to understand how to navigate formal ethical processes. However, it is even more important that you understand the fundamental issues involved, regardless of institutional formalities, since this can equip you to design and conduct research that not only avoids harm but also potentially benefits informants and their communities as well as enhances your own understanding of your encounters in the field and the knowledge they produce.

To navigate formal ethical clearance procedures and also to take ownership of your own ethical dilemmas, you need a clear understanding of the ethical issues at stake in fieldwork: these are the questions all fieldworkers need to consider. This next section sets out a series of ethical questions that have been raised in the geographical literature, questions that you will need to ask about your own research. The following section then explains how you can use this understanding to design ethically sound field projects and gain the formal ethical clearance that will be required before you begin.

ETHICAL QUESTIONS

Your fieldwork is likely to make some kind of difference to a series of individuals, groups and/ or organisations: these are the people you will meet in the field, some of whom will give of their time in order to answer your questions or help out with your projects, while others may just see you snooping round their neighbourhood and wonder, indeed perhaps worry, about what exactly you are up to. The first step in anticipating the possible consequences of your fieldwork is to identify those who might be affected by it: most directly, this will be your informants. You can then begin to explore the possible intended and unintended consequences as regards their 'dignity, privacy and basic rights' (Momsen 2006: 47). The most important ethical questions you must ask are as follows.

Is there a risk that your fieldwork will harm informants? What steps can be taken either to prevent or to mitigate this harm?

These concerns are particularly acute where vulnerable people are involved, so researchers interested in groups such as street children, political dissidents and homeless people tend to pay more attention to ethical questions than others whose research involves less sensitive groups such as business leaders and people in public office. Imagine, for example, that you are interested in observing and/or interviewing undocumented workers. Might this cause anxiety to these individuals, who may perhaps worry that you are working for the immigration authorities or police? Or might it put them in danger, if their employers see them cooperating with you? Furthermore, you may not only risk the safety or wellbeing of individuals, but also that of their families and communities. To avoid harming informants you may have to rethink your project completely, or it might be enough to modify your data collection methods or the ways in which you write up and circulate findings. Kim England, who had begun research on lesbian-positive and lesbian-owned businesses in Toronto, became concerned that her findings could harm members of these groups if these got into the wrong hands: as a result she decided not to publish them (Nast 1994; Staeheli and Lawson 1994). In other cases, it may be sufficient to preserve the anonymity of informants by using pseudonyms (made-up names) and generic identities (for example, age, gender or occupation). Where visual images are used individual identities may need to be protected by obscuring the faces of those depicted or, once again, by withholding or destroying data (Johnsen et al. 2008). It is generally assumed that informants and other individuals named or depicted in the context of research will be anonymous unless they explicitly waive this option or choose to be named. This is explained in more detail in the second part of this chapter.

Is your research potentially exploitative? Who or what is your research for?

Addressing the question of whether and how you can justify fieldwork, in Chapter 2, we focused upon the potential benefits to you and set to one side broader questions about how your research might impact upon others. Dina Abbott (2006) challenges us to frame the 'why' question more broadly by interrogating the politics and legitimacy of fieldwork. Tariq Jazeel and Colin McFarlane present this as a question of responsibility, of asking 'what is at stake when a group, a place or a topic is researched, spoken and written about?' (2007: 782). The most tangible way to approach this challenge is to ask whether fieldwork has been designed for your personal gain alone or whether you have balanced this with the interests of participants. Your interests, as we discussed in Chapter 2, will include gaining academic and employment skills; obtaining credits and grades; satisfying your curiosity; and even generating intellectual property that may have some commercial value. Illustrating this, Cindi Katz has reflected on her own motives and interests in conducting fieldwork – in Sudan and New York – and admitted that career interests have shaped the ways in which she has worked and published. She has also acknowledged that her 'field projects all have probably been more beneficial to [her] than to [the participants]' (Katz 1994: 71–72).

What effects would you like your fieldwork to have upon stakeholders?

The literature on fieldwork – particularly in the Global South and/or among vulnerable and/or disadvantaged communities – illustrates how a growing number of researchers have not only tried not to harm informants and other stakeholders, but have also actively sought to benefit them. This can mean interrogating each aspect of fieldwork, not only your relationships with participants but also those with others in the field who support your trip, for example by cooking for you and driving you around (see Powell 2008; see also Postcard 4.1 below). Katz, for example, tried to balance her own self interests in conducting research with the interests of informants and their families and communities by providing information that might underpin changes in agricultural practices and development planning (Katz 1994; Brydon 2006).

As an undergraduate conducting a small field project you may feel sceptical about whether you can really give anything back to informants and you should be realistic rather than overly ambitious about this, as we explain in Chapter 8 in our discussion of Action Research. You are not alone. Others have reflected on the difficulty of 'giving something back'. As regards their research in Vietnam, Steffanie Scott, Fiona Miller and Kate Lloyd (2006: 32) reflected that 'we were all keenly aware of the burden imposed in asking for people's time for an interview without being able to offer much specific benefit in return'. They also noted that it was not only ethically desirable to give something back to participants; promising to do so also pays off, encouraging potential beneficiaries to invest time and energy in the research. Consequently, the business community, investors, foreign aid providers and project collaborators can sometimes face a warmer reception than social science researchers (Scott et al. 2006: 35).

Reciprocity is therefore not only ethically but also practically desirable and this is reflected in the propensity of participants to make long-term commitments to research projects. Stan Stevens, a professor who has been privileged to spend many years conducting sustained fieldwork among indigenous peoples in Nepal, suggests that 'short-term researchers may get away with carrying out grab-and-run research, taking what they can and clearing out with little regard for reciprocity and responsibility', whereas longer-term fieldwork tends to be more responsible, if only by necessity. The latter 'necessitates locally responsive research, listening to and responding to what indigenous people think is important and working on behalf of their interests and concerns' (2001: 72). For Stevens, then, responsible research means engaging with researched communities throughout the fieldwork process, allowing respondents to help shape the research agenda, and it also means feeding the findings back in an accessible and meaningful form. This is something you can do, whatever the scale of your project. For example, you can send copies of your field report to the communities who helped you with your research and previous experience suggests that this will be well received. If this is too technical or long, you could write a summary report in appropriate language and send that instead. Other examples of previous research illustrate some imaginative solutions to this general problem of how to give something back and work towards some kind of reciprocity. Elizabeth Chacko, conducting interviews with villagers in India, noticed that few people had access to cameras, and so she made gifts of her photographs which were both received and 'cherished' (2004: 60).

Reciprocity can be brought into fieldwork in more fundamental ways too. Chacko looked for ways to make her interviews less one-sided: 'Women also asked me questions during the interview itself, and in the spirit of reciprocity and equalising the power balance, I often let the respondent take on the role of interviewer' (2004: 60). Others suggest that fieldwork should ideally involve reciprocal learning processes: 'research partnerships' involving 'mutually beneficial opportunities for shared learning, exchange of ideas and the advancement of knowledge' (Scott et al. 2006: 31). In Postcard 4.1 below, Bill Gould illustrates how this kind of knowledge exchange is possible, describing how students from the UK interacted with their counterparts in Tanzania during a fieldtrip there.

What sort of relationships would you like to cultivate with research participants? What can you learn from these relationships?

If reciprocity is a research ideal, so is fieldwork in which the power differentials between researchers and informants are ethically navigated. Western academic researchers tend to approach the field from positions of relative power. Sarah McLafferty argues that, 'except in rare cases, the researcher holds a "privileged" position – by deciding what questions to ask, directing the flow of discourse, interpreting interview and observational material, and deciding where and in what form it should be presented' (cited in Rose 1997: 307). This privilege may be compounded by the researcher's relative wealth and power: Tariq Jazeel and Colin McFarlane (2009: 110) reflected on how their own 'metropolitan privilege' shaped their research in the Global South, while others have referred to the privilege associated with professional status and class (Dowling 2005). Undergraduates, many of whom will be running up debts in order to take fieldtrips, and who may be young and without paid employment, may not recognise the picture of themselves as privileged. Certainly, this description applies more to professional academics and funded postgraduates. Nevertheless, it helps to understand that on some level even undergraduates will conduct fieldwork within the context of an uneven field. In some cases you may have the upper hand in field encounters, since it is you who will be asking the questions and setting the agenda and this will shape the knowledge that is produced and the uses to which it is put. On the other hand the opposite can sometimes be true and you may feel intimidated or wrong-footed, for example if you are interviewing elites, if you are a female student interviewing a man, or if you feel disadvantaged by knowing less about the subject than the people you are researching.

Robyn Dowling (2005: 27) argues that it is best to begin by acknowledging the realities of power in the field and interrogating this by asking 'what sort of power dynamics you expect between yourself and your informants'. These dynamics can be very challenging, so much so that some commentators would counsel against fieldwork in which the power differentials are too great. Abbott, for example, is severely critical of a British university's fieldtrip to the small West African state of Gambia, which she argues re-enacts racialised colonial relationships. She asks: 'How can I, as a non-white person, reinforce a geographical tradition of fieldwork that exposes myself and students (mostly white) to the "history of slavery" re-enacted within a framework of skewed power relations?' (Abbott 2006: 331). Gillian Rose's prognosis for fieldwork is equally negative, arguing that this geographical tradition is too closely associated with macho ('masculinist') and imperialist practices, white European men striding round the world and lording it over others, always seeking out 'the exotic, spectacular and remote' (Rose 1993: 70, quoting Stoddart 1986: 55).

Sometimes, however, you might be able to navigate power differences in ethical ways. Reflecting on her fieldwork in Central America, Julie Cupples presents an engaging example of how this might be done. She describes a 'heightened state of awareness and stimulation' including 'intellectual stimulation but also sexual desire' (2002: 385). She does not rush to any moral or ethical conclusions but is concerned in the first instance with understanding her own feelings and locating these within an understanding of power dynamics in the field: it is then that she comes to make her own judgements about how to navigate all of this. These inform her decision about whether and how a sexual dimension might be allowed to enter her relationships with research participants. This raises complex ethical issues: what anthropologists have called 'sex with the natives' is widely seen as unethical (2002: 382; Whitehead and Conway 1986), even though some researchers have described and tried to justify such encounters (Rubinstein 2004). Sex in the field as elsewhere is also potentially risky; 'the fieldworker is open both to the pleasure of sexual intimacy and to the violence of sexual intimidation' (Coffey 2005: 425). On the other hand, the fieldworker cannot leave their sexuality at home even if they wished to, since whether we like it or not 'we are also positioned by those whom we research' (Cupples 2002: 383). Julie Cupples has reflected on her relationships with participants and others in the field: 'at times, men feigned interest in my research project in an attempt to spend time with me. I did, however, sometimes take advantage of such interest and used them to further my research and make connections with places and people' (2002: 386). Thus while certain expressions of sexuality may be unethical in fieldwork Amanda Coffey argues that we have much to learn, through sexuality, about the wider set of social and power dynamics that exist within the field, including 'the relationships between fieldworker (whose reception will be a function of his or her age, gender, race, sexuality, and other forms of identity); the relational nature of the research process (establishing and negotiating field roles, relationships, boundaries); and the possible emotions of fieldwork (love, hate, excitement, risk, power, belonging, alienation)' (Coffey 2005: 410).

Understanding your fieldwork in this way – as a series of encounters between yourself as an outsider and the people and places that make up a field – you begin to think more explicitly and critically about your own presence in the field: how you behave and are perceived and how this affects the kinds of encounters you have and what you find out. As McDowell put it, 'we must recognize and take account of our position, as well as that of our research participants, and write this into our research practice' (1992: 409). In fieldwork as in other forms of geographical research our circumstances will shape what we can find out and know. Acknowledging our 'positionality', it is possible to be explicit about the limits of what we know – since 'all knowledge is produced in specific circumstances and that those circumstances shape it in some way' (Rose 1997: 305). This is partly a matter of intellectual rigour – understanding the limits of our knowledge – and partly of ethics, since it allows us to interrogate the uneven power relations through which knowledge is generally produced.

Postcard 4.1: Sustainable Development in Tanzania, by Bill Gould (this illustrates how ethical principles including reciprocity and the full consideration of informants and stakeholder groups can be incorporated into the heart of fieldwork research design and methodology)

Liverpool University geography students have had the opportunity to take a seven-week-long field course entitled 'Sustainable Development in Tanzania'. This was readily taken up, despite the expectation that students would need to seek sponsorship (£1500 in 2000) to support themselves and also one Tanzanian student's participation in the course. The course originated as the optional field work component of an existing module in the Department of Geography in Dar es Salaam, but that had been severely hampered by lack of finance. In this partnership the British students directly supported the field experience of their Tanzanian counterparts. The course was delivered and assessed by members of the Department of Geography in the University of Dar es Salaam, with occasional inputs from Liverpool staff and a post-graduate in the field, and the travel arrangements, general infrastructure and social programme were facilitated in Tanzania by the established gap-year and young people's NGO, Students Partnership Worldwide (SPW).

(Continued)

(Continued)

The primary academic rationale for the course was to give the British students direct field experience of how farmers and communities sought to achieve – or failed to achieve – sustainable livelihoods. Students were exposed to local experiences in such matters as water management (notably in the irrigation furrow system on Mount Kilmanjaro), crop management to minimise risk (including experience of multi-cropping of ground vegetable, fruit and tree crops on shamba plots), and innovation in new intermediate technologies (e.g. wind power, low-energy stoves, renewable bio-energy). Direct field experience contributed to students' broader understandings of 'development'.

Much more fundamental to student learning, however, but clearly much less amenable to assessment or measurement, was the direct experience of living and working day to day in one of the poorest counties in the world. This was facilitated in no small measure by the continuous presence of a local SPW staff member, Andrew Kalinga, himself much the same age as the students, on all of these courses. Andrew's formal role was primarily administrative – to make sure the buses were there at the right time and the accommodation was secured – but critically it was also social, to give the students confidence about being in this new and strange environment. This included teaching them some simple but useful Swahili and also introducing students very directly and personally to such every-day activities as the hazards of travelling on a dala-dala (shared mini-bus), buying a beer or chips at a not-very-attractive local stall, ordering and eating food in a local restaurant, using a traditional toilet, and going to a public beach in Dar es Salaam. Gaining confidence in such basic activities at an early stage was important for establishing students' interactions and empathy with Tanzanians. Such an experiential introduction to living in the Third World, to the lived experience of most people, is not necessarily easily or quickly gained even with normal gap-year travel, and neither is it always available though standard 'island' field classes to such destinations. However, in this partnership format, with its local social as well as academic leadership, it assumed a prominence that added greatly to the actual and perceived value of the experience.

A further advantage to this partnership format was that the Liverpool students worked and lived alongside their Tanzanian counterparts in roughly equal numbers over the whole six weeks of

(Continued)

(Continued)

teaching, travelling, and field working. The courses began with some introductory work at the University of Dar es Salaam, with students living in the halls of residence (it was vacation time) before going into the field. Since some of the Tanzanians had had very little field experience in their own country and themselves had a distinct bias to urban and relatively wealthy backgrounds, the Liverpool students were at no major knowledge disadvantage in rural settings. The relationships between the Liverpool and Tanzania groups were not always easy (the Tanzanians were overwhelmingly male, generally older, and less outgoing), but they did work together in groups, where there was a lot of mutual learning and support, and this extended beyond the course work and directly into field accommodation in schools and other educational establishments, such as the Coffee Co-operative College in Moshi, and general off-course activities. The students lived, ate and socialised together, as well as working on, field presenting and writing up group projects, with the work groups deliberately formed to include students from both universities.

   The students acknowledged not only the academic merits of the course, but also the social and personal value of the experience and how it had been constructed. Andrew Kalinga become an iconic figure within the student community and when he visited Liverpool in 2000 the students from each of the cohorts he had been involved with welcomed him with great affection. They had begun to learn how to look at impoverished communities from the inside, from the lived experience of their members, from their lives of struggle as well as their cultures of fulfilment and joy, rather from the outside as technical development practitioners seeking only to alleviate poverty. Such learning can only grow out of a directed field experience.

DOING ETHICAL FIELDWORK: COMPLYING WITH ETHICAL SCRUTINY PROCEDURES

This chapter will now take a more practical turn, setting out the primary ethical considerations that undergraduate geography students engaged in fieldwork need to consider. This includes guidance on satisfying formal ethical review procedures which universities are increasingly imposing upon major projects including dissertations and fieldwork. These formal policies require students to understand the ethical dimensions of their research in order to satisfy the minimum ethical standard: not doing harm to the people or places involved in the research. As the previous sections have explained this is indeed a bare minimum and an understanding of ethical issues and debates can be more than a matter of formality and institutional bureaucracy; it can open up research agendas in imaginative and positive ways.

Ideas about ethical research have been formalised, through research agencies and funding bodies, and through disciplinary bodies and universities, such that formal codes of practice define ethical standards, with which researchers at all levels – from undergraduates to professors – are typically required to comply (Brydon 2006). These procedures apply most directly to discrete, substantial projects such as dissertations and also to individual and group research projects that are central to some fieldwork. They apply less directly to other kinds of fieldwork, such as site visits involving large numbers of students and field assignments that may be prescribed by the field leaders who may therefore take responsibility for considering the ethics of the fieldwork in question. Even in these cases, however, it is important for students to apply an understanding of the ethical issues set out above, thereby ensuring that your encounters with others and with each other are ethically sound and defensible.

Ethical procedures will vary between organisations and institutions as well as between countries and over time, but they do have a number of things in common. As Australian geographer Hilary Winchester has pointed out, these 'are not trivial matters, involving in my own university the completion of a substantial form and submission of the project design, consent form, and survey instrument' (1996: 117). The content and form of most ethical codes can be illustrated with reference to the 'ethics policy' used by the Royal Geographical Society (RGS), with respect to projects supported through one of its funding schemes. The RGS ethics code includes several themes that are particularly relevant to undergraduate fieldwork, so these are explained in detail in the following paragraphs (see italicised text).

The RGS-IBG requires the research it funds to be conducted in an ethical manner. The following considerations should therefore apply to all research supported by the RGS-IBG, whether through financial support, or implicit support through presentation at RGS-IBG, Research Group conferences, or other RGS-IBG events or publication in RGS-IBG journals:

- accurate reporting of findings, and a commitment to enabling others to replicate results where possible;

- fair dealing in respect of other researchers and their intellectual property;

- *confidentiality of information supplied by research subjects and anonymity of respondents (unless otherwise agreed with research subjects and respondents).*

Additionally, proposals may raise one or more of the following considerations:

- *the involvement of human participants;*

- research that may result in damage to natural or historic environments and artefacts; and

- the use of sensitive social, economic or political data.

The review process should be proportional to the likely risk (for example, research on vulnerable groups or at-risk populations demands more careful attention than other forms of research). Wherever necessary, appropriate consent should be obtained from or on behalf of participants or others affected by the research. (http://www.rgs.org last accessed 17 July 2010; emphasis added)

It is useful for students to see the RGS code because it identifies ethical issues that are relevant to Geography as a discipline, but undergraduates on fieldtrips are more likely to be required to conform to ethics policies that are published and enforced by individual institutions, namely universities and colleges. The following paragraphs explain the codes and criteria that are most relevant to you as a student. These revolve around ethical approaches to research involving human participants. Before focusing upon these issues, however, it is important to briefly acknowledge two other issues which the RGS ethics statement raises. First, ethical issues are not restricted to research directly involving human subjects but also relate to the collection and analysis of secondary data. In some cases strict rules will apply which you will be forced to respect. When using archives, for example, you will be required to specify what you wish to do with the data you collect and you may be prevented from quoting and reproducing what you find. And you will not be able to access certain forms of census data if there is a risk that individual households may be identified through these. Second, the RGS website refers to potential damage to the environment and to artefacts. Concerns about the immediate environmental consequences of research are generally more acute in physical rather than human geography, given the intrusive nature of some physical geography research: digging soil pits, for example, or removing samples from the natural environment (Maskall and Stokes 2008: 28–29). Still, human geographers also need to be aware of the potential environmental impacts of your work in the field. We have already raised the issue of fieldwork's carbon footprint in Chapter 1. Your fieldwork can also impact negatively on human environments, particularly when large numbers of students descend upon small communities or when fieldtrips repeatedly return to the same places (Livingstone et al. 1988). This may not only disrupt local life, it might also result in a saturation of the research environment, undermining the research as potential respondents become reluctant to participate or conditioned to respond in particular ways.

Codes governing appropriate conduct in particular localities may be formalised and enforced through laws and regulations or they may take the form of informal and/or unwritten cultural codes. These could, for example, relate to questions of clothing and manners. Denis Cosgrove used to tell an anecdote about how he managed to cause a stir in Tel Aviv's Ben Gurion Airport when dressed in a rather too short pair of shorts! And students we accompanied on a walking tour in the deprived Downtown Eastside of Vancouver have commented that they felt they were trespassing and peering unethically into other peoples' lives (see Figure 1.2). Their anxieties were not unfounded: one man shouted at the notebook- and camera-wielding group, asking if we would like to watch him 'shooting up'. In each of these examples ethical conduct is not simply a matter of students following rules laid down by others, but rather about becoming sensitive to ethical issues and taking responsibility for moral judgements on how to conduct fieldwork.

Human participants

The RGS ethics statement flags up the need for ethical scrutiny in research with 'The involvement of human participants'. Institutional ethical clearance procedures typically elaborate on this by asking the following questions. Any positive answer will flag up the study as requiring detailed scrutiny and possible rejection or modification.

- Does the study involve participants who are particularly vulnerable or unable to give informed consent (e.g. children, people with learning or communication disabilities, people in custody, people engaged in illegal activities such as drug-taking, your own students in an educational capacity)?

- Will the study require the co-operation of a gatekeeper for initial access to the groups or individuals to be recruited (e.g. students at school, members of a self-help group, residents of a nursing home)?

- Will it be necessary for participants, whose consent to participate in the study will be required, to take part without their knowledge at the time (e.g. covert observation using photography or video recording)?

- Does the study involve deliberately misleading the participants?

- Will the study require the discussion of sensitive topics that may cause distress or embarrassment to the participant or potential risk of disclosure to the researcher of criminal activity or child protection issues (e.g. sexual activity, criminal activity)?

- Could the study induce psychological stress or anxiety or cause harm or negative consequences beyond the risks encountered in normal life?

Communication

The key to ethical research involving human participants is clear communication: 'An ethical researcher' should be 'context-sensitive, honest and "up front" about her/his own interests and how they affect the research and the kinds of relationship s/he has with members of the research(ed) community' (Brydon 2006: 28). Good communication is likely to involve written and/or spoken explanations of the project, which would make it clear that participation would be voluntary and that a participant would be free to withdraw at any time; would explain what this participation entails; would seek informed consent, in writing if appropriate, from relevant individuals or communities; would offer to provide feedback on any findings when the study is complete. These principles should not be applied too rigidly, since most are appropriate to or feasible in some contexts but not others. Figure 4.1 offers a flowchart to guide your thinking as you design your research and consider its ethical impacts. As you will see, your project idea might require some adaptation in order to effectively respond to any ethical dilemmas you may face.

Ethical criteria are not simply a checklist to be addressed mechanically, but are a series of issues that the researcher must be sensitive to and must generally think through contextually. For example, it may not be appropriate to gain individuals' consent for ethnographic projects in which the sample of participants is not defined in advance and in which groups rather than individuals are being observed (Chapter 8 explains this technique in more detail). If you were researching a music festival or street demonstration, imagine trying to explain your project to everyone present or everyone you meet however briefly: 'If they do not think you have lost a few screws, they will certainly become bored and embarrassed by the spiel' (Hoggart et al. 2002: 271). And while transparency is generally desirable and safer for the researcher there may be instances in which it is ethically defensible to conduct covert research, in which researchers will either not explain or will actively conceal the nature and purpose of their research (McDowell 1997).

How, then, can you explain your project and recruit participants? It may be enough for you to devise a short spoken explanation which you can simply deliver when it is needed, perhaps over the phone or in person. Ethics committees will sometimes require evidence of this, for example in the form of a taped conversation (Scheyvens et al. 2003: 144). In other cases, it may be too formal to tape verbal permissions. Elizabeth Chaplin, whose research involves taking pictures of people, explains that in her experience it is enough simply to ask someone whether they are willing to be photographed and then to seek written permission before publishing the photograph (2004: 45). For most fieldwork projects you will need to devise a written statement that will vary from a few sentences you can include in an email to a longer and more formal statement. Or you may need both a spoken and written explanation (in appropriate local languages). In each case you will need to tailor your statement to your particular audience, considering for example their age and literacy and requesting 'informed consent' which has been defined as follows:

> Informed consent is when a potential participant freely and with full understanding of the research agrees to be part of the project. It is premised on the notion that the person has a complete and thorough understanding of the aims and processes of the research project, what the research will be used for, such as policy formation and publications, and who will have access to the information gathered. Knowledge of the research comes from the researcher fully and honestly explaining what the research is about and providing an opportunity for the participant to ask questions about the research at any time. (Scheyvens et al. 2003: 142)

All of this should be explained in clear and simple language so that the implications of taking part are understood both by potential participants and, where applicable, by their guardians (such as parents, teachers, and caregivers). The following extracts, taken from one particular university's ethics policy, provide useful and more generally helpful guidance on preparing a Participant Information Sheet (see Figure 4.2). Note that these guidelines are detailed and suggest more information than you are likely to require in a typical undergraduate field project. They are included for the sake of completeness – so that you can pick out those sections that are relevant to your particular project and because this can be helpful for your broader research skills training, which you may need to draw upon later in your studies or when you are employed.

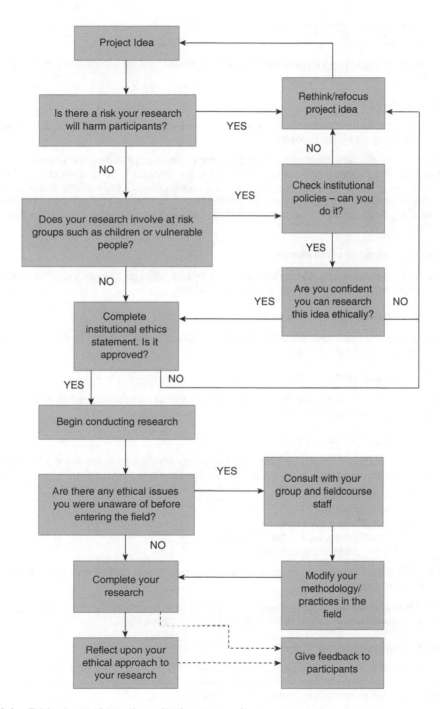

Figure 4.1   Ethical considerations in the research process

1 **Title of Study**

Your study title should be the same on all related documents and explain the study in simple English.

2 **Invitation Paragraph**

Invite the participant to take part in the study and be careful to make sure that it does not sound as if they are being pressured or coerced:

e.g. You are being invited to participate in a research study. Before you decide whether to participate, it is important for you to understand why the research is being done and what it will involve. Please take time to read the following information carefully and feel free to ask us if you would like more information or if there is anything that you do not understand. We would like to stress that you do not have to accept this invitation and should only agree to take part if you want to.

3 **What is the purpose of the study?**

In lay terms, with all technical terms and acronyms defined, you should explain why the study is being done, e.g. the background, aims and objectives, etc.

4 **Why have I been chosen to take part?**

Briefly explain the reasons why and how you have chosen to invite participants and also how many others will be taking part.

5 **Do I have to take part?**

It should be made clear that participation is voluntary and that participants are free to withdraw at anytime without explanation and without incurring a disadvantage.

6 **What will happen if I take part?**

In lay terms, you should provide an explanation of exactly what will be asked of the participant and what will happen during the research. For example, you should explain clearly:

- what the methods are.
- who the researchers are.
- who will be carrying out the tests.
- what the duration/frequency of the tests will be.
- what the participant's responsibilities are.

When writing this section, think about what details you would want to know if you were to take part in a research study.

Participants should also be made aware if the research involves any audio/visual recording and this should be made clear in both the information sheet and consent form.

7 **Are there any risks to taking part?**

Please explain whether there are any perceived disadvantages or risks involved. Explain that if the participant should experience any discomfort or disadvantage as part of the research that this should be made known to the researcher(s) immediately.

8 **Are there any benefits in taking part?**

Any benefits (at the time of participation or in the future) should be explained. If there is no intended benefit this should also be made clear.

9 **Will my participation be kept confidential?**

You should inform the participant how the data are to be collected, how these will be stored securely, and whether these will be anonymised, what they will be used for (whether for this specific project or also for future research), who will have access to the data, how long they will be stored for (please make sure you consult funder-specific guidance if applicable), and how they will be disposed of.

10 **What will happen to the results of the study?**

Detail how the results will be made available to the participants and whether the results are to be published. If the results are to be published, detail how and where they will be accessible. Tell participants that they will not be identifiable from the results unless they have consented to this.

11 **What will happen if I want to stop taking part?**

Participants should be informed that they can withdraw at anytime, without explanation. Results up to the period of withdrawal may be used, if they are happy for this to be done. Otherwise they may request that these are destroyed and no further use is made of them.

12 **Who can I contact if I have further questions?**

You should give the name, university address, and email number of the students conducting the project.

Figure 4.2 Participant Information Sheet

Source: Adapted from www.liv.ac.uk/researchethics (last accessed 17 July 2010).

An important theme raised by this Participant Information Sheet is confidentiality. This 'recognises that a researcher may be entrusted with private information' and makes explicit the planned use of this information (Scheyvens et al. 2003: 146). The RGS requires: 'Confidentiality of information supplied by research subjects and anonymity of respondents (unless otherwise agreed with research subjects and respondents)'. When conducting field-work you will need to start with the assumption that the anonymity and privacy of partici-pants will be maintained wherever possible, except in those cases where respondents explicitly waive their right to this or assert their desire to be named. True anonymity is not always feasible since it may sometimes be possible to guess who respondents are: for example, if the researched community is small and the background information gives individuals away. In such cases it may be necessary to warn respondents that their anonymity may not be watertight.

Similarly, you may decide not to use material that may compromise your sources if it becomes clear that your doing so – even if this is permitted within the terms of your research – may harm informants. As mentioned above, Kim England decided to withhold data she had collected on lesbians in Toronto on the grounds that it might harm members of these communities. Decisions about confidentiality – about what to include in a report and what to withhold – are usually a matter of judgement which you will have to make rather than leave to ethics committees to adjudicate on. Garth Myers, who conducted ethnographic research in East Africa, reflected that writing was 'a delicate matter' of differentiating 'anybody's business' from 'nobody's business' (2001: 198). He suggested that, where sensitive or personal information was involved, it would be a good idea to involve the research participants in making decisions about what to include and how to do this.

It is important to note that, while published studies by professional academics can provide valuable lessons for your own undergraduate studies, there are of course significant differences between the two. You can learn from professional research but you will not have the experience or resources to match its scope. As a result you will need to adapt rather than duplicate ethical procedures, such as the model Consent Form shown in Figure 4.3. This model will help you devise your own documentation if you decide that all or part of it is appropriate and/or if your university or college requires it. This includes statements on confidentiality and allows respondents to decide whether or not they wish to remain anonymous.

SUMMARY

This chapter has discussed the ethical issues surrounding being in the field and offered experiences from a number of researchers. A common theme in all approaches is the desire to seriously anticipate and monitor the impacts that research has on others. The key points of the chapter were:

- Fieldwork will always present some dilemmas. You do not have to travel to the Global South to encounter these. Regardless of the geographical location of your fieldwork, a consideration of the ethics involved should be made.

- You will need to consider whether your research has the potential to harm others (a serious rethink will be required if this is the case); if the research is potentially exploitative (more rethinking is needed here); how the research may benefit stakeholders; what sort of relationships you would like to cultivate with the research participants.

- The process of completing an ethics form will vary according to individual institutions, so we have outlined some generic guidelines and consideration points. Such form-filling may seem onerous but as this chapter demonstrates it is of primary importance in research planning. Indeed ethical considerations do not end with receiving institutional approval. They continue throughout the research process and may even inform how you come to think about a variety of issues into later life.

YOUR UNIVERSITY LOGO HERE	
MODEL CONSENT FORM	
Title of Project:	
Researcher(s):	
	Please initial box
1 I confirm that I have read and have understood the information sheet dated [DATE] for the above study. I have had the opportunity to consider the information, ask questions, and have had these answered satisfactorily.	
2 I understand that my participation is voluntary and that I am free to withdraw at any time without giving any reason, without my rights being affected.	
3 I understand that, under the Data Protection Act, I can at any time ask for access to the information I provide and I can also request the destruction of that information if I wish.	
4 I agree to take part in the above study.	
5 I give permission for the transcript of my interview/research to be used for research purposes only (including research publications and reports)	
6 I understand that such information will be treated as strictly confidential. I understand that I have the right to anonymity. I assign copyright of my transcript to [names of student researchers], who may quote the transcript either with strict preservation of anonymity or under my own name [please delete as applicable].	

_____   _____   _____

Participant Name   Date   Signature

_____   _____   _____

Researcher(s)   Date   Signature

The contact details of the Researcher are:

Figure 4.3   Model Consent Form

Source: Adapted from www.liv.ac.uk/researchethics (last accessed 17 July 2010).

CONCLUSION

This chapter began with a series of ethical dilemmas and then provided some structure through which to address them, illustrated with examples in which researchers have confronted similar issues and come to their own conclusions about how to address them. To return to the original dilemmas: should you attempt to contact members of an Aboriginal Settlement in Australia? Should you flirt with participants? Should you impose upon the time of business leaders? Should you embark on what might seem to be a 'tropical jolly'? There are no definitive answers to any of these dilemmas. We have illustrated for example how some researchers can justify sexual encounters with participants, while others cannot; how some have felt extremely uncomfortable walking in the footsteps of white, heroic colonial travellers and explorers whilst others have been able to reposition themselves as they conduct fieldwork in the tropics. In most cases, ethical issues are a matter of judgement which you will need to resolve for yourself by identifying the issues at stake and making informed decisions through discussions with other students and with field leaders. In some cases, particularly those involving at-risk groups, these decisions may well be taken out of your hands as you are forced to rethink your research by university ethics committees, but these cases are the exceptions.

Therefore the onus is on you. While we can guide you through systems of ethical scrutiny and explain the ethical standards that researchers are now required to follow, we must ultimately direct the important ethical questions back to you and to your own ethical judgements and values. Linda McDowell concludes simply that 'you must hold on to your own standards of ethical behaviour and decency and to treat others as you would prefer to be treated yourself if the relationship between the researcher and the reverse were to be reversed' (McDowell 1997: 393).

Advancing an ethical project should be a reward in itself but more than this an understanding of ethical issues can also deepen your understanding of some of the broader issues concerning the constitution and limits of geographical knowledge. Ethical reflection brings us back to questions of responsibility: why we do fieldwork in the first place and what we hope to get out of it for ourselves and for others.

FURTHER READING/KEY TEXT(S)

- Dowling, R. (2005) 'Power, subjectivity and ethics in qualitative research'. In I. Hay (ed.) *Qualitative Research Methods in Human Geography.* Melbourne: Oxford University Press, 19–29. This proposes a preliminary set of prompts for students, entitled 'How to be critically reflexive in research'.

- Scheyvens, R., Nowak, B. and Scheyvens, H. (2003) 'Ethical issues'. In R. Scheyvens and D. Storey (eds), *Development Fieldwork: A Practical Guide.* London: SAGE, 139–166. Though specifically concerned with development geography, this is an excellent general text on research ethics with many references to fieldwork.

5

WORKING IN GROUPS AND TRAVELLING TOGETHER

OVERVIEW

This chapter addresses the following questions:

- Why might you be required to complete work in groups?
- How can you most effectively work with others in your group?
- What problems might you face and how can you overcome them?
- How can you make sure that your fieldtrip is as inclusive as possible?
- What can you learn from working and travelling with others?

The chapter offers practical advice on how to overcome some common challenges that may arise when working in groups. It then goes on to examine fieldwork as a social experience. As previous chapters have emphasised, critical reflection is necessary when considering and managing your relationships with others in the field.

Fieldwork involves working together and also travelling as part of a group, sleeping and eating in close proximity, and spending spare time in each other's company. These interactions with each other take two forms, first a formal structured time spent in groups with or without staff guidance, and second an informal social time that is not 'timetabled' or supervised. As Chapter 2 stressed, fieldwork is an opportunity to develop practical teamwork and communication skills but this is not without its challenges as fieldwork offers a specific – and often intense – environment in which to conduct group work. This chapter therefore provides some guidance on how to survive and prosper in a group. The social dynamics of fieldwork also raise another set of ethical issues and challenges above and beyond those associated with the relationships between researchers and researched communities which were examined in the previous chapter. This chapter begins with suggestions on how to work efficiently and happily as part of a group before moving on to discuss the broader issue of how to interact ethically with others on the fieldtrip.

Figure 5.1   Working together: two students plan how they will approach the company in the background for their research on the film industry, and discuss the role each will perform in an interview. Photograph by Jennifer Johns

WHY DO I HAVE TO WORK IN A GROUP?

It is now commonplace for fieldtrips to include elements of group work and often groups will be required to produce output (such as a presentation, a tour, or a piece of written work) that may be formally assessed. Increasingly, learning in small groups has become regular part of the student fieldwork experience as it is acknowledged that active participation in group processes can produce different kinds of academic and skills-based learning. As David Jacque and Gilly Salmon suggest, 'group interaction allows students to negotiate meanings, to express themselves in the language of the subject and to establish a more intimate and dialectical contact with academic and teaching staff than more formal methods permit' (2007: 1). Collaborative work is often incorporated in fieldcourses for a number of reasons including practical concerns (being able to safely collect data), the facilitation of in-depth studies (working together on a project allows the combined output to be more substantial), and to allow students to learn from each other whilst receiving greater levels of formative feedback and support from staff. In addition, as suggested in Chapter 2, there are obvious life-long learning opportunities to be gained from group working with peers. A study commissioned by the British government identified a demand for skills that can be acquired through group fieldwork as employers highlighted shortages in team, communication and management skills (DfES 1999). Developing and being able to demonstrate the possession of such skills can provide graduates with a way of distinguishing themselves from others in increasingly competitive graduate labour markets.

It is important to emphasise that such skills are not automatically generated by just being a passive member of a group! To gain genuine academic and skills-based experience active participation in the group task is required, and often challenges (either intellectual or practical) must be overcome as part of this. Even if you have worked in many small group situations before, you may find that group work in the field is particularly intense as the group will often be required to spend a lot of time together, both while working and in shared accommodation. It may be that you feel that you are better equipped to tackle fieldtrip tasks on your own. This is a fairly common feeling amongst students, in part due to the culture of individual achievement that many education systems create. You compete as an individual to gain your university place and upon graduation when you enter the job market. It is therefore understandable that some students will shy away from group work in favour of working autonomously as they do not wish to be dependent upon the cooperation of others. However, it is highly unlikely that you will be able to participate on a fieldcourse without engaging in collaborative work. The onus therefore is upon each individual to embrace the experience of working and living with others and attempt to discern the benefits rather than the challenges.

Postard 5.1: Working in Groups, by Eric Pawson (a champion of Problem Based Learning or PBL)

Group work can be hard but it does have its rewards: 'My skills base has changed considerably. I'm more of a free thinker. I'm more open to hearing other people's opinions', said a recent student. Another commented that 'I have always been a good individual studier. However, now through this experience I have gained skills about group work and dynamics and [feel better adapted] for entering the working world'. These are exciting and potentially life-changing discoveries.

(Continued)

(Continued)

How to work together to do this is a subject which is avoided by most books on research methodology. It's not unusual for group members not to know each other very well, or maybe initially not even like each other all that much! In fact, you may find yourself in a group where the lecturers have intentionally broken up pre-formed allegiances in order to force negotiations into the open. Thus the backgrounds of group members can be very varied. I worked alongside a recent group in a service-learning course whose ages ranged from the early twenties to the mid thirties, and included a Pasifika woman, a Serbian immigrant man, an American student, a recently qualified teacher, and a young New Zealander. They quickly discovered that one or two of them had a talent for baking, so their meetings became light-hearted competitions to see which of them could provide good cakes and biscuits for the group. They all became great friends.

In other cases, however, it will not be quite so simple. There is an oft-repeated model that describes the development of group dynamics over time, interestingly originally derived from a wholly atypical population, that of American psychiatric patients in the 1950s. It is known as 'forming-storming-norming-performing' (Tuckman 1965). These four stages do not inevitably follow on from each other. But the model does have the advantage of pointing out that it is quite common for groups to argue and fall out. This can be a very good thing. Time and energy spent getting to know each other through storming will help a group to 'norm' into a functional unit that will then really begin to 'perform'. Sometimes without the storming, a group will never uncover any real insight into its topic. There are all sorts of sources on the web, and in print, that can be used to diagnose and resolve group 'storming' and 'norming' issues.

In many respects, group work is like a relationship: the more you are willing to put into it, the more you'll get out of it. The more preparation you do, the better the end result will probably be. The greater the respect you have for your partner or partners, and the more you learn the risks and benefits of compromise, the bigger the rewards in self-discovery and uncovering the joys of being with the other. This may all sound a bit dramatic but most students will find group work quite intense, something very different from the singular focus of much individual work. And it is an experience that provides a really good basis for engaging with those lifelong learning skills that can prove so valuable in the workplace.

FORMING GROUPS AND BECOMING A TEAM

Your fieldwork groups will either be determined for you by field class staff, or you will be free to form your own groups. In the latter case, you should think first about whether you want to base your groups on pre-existing friendships or your academic interests (which may not overlap). As group work is not always straightforward our initial reaction is often to choose to work with individuals that we already know. However, groups formed by staff will often attempt to break up cliques and ensure as heterogeneous a mix as possible. This is to ensure that groups are balanced in terms of abilities and background to prevent individual students being isolated and to encourage the development of teambuilding communication skills. Mixed ability groups (and those which are culturally diverse) are often more productive and successful than groups formed using more selective criteria. Your fieldwork group is not permanent, with individuals only required to work together for as long as it takes to complete the required tasks. The temporary nature of such groups is not necessarily a weakness and can, in fact, bring about conditions of trust, experimentation, novelty, and productivity. When working in shorter projects, group members may take more chances and put up with more discomfort than they might in a long-term group (Miles 1964). They might also work harder (Ephross and Vassit 2005). Fieldwork group projects therefore create an environment in which students can develop interesting ideas and work together to research their topic. Working with people we didn't previously know can be liberating and provide opportunities for us to work in new ways. In addition it may well provide us with experiences of project work that will be highly valued by future employers.

As this chapter seeks to illustrate, the rewards of challenging ourselves to work effectively with others can be significant (and this can even be fun). Indeed, we should not make assumptions about others before, or even during, group tasks. Students can be guilty of categorising each other according to perceived ability levels, resulting in those who consider themselves to have high IQs becoming nervous about working with those who are less 'IQ-clever' and vice versa. In fact, research by management theorists shows that teams composed of individuals ranked highest in mental ability tests were no more likely to succeed over other teams. Clearly there is much more to creating a successful team than bringing together intelligent individuals.

MAKING THE TRANSITION FROM A GROUP TO A TEAM

Communicating with others should begin early on in your fieldwork experience. There are a number of 'ground rules' that can be established in order to create some structure to how your group works together.

- Realise what you are trying to achieve. What are your shared goals?

- Developing a 'group ethos' can be crucial to the success of your project. The amount of time you have to work together before entering the field can vary, but even if you find yourselves grouped together and sent into the field immediately, you should set aside some time to discuss what the project is and what you aim to achieve.

- Decide how the group will communicate with each other (i.e. phone, email, face-to-face) and agree how often you need to do so or when to meet.

- Coordinating a group of individuals whilst in the field is complex. You will not all be doing the same tasks at the same time so effective communication and planning is essential. It is vital that everyone understands what is going on and what is expected of them. Never leave a meeting without all group members being entirely certain about what they need to go away and do. Also include set meeting times and places in your research schedule – it is easier to cancel a pre-arranged meeting if it is not required than to negotiate new meetings while busy coordinating your research activities. It is worthwhile to agree a default form of communication. Do not necessarily assume that all group members can use their mobile phones to communicate. One student on a recent fieldtrip appeared not to be engaging with the project and missed a group meeting. She eventually admitted that she hadn't brought her mobile phone on the fieldtrip as she couldn't afford the charges to use it abroad. The group had been texting her, entirely unaware that she was not receiving their messages.

- Frequent group meetings are important, but do not assume that these will always result in easily-reached decisions. Research in the field is difficult and your group may have to make some difficult decisions and/or compromises. How will your group make a decision if there is conflict? Does your group ethos include the need for a consensus to be reached? Do all group members need to be happy with a decision before it is acted upon? There are no right or wrong answers to this. It is also important to establish the degree to which individuals or smaller teams within the group are able to make decision while collecting data. If you are in an agreed location to conduct participant observation how will the rest of the group react if you decide that a different location is more appropriate and collect data there instead? How much flexibility do individuals have within the group?

Difficulties can result when group members have different ideas about what they want to achieve, how they are going to do this, and when this is going to happen. Two members of a five person group we supervised were reluctant to collect data in the evenings. They revealed that they had obtained tickets for several sporting events, not realising that this could interfere with their project work. To the rest of the group they seemed to be prioritising their social activities and viewing the fieldtrip as a holiday. A compromise was reached when the two students expressed their commitment to the project and offered to compensate for their absence by collecting data on their day off. Similarly, it is essential to reiterate and reaffirm the project objectives through frequent communication. As an example, one group of six students decided to separate into two groups of three, each taking responsibility for interviews on opposite sides of the city. The group had agreed on the project research questions and aims and, feeling confident in their plans, felt it was only necessary to hold a group meeting after three days of data collection. When the group finally met, it became clear that the two teams had been using their interview schedules very differently and one team had not made any notes during the interview, relying solely on a dictaphone to record the interview. The different emphases placed on the data collection resulted in data that were hard to compare across the two teams and the lack of notes for half the interviews made initial discussion and analysis in the field much more difficult. The group realised that they should have met every day to review their progress, discuss and share the data being yielded from the interviews, and to agree on the practical aspects of record-keeping.

Peter Levin (2005) suggests that you keep ground rules under review as they may need to change as the project develops. This is particularly relevant to fieldwork as the pressures on your time will vary and it will be difficult to accurately assess the length of time specific tasks will take. You may also find that you need to meet more frequently in the field, or that some tasks need to be reallocated once you have a better idea of how time consuming they are. If the group are all aware that the ground rules can change they will be better equipped as a group to respond to the unpredictable field environment.

UNDERSTANDING TEAM ROLES AND OVERCOMING GROUP PROBLEMS

Group composition is important but it does not determine what exactly takes place in a group – that is decided by the actions of the students involved. Understanding the strengths and weaknesses of individuals involved in a group can provide useful insights that will help them to work together more effectively. Often based on psychological profiles developed for business and management recruitment and planning, there are a plethora of different methods for measuring and categorising individuals into 'types' of group members. This section uses a more student-friendly typology adapted from the work of Belbin (1981). It does not require each group member to complete a lengthy, probing questionnaire! Rather, a short period of individual reflection and group discussion will usually enable the composition of the group in terms of team roles to be established. Table 5.1 outlines eight team roles and the strengths and potential weaknesses of each of these.

As Table 5.1 shows, each team role offers a different set of skills and contributions to the completion of a group task. It is important to note here that no one team role is more important than

Table 5.1 Team roles for project teams

Team Roles	Strengths	Potential drawbacks
Innovator	Produces ideas, ready to challenge inertia and complacency. May be invaluable if you are developing your own group research idea. May also help develop solutions to problems with data collection in the field.	Ignores details, can be impatient, over-sensitive. May struggle to plan how and where to collect data in the field.
Resource investigator	Can find people, brings new information to the team, responds to challenge, enthusiastic. Will be valuable when planning data collection, contacting potential research participants and documentary and secondary data.	Can be too optimistic, may lose interest once initial interest has passed. Will need support from team whilst in the field to keep their concentration on the task. May become disillusioned with setbacks in the field.
Chair/coordinator	Self-confident, positive, good at guiding team, promotes decision making.	Can be bossy or manipulative, can be inflexible.
Implementer/shaper	Makes things happen, changes ideas into plans, careful and efficient, needs to succeed. 'Can do' attitude will be valuable in the field.	May be impatient if things don't go the 'right' way. This is particularly likely to happen in the field.
Monitor/evaluator	Careful, looks at all the options, tests out ideas, thinks strategically.	Can be distant, over-critical, doesn't inspire others.
Team worker	Shows an interest in others' ideas, listens, concerned with social interaction, places teams above personal concerns. Aims to have a happy team and will work to achieve this.	May be indecisive when most needed, e.g. when urgent action is required.
Plant	Creative and imaginative, unorthodox. May provide a novel solution if research problems arise.	Ignores practical details making their contribution in the field potentially problematic. May need to be convinced about the unfeasibility of their ideas.
Completer/finisher	Follows through, conscientious, works hard to finish things properly. Will not run out of enthusiasm so role in writing up may be invaluable.	Can be over-anxious about detail and perfectionist, doesn't like to delegate. This will be challenging in the field where delegation is essential.

Source: Adapted from Jacques and Salmon (2007: see Table 6.1; based on Belbin 1981)

another and that it is not necessary to have individuals fulfilling every role in the group. What is clear, however, is that the different functions of group work provide opportunities for different individuals to make unique contributions. For example, having an 'innovator' or 'plant' in your group may prove to be invaluable when your group brainstorms to come up with a research idea. Similarly, a 'completer/finisher' may come into their own once you return from the field and are faced with the task of writing up your project. So, not only do different individuals have specific contributions to make, the strength of their most crucial involvement may also occur at different points in the fieldwork process. By understanding yourself, and your other group members, it may be possible to plan your project more efficiently and, through early acknowledgement of the potential drawbacks of each team role, avoid or mitigate any group work problems. Postcard 5.2 below describes an important, early stage in the formation of fieldwork groups in which group members identified the strengths that they had brought with them. Rachel Spronken-Smith shows how her students identified complementarities to decide which roles each student could perform.

Postcard 5.2: Identifying Skills, Strengths and Roles, by Rachel Spronken-Smith (with a questionnaire devised by Ruth Panelli)

Geography students at the University of Otago, New Zealand, regularly work in groups which are facilitated by tutors. In one module, the group has first to generate a research question, then design a research methodology to address the question and conduct their fieldwork and analyses, and finally communicate their findings. One student explains how his group got going:

'In our first group meeting – of six students and our tutor – we introduced ourselves and then had to fill out a skills matrix that considered aspects such as work habits/skills, group roles, and technical and research skills. Then we compared our profiles to see where the group strengths and weaknesses were. Our tutor also asked us whether there were any particular skills we wanted to develop. Then we discussed how our group was going to operate. We decided that we would have both a rotating chair and secretary (who would take minutes and post online). This way we would all develop skills in chairing and recording meetings. Our tutor also asked us about what we thought her role as tutor should involve. Although some of us hoped it would be to tell us what we wanted to know, the reality was she was there to guide

(Continued)

(Continued)

our learning – the onus would be on us! This soon became apparent as when we were stuck in later meetings we would turn to her for advice and often our "look" would be thrown back at us! While this was frustrating at the time, I later came to realise the benefits of us floundering around and finding our own way. Don't get me wrong – if we were way off track, we would gently be nudged back on!'

The skills matrix can take the form of a questionnaire, which group members complete and share with each other. The following questionnaire, developed by Ruth Panelli, could be useful for any students, whether or not you have been formally required to complete it.

Getting to know your group: self introduction

A project team will always work better when team members have a sense of each other's backgrounds and work styles. Fill in the following questions in ways you are happy to share with your group. Then discuss them in terms of what the group perceives its initial team strengths and challenges to be (i.e. attributes that as a group you may need to watch and enhance during the course of the research).

1 Name _____

2 Contact details
  - *term telephone (and best times to ring)* _____
  - *email:* _____

3 Background
  - *home area/town* _____
  - *past contact/experience in topic (if any)* _____
  _____

4 Subjects enrolled in this year _____

5 Work habits/skills (circle one star in each row to describe your work habits/skills)

	Super organized				Super chaotic
Organization	organized	*	*	*	*	chaotic

(Continued)

(Continued)

Forward Planning	Always plan in advance	*	*	*	*	*		Never plan ahead
Time keeping	Always early or on time	*	*	*	*	*		Always late
Writing skills	1st rate written skills	*	*	*	*	*		Writing is not my forte
Small gp oral skills	Confident talker *	*	*	*	*			Shy + quiet
Formal oral Presentations	Enjoy public speaking	*	*	*	*	*		Find this un-nerving

6 Technical skills (circle one star in each row to rate your skills in the different areas)

	Great	Good	Some	Poor	None
Instrumentation and data loggers	*	*	*	*	*
GPS and surveying equipment	*	*	*	*	*
Excel spreadsheets	*	*	*	*	*
Statistics	*	*	*	*	*
GIS	*	*	*	*	*
Cartography/photoshop/graphics	*	*	*	*	*

7 Group roles (circle one star in each row to indicate your experience with different roles)

	Always	Often	S/times	Rarely	N.A.
Leader: Happy to be a spokesperson and a high profile group member	*	*	*	*	*
Decision-maker: Happy to identify group tasks + challenges and make decisions about them	*	*	*	*	*
Organizer: Happy to make sure group is organized to be able to achieve goals	*	*	*	*	*
Logistics/Gofer: Happy to do the work that keeps things rolling smoothly	*	*	*	*	*

(Continued)

(Continued)

Carer: Happy to look out for group   *   *   *   *   *
dynamics and encourage consensus
and good relations

Outsider: Find it hard to speak up   *   *   *   *   *
in groups and/or find group work
offputting

8 Group work experience to date
  a In your opinion, what is the best thing about group work?
  b In your opinion, what is the worst thing about group work?
  c What do you think you can contribute to the group research
    experience?

While we can seek to understand how individuals work in teams, there are some broader cultural and societal factors that can influence or determine how group members interact. As suggested above, groups that are culturally diverse are often more innovative and can out-perform more hemogenous teams. However, where groups are composed of people from different countries or ethnic backgrounds, misunderstandings can arise. Peter Levin (2005) identifies five aspects of culture and cultural differences and how these can give rise to mis-understandings:

1 *Individualism versus collectivism.* Culture can affect how people view their individual positions within groups and society in general.

   • Action: all group members should aim to adopt a compromise position whereby individual thoughts and ideas are voiced, but a consensus for action is also found that the whole group is happy with.

2 *Tolerance of uncertainty.* This refers to the degree to which an individual's education has emphasised learning by rote or critical thinking. People will have different levels of confidence in their ability to challenge ideas and work independently.

   • Action: the whole group should aim to provide sufficient structure to the group project – defining the group aims and ground rules would certainly help here – so that any uncertainty is reduced.

3 *Issues of embarrassment and 'loss of face'.* There are cultural reasons why certain situations will be viewed (and felt) differently. In group scenarios there can be very different

understandings of what is polite, humorous, or embarrassing. For example, in some cultures it may be very difficult, if not impossible, to admit that you are unable to perform a particular task.

- Action: individuals should take time to think before they speak or act if they find themselves in a heterogeneous group.

4 *Issues of gender.* In relation to group work, gender issues can be manifested in a miscommunication between how individuals expect to be treated according to their gender. For example, some women would expect to be treated the same as male members of the group and would be angered if they thought they were being excluded from particular discussions and/or tasks.

- Action: conflict in group work in relation to the issue of gender can be avoided through an awareness of and sensitivity towards others (this should be considered alongside the discussions made in Chapter 4).

5 *Codes of behaviour.* There are cultural differences in what kind of behaviour is acceptable, and given the amount of time your group may spend together in the field, problems can manifest themselves through frustration at the behaviour of others.

- Action: think about how you communicate with others, specifically in relation to personal space and boundaries, if you are interrupting people when they are talking, voicing your impatience, or expressing yourself while disagreeing with one or more group members.

The cultural issues highlighted above can impact on group work so it is up to individual group members to think about the composition of their group and to attempt to keep misunderstandings to a minimum. In the majority of cases cultural differences in group work will contribute positively rather than negatively, so it is best not to enter group work with the expectation that you will encounter difficulties. In fact, your awareness and experience of cultural differences in behaviour and attitudes to group work can help prepare you for your relationships with the whole fieldwork group (discussed below), in your encounters with others in the field (as discussed in Chapter 4), and also with particular research activities (for example, in interviewing research respondents from different cultural backgrounds: see Chapter 7).

CONFLICT RESOLUTION

In a perfect world, group work would be easy and enjoyable. There would be no conflict, no slacking, everyone would contribute, and things would run smoothly according to schedule. However, this is rarely the case and sometimes groups have to work hard to ensure that problems do not hinder the completion of their work. There will be some issues that, when they arise, will cause particular distress for group members and could perhaps seriously compromise the integrity of the group and its ability to function. One such issue is that of the 'free rider' – where one or more group members refrain from contributing fully to the task, safe in the knowledge that they will benefit from the work of the rest of the 'team'.

The free-rider issue is something that your fieldwork staff will be aware of, and your institution may have introduced some measures that will attempt to mitigate the effects of such 'social loafers' in group work. For example, you may be required to complete a form when you submit your work which identifies the roles performed by each member and/or there may be mechanisms for rewarding (or penalising) particular group members when your group work is assessed. In the absence of such mechanisms, there are certain strategies that can be adopted by the group as a response to this problem.

First, both staff and students can play a role in reducing the incentive to free ride. Staff can communicate the challenges of group work and the potential rewards and discuss the drawbacks of individualist views of working. The group itself can also establish ground rules so that expectations are synchronised, different cultural backgrounds are acknowledged, differences are discussed where necessary, and all viewpoints are considered. Individuals will have a stronger incentive to contribute to the work of the group if they feel that their contribution is valued (West 1994).

Second, as Peter Levin (2003) highlights, there is a difference between unintended and deliberate free riding. The former can occur when a student becomes overwhelmed with the pressures of their academic work and begins to make changes to how they allocate their time. They would therefore appear to be backing out of work but would have no deliberate intention of taking advantage of others. Similarly, if a student felt unable to decline a task they were allocated (due to the over-dominance of other team members or because of cultural reasons) they may then feel ill-equipped to fulfil it. Failure to complete the work is then a consequence of that individual floundering rather than deliberately free riding. If this situation occurs, open and constructive discussion with the rest of the group about how to overcome the difficulties may be all that is needed to bring the individual back into the group and contribute to its progress.

Third, in the case of deliberate free-riding you may feel that it is appropriate to consult a member of staff. You may also feel however that this is 'telling tales', but if you are struggling to overcome a genuine case of a group member taking advantage of the rest of the team it is advisable to let staff know sooner rather than later. Unfortunately, if the free riding is a conscious act by an individual, there may be little that the rest of the group can do to change the situation. Initial steps would include meeting with the individual to discuss whether there are any problems that the group is unaware of. These may be challenges in completing the work due to insufficient information or resources (does the group have a solution?), or personal problems that are impacting on the capacity of the individual to produce (it is not the responsibility of the group to intervene in personal problems, although some sympathy and understanding may help the individual feel supported rather than persecuted by the group). The next stage is for the group to develop a contingency plan that can respond flexibly if the individual does not produce the required work, or indeed, in the event they do. In the context of field-work where many project tasks are of a practical nature, such as collecting data, it may be that free riding occurs less often while in the field. The problem is more likely to happen in the planning and writing-up stages of the fieldwork project when staff supervision is less and there are much lower levels of group contact.

Finally, as with many of the challenges of group work, coping with and responding to prob-lems such as free riding can become worthwhile learning experiences. Free riding is not lim-ited to university projects – it occurs (perhaps more frequently) in the world of work and potential employers will value candidates with some experience of how to manage free riding. It is also valuable for all individuals to develop an ability to communicate with others in con-structive ways and develop solutions that allow them to consider perspectives other than their own. The principle of inclusiveness is important in fieldwork group work, and indeed, in the broader context of the fieldtrip as you will be travelling, sharing living space and socialising with others.

Postcard 5.3 'Fairytale of New York': Alcohol and Fieldtrips,
by Mark Jayne

For the past five years I have been the co-ordinator for a fieldtrip to New York and I am happy to admit to feeling 'at home' during our annual visit. Indeed, I am sitting writing this postcard in a pleasant Irish bar on a Sunday afternoon enjoying a few pints of Brooklyn Beer.
   Now the first thing that it is important to clarify is that the fieldtrip is not a boozy holiday. I can see that for some students a fieldtrip to an exciting location can cause conflicting priorities – on one hand they have been constantly reminded that the week is not a vacation and that there is challenging assessed work to complete. On the other hand there are so many cool things to do – shopping, sightseeing, hanging-out in Central Park, more shopping, music, sporting events, Broadway shows and of course, drinking (and did I mention shopping?).
   One of the oft-used terms that I have heard staff remind each other of when talking about fieldtrips is that the relationship between staff and students is not in loco parentis – 'in the place of a parent' – referring to the legal responsibility of a person or organisation to take on the functions and responsibilities of a parent. Being over 18 years of age students are afforded the responsibilities of adulthood. However,

(Continued)

(Continued)

the most obvious problem for them is that the legal age for alcohol consumption in the USA is generally 21. Having enjoyed a legal drink since the age of 18 in the UK, students will tend to fall back on tried and tested experiences of buying alcohol when underage. Fake IDs, dressing to look older, or finding venues that will turn a blind eye all takes up a lot of time and energy during the week, and for some, these strategies will ultimately fail. Although I have not undertaken ethnographic work with students there are nonetheless signs and practices that give away the pleasures and consequences of drinking – noisy late-night conversations in hallways, the onset of 'travel sickness' during bus trips, blurry eyes, un-responsiveness, and generally grumpy behaviour.

While a small number of students who are tee-total have had to negotiate their presence or absence from nights including alcohol – touch wood, oh no! I've made my table wobble and spilt my beer! – I am happy to say that there have been no major alcohol-related incidents of illness, violence, or disorderly behaviour (that I am aware of) with students responding to calls to ensure a collective responsibility for themselves and their friends as well as residents and other visitors to the city. However, I have heard numerous stories of fun and 'interesting' conversations with strangers, various personal belongings being lost, students getting themselves lost on the subway, and sexual encounters, as well as laments about waking up in the previous night's clothes and make-up and minor bumps and bruises being put down to alcohol, dancing, and 'messing about'. Of course, the recounting of these experiences amongst students (and amongst staff also) is not a feature that can be solely associated with fieldtrips but it does characterise the sociability, reciprocity, and friendship that are bound up with seeing people at their best and indeed sometimes their worst after drinking alcohol. Stories and photos will also invariably find their way onto social networking sites even before the next day's hangovers have taken hold.

During the fieldtrip week there will usually be a couple of nights when staff and students will meet and mingle away from formal or professional settings. Discovering a happy medium of finding out about each others' lives or discussing the marks received (either disappointing or rewarding) is an important part of fieldtrips. Staff and students interacting in the informal situation of a pub, bar or restaurant is

(Continued)

(Continued)

nonetheless an important shared moment that for staff means an engagement with students that goes beyond standing in front of a sea of faces in large lecture theatres or the restricted contact with personal tutees or dissertation students: for students it offers an opportunity to get to know the personalities beyond more remote teachers, administrators, and assessors.

For staff, however, various unanswerable questions remain about when exactly during a field course they are officially 'off duty' and allowed time to relax. Indeed having a drink with colleagues, after a tiring day of walking tours or student consultations, is in part a way to unwind and deal with the jet-lag. Following the one alcoholic drink (with an evening meal) that has been officially sanctioned as university expenses, evenings encompassing chatting, lovely food, and more alcohol, will often lead to candid conversations – 'talking shop', putting to rights the world of academia and the state of universities, gossiping about colleagues, and of course being highly entertained by the behaviour of students (whether drunk or not) are part of the fieldtrip experience. Dealing with your own and other staff members' hangovers, tiredness and grumpiness is also part of the team-building nature of fieldtrips.

As I am finishing my final beer of the day I am challenging myself to pick some highlights from the many fun times I have enjoyed during the fieldtrips to NYC. Amongst the alcohol-related highlights of being in one of the great cities of the world are many memorable and less easily remembered nights out. Dancing to Northern Soul music at a club and listening to jazz at the iconic Village Vanguard were both great experiences, as was seeing The Pogues play on St Patrick's Day and later on dancing in Central Park while singing 'The Fairytale of New York'. However, without a doubt the best evening I have the pleasure to remember was when watching Wales beat France to secure the 2008 Six Nations Grand Slam. I'm not sure what some New Yorkers thought of raucous choruses of 'Bread of Heaven', sung with a small bunch of other Taffs I'd met in the Irish pub which was screening the match. But for a short time our singing could be heard above the hooting of car horns on Broadway as we celebrated in New York City.

TRAVELLING TOGETHER

The social experience of fieldwork can also be marked by various differences within the group. An ethical critique of fieldwork, spearheaded by feminist geographers, has shown that fieldwork has privileged some students at the expense of others. Through a range of traditions and practices, from demanding walks to alcohol-fuelled socialising, fieldwork experiences have been structured by age, sexuality, physical ability, and cultural background. Some students – particularly able-bodied young heterosexual men – have been at the centre of things, while others have been marginalised or left behind. This raises an important question: how can you learn critical lessons about the exclusionary tradition of fieldwork in geography, by becoming sensitive to ethical issues surrounding relationships within the field class, and by ensuring that your own fieldwork is as inclusive as possible? How can this enhance your learning experience?

Gillian Rose's path-breaking (1993) critique of academic geography, *Feminism and Geography*, issued a challenge to academic geography in general and its fieldwork tradition in particular.

Figure 5.2   Heroic fieldwork: British university's brochure presents geographical fieldwork as the preserve of young able-bodied men.

Source: Hall et al. (2004: 260; see Figure 1)

Rose argued that academic geography had been characterised by 'geographical masculinities in action' (1993: 65) through discourses and practices such as surveying, map-making, lecturing, and fieldwork. 'Fieldwork,' she suggested, 'is a performance which enacts some of the discipline's underlying masculinist assumptions about its knowledge of the world' (1993: 65). These assumptions are illustrated in some recent depictions of fieldwork on British universities' websites and departmental brochures (see Figure 5.2). As explained in Chapter 1, fieldwork has often been seen as a disciplinary initiation ritual and Rose argues that this produces and rewards heroically masculine geographers and marginalises others. This initiation ritual involves challenging walks and other physical endurance tests and while these are most pronounced in the physical side of the discipline they are also important in human geography. Masculinity is performed not only in the content of fieldwork but also in socialising, in which captive audiences of students will variously choose and feel obliged to participate. Rose argues that 'fieldwork also involves the necessary amount of drinking in order to prove how manly the fieldworker is' (1993: 70). It is necessary here to interrogate claims such as these in which there are obvious holes. It is, for example, far too simplistic to portray drinking simply as a masculinist or male preserve. Mark Jayne presents a more nuanced and light-hearted – but not uncritical – picture of the role of alcohol on fieldtrips in Postcard 5.3. An image of students socialising during a fieldtrip in Berlin, meanwhile, illustrates the presence and prominence of alcohol but not necessarily of drunken or laddish behaviour in the field (Figure 5.3).

Figure 5.3   Students in a cafe in Friedrichsain, Berlin. Photo by Tinho DaCruz

Yet some studies do show that female (and some other) students have often felt marginalised and intimidated by fieldwork. Female students are more likely than their male counterparts to worry that they are not sufficiently fit for fieldwork and may not be able to keep up. These concerns, though generally unfounded, have been shown to reduce female students' enjoyment of fieldwork and discourage them from taking fieldwork where it is optional (Maguire 1998). A study conducted in Singapore found that female students tended to opt out of a fieldwork module which involved spending up to a month in the paddy fields of Malaysia, with the consequence that an important component of honours geography was overwhelmingly male dominated (Goh Kim Chuan and Wong Poh Poh 2000: 109).

Arguments about the male domination of fieldwork have been supplemented with other claims about the ways in which fieldwork excludes and marginalises some other students. Julie Cupples (2002), whose research in Nicaragua is discussed in Chapter 4, argues that fieldworkers cannot leave their sexualities at home, regardless of whether they might wish to. This is important, not only for relationships with researched communities but also for dynamics within the student group. Sexuality is sometimes expressed directly, through currents of desire and actual relationships between students, though from what we have seen on fieldtrips this is relatively rare and less important for most students than the ways in which sexualities shape wider relationships and group dynamics. The intimacy of fieldwork brings sexuality into focus, making this more significant than it might be in the classroom or seminar group. Sharing accommodation, including dormitories and bathrooms, is all part of the fun for many, but it can be an issue for some students who will feel their privacy is being threatened, and this may also be particularly acute for those whose religious or cultural backgrounds prescribe specific forms of bodily privacy and/or for those who feel uncomfortable with conventional forms of gender segregation, perhaps because they are gay or lesbian, or because they have had no previous experience of living alongside others who are gay or lesbian. Karen Nairn (2003: 69) interviewed academic staff and students on fieldwork and found evidence that for some students and also staff fieldwork brought their sexuality into focus and frequently in uncomfortable ways. A gay-identified staff member admitted to feeling 'very uncomfortable about the overnight business' and speculated that 'as a student I think I would have felt so uncomfortable as to avoid any course that had a field trip'. Nairn argues 'that the separation of the sexes (in this case of five fieldtrips where this was enacted or at least attempted) was premised on fieldtrip organisers' unspoken assumptions that the field trip participants were heterosexual and separation might manage/control heterosexual desire and/or embarrassment' (2003: 71). Like Rose's generalisations about the relationships between masculinity and drinking, Nairn's assertion that 'sexuality in the classroom tends to be denied' (2003: 69) and her conclusions about the marginalisation of gay and lesbian students can be usefully interrogated. Our experiences suggest that things are not quite so clear-cut, and that an opening-up of the discipline to a 'complex of marginal people' including 'women, or people of colour, or gays, or lesbians', which Audrey Kobayashi (1994: 73) has noted and welcomed, might be finding expression in fieldwork.

Images of heroic fieldwork (see Figure 5.2) underline not only the gender but also the age, race, and physicality of the fieldworker, who is commonly depicted as young, white, and able-bodied. Studies have shown that older and less able students can be left feeling marginalised and in some cases excluded by 'the taken-for-granted notion that everyone is physically able': physically mobile, able to see, and able to cope physically and mentally with long days in the field and in some cases with long flights and late nights (Nairn 1999: 274). These assumptions are, to some extent, self-fulfilling in the sense that they exclude people with disabilities: including those who rely on wheelchairs and/or are blind or visually-impaired, as well as those with conditions ranging from dyslexia, diabetes, and dietary disorders to epilepsy, asthma, and allergies (Hall et al. 2004: 266). In this way, fieldwork has been guilty of compounding the discrimination and deprivation that people with disabilities face in the wider society and in education.

Some disabilities are more prevalent among older students, some of whom find it hard to keep up with physically demanding fieldwork, while also coping with the demands of fitting in socially with students who may be much younger. Typically, an older male student interviewed by Karen Nairn said that he struggled with the physical demands of fieldwork while he also felt like an outsider on the trip and 'perceived that his age shaped how he chose to relate to the younger students as well as how the students might relate to him' (Nairn 1999: 278-9). A student interviewed by Sarah Maguire corroborated this, generalising that 'Older women or men, I believe, felt insecure about going. It is a new thing for a middle-aged person to away with a younger bunch of people'(1998: 212). The tendency for older students to struggle physically on fieldtrips, and thus for discrimination on grounds of age to intersect with that of physical ability or disability, points to a broader set of relationships between various forms of difference and vectors of discrimination. In other words, not only have young, male, able-bodied, white students been feted as the ultimate fieldworkers; other students have also been doubly marginalised, perhaps because they are both old and less fit or because they are both female and belong to a minority religious or cultural group (which may have particular customs regarding gender segregation or alcohol consumption) Their marginality can then be compounded, sometimes to the point that they opt out of or are excluded from a fieldtrip (Nairn 2003).

WHAT CAN YOU DO ABOUT THIS?

But what can you as a student do about any of this? Perhaps not as much as your university and fieldwork leaders, who are increasingly required under the law to make their provisions more inclusive (Hall et al. 2004), and – through the sort of criticisms reviewed here – are also becoming informed and motivated about effecting these changes. In the UK, for example, the Special Education Needs and Disability Act 2001 requires education providers to 'make reasonable adjustment to any arrangements, including physical features of premises, for services that place the disabled student at a substantial disadvantage in comparison to persons who are not disabled' (Department for Education and Employment, quoted by Hall et al. 2004: 256). The emphasis to date has been on what governments, institutions, and fieldtrip leaders can do in practical ways to make provision for students with disabilities . The QAA, for example, stated that 'institutions should ensure that, wherever possible, disabled students should have access [to] fieldtrips' (QAA 2000, Benchmark Statement for Geography, Precept 11, quoted by Hall et al. 2004: 255; see Chapter 2 for a broader discussion of benchmark statements). In addition the Geography Discipline Group published a practical guide to *Providing Learning Support for Students with Hidden Disabilities and Dyslexia Undertaking Fieldwork and Related Activities* (Chalkley and Waterfield 2001), which devoted just one of its 25 pages to 'the student voice'; the rest were concerned with anticipating the needs of students and making provisions for them. Hall et al. (2004: 270) found that universities and fieldtrip leaders have made many different sorts of provisions, ranging from the 'tailoring of field locations' to ensuring that certain students 'get a rest in the afternoons'. But legal obligations and top-down provisions do not absolve students of some responsibility to conduct fieldwork ethically and/or to challenge unethical fieldwork practices. Some students, reading the likes of Rose, may conclude that fieldwork is a rather misogynistic anachronism that is best relegated to the past. Others, however, will want to find ways of working that challenge some of the assumptions about what fieldwork should entail and about who can – and cannot – be a good fieldworker.

Studies of fieldwork have shown that some female students have been happy to throw themselves into practices that are sometimes represented as masculinist. This unsettles generalisations 'that women don't enjoy being outside, getting dirty or taking part in strenuous challenges' (Bracken and Mawdsley 2004: 281). Meanwhile, others have explored ways of doing fieldwork differently and equally of changing perceptions about how fieldwork should be done. For example, they have contested the assumption that fieldwork necessarily 'involves arduous activity; long stays in remote, inhospitable and often hazardous environments; specialist clothing and equipment; and being part of mainly-male teams, whose social culture may involve heavy drinking and general homo-sociability which can be exclusionary to women' (and some men) (2004: 282). In fact, it does not. For example, the heroic image of fieldwork contrasts with actual experiences in which fieldworkers will commonly participate in small groups which can prove to be 'supportive' rather than competitive (2004: 283). This means making choices about how fieldwork is done and how it is represented. For students this can require a series of small choices about whether to take optional fieldwork modules and then about how to participate in the fieldwork they have signed up for.

This means that as a student you can still play a part in finding solutions to the problems and tensions identified above. In one fieldtrip we ran, which involved a residential stay in a hostel that permitted mixed-sex room sharing, in rooms of different sizes, we asked students to decide among themselves how they wished to share. The only rule was that each student must be entirely comfortable with their arrangement. This can have mixed results. Sometimes rooms will be entirely gender segregated; on other occasions male and female students will mix together. One year, for example, a gay-identified male student agreed to share with four female students and all those concerned said they were happy with this arrangement which we would not have imposed ourselves.

In other ways students have also been solving or mitigating some of the exclusionary practices and attitudes that have been implicit in a great deal fieldwork, including discriminatory attitudes towards students with disabilities. Studies of fieldwork in higher education report something that fieldwork leaders can neither enforce nor take credit for: generally good relations between disabled and non-disabled students (Ash et al. 1997). Needless to say, this is not always the case: friendship and other social contacts between disabled and non-disabled students tend to be low outside the classroom and some able-bodied students do play a part in marginalising their disabled peers (Low 1996; Ash et al. 1997; Nairn 1999). So it is incumbent on students, as well as staff and institutions, to 'be more self-reflective and self-critical of [your] social practices while on fieldwork' (Hall et al. 2004: 275), to identify discrimination where it does exist, and to find creative ways of making fieldwork more inclusive as well as ethically sound.

By understanding how fieldwork has marginalised and excluded some students, and how it is being reinvented as a more inclusive and self-reflexive set of practices, you can not only avoid some of the pitfalls that characterised fieldwork in the past, you can also learn positive lessons about the making of geographical knowledge. Fieldwork and the knowledge it produces are fundamentally embodied. As Karen Nairn puts it, 'the body as well as the mind works on a residential field trip' (Nairn 1999: 272). Traditionally the fieldtrip has involved 'geography work (which tends to privilege the mind, the eyes, and the hands)' and 'body work (the eating, drinking, walking, sleeping "like a geographer")' (Nairn 1999: 272). But as these assumptions are unsettled it is not only possible to acknowledge and value different bodies in fieldwork, it is also possible to gain insights about how fieldwork and the knowledge it produces are fundamentally 'embodied'.

If we are aware that fieldwork is indeed an embodied practice we might explore forms of this that dispense with assumptions about what the body can do and which bodily capabilities should be mobilised in the field. We might, for instance, develop non-visual field methods and/ or approach the field through the other senses. Nairn suggests conducting fieldwork in which, for example, students 'take notes about the smells and tastes they experience on field trips' (1999: 281; see also the various discussions of these methods in Chapters 6 and 9). We might also work with the ways in which geographers have different physical abilities with the potential to conduct different kinds of embodied fieldwork. In being sensitised to questions about the body, disability and geography, we might also study disability and space as a subject in its own right (Gleeson 1998). The question of how to do embodied research better is also one with a collective dimension to it, given that students have different bodies and bodily capabilities. Hall et al. suggest that part of the solution to designing more inclusive fieldwork will be to 'rethink specific projects from the perspectives of the different student "bodies" and ask if they are able to achieve their learning outcomes in ways that are inclusive of this diversity' (Hall et al. 2004: 275).

But how can his be done? Students with physical and learning disabilities have demonstrated an understanding of how different abilities need not slow fieldwork down; more positively, they can feed into more diverse and productive ways of working in the field. Robert, a final year geography student with dyslexia, interviewed for a study of fieldwork involving students with disabilities (Chalkley and Waterfield 2001: 18), believed he could work alongside others in group projects, assuming a distinctive and complementary role: 'In group work I like to lead but I am not so good at fine-tuning the report. That's for others'. The authors of this report reinforced Robert's point, generalising that:

> Students with dyslexia often have counter-balancing strengths in other areas and feel disadvantaged by assessment systems which rely very heavily on essays. Fieldwork can be used as an opportunity to recognise strengths in areas such as verbal presentations and thereby help to level the assessment playing field. (Chalkley and Waterfield 2001: 18)

James Robertson, a student with cerebral palsy, reflecting on his disability in the context of education, described a 'buddy system' in which students were paired up according to the complementarity of their abilities and needs: a student who could cook but could not carry pots, for example, would be paired with another person who could carry but not cook. 'I think the buddy system is an invaluable resource for students with disabilities', he concluded, 'because it provides them with the means to be more independent, and also a friend with similar interests and background who can help if they get into difficulty' (Robertson 2002: 31). The positive thing about James's intervention was that despite the conventional wisdom that disabled students should be provided for and that ethical considerations should be anticipated and resolved by academic staff this student demonstrated the important part that students themselves can play in the identification and resolution of ethical issues, and he also illustrated how this can not only enhance the learning experience for students with disabilities but can also do the same for others as well.

SUMMARY

This chapter has discussed the challenges of living and working with others in the field. While some general principles of group work and ethical practices in our encounters with others apply, the intensity of fieldwork means that particular aspects of both need to be considered before, during, and after our fieldwork experiences. The key points of the chapter were:

- The field is a challenging environment to work and socialise in but many potential frustrations and difficulties can be overcome through the relatively simple process of each individual taking some time to think about the impact of their actions.

- Group work may not be enthusiastically embraced by all but its use in fieldwork is often essential and this chapter offers guidance on how to establish group ground rules, understand the variety of team roles that can make up a group, and overcome any difficulties that might arise when working together.

- Individuals interact not only within project groups but also as part of the whole fieldtrip group. This chapter has discussed the ways in which fieldwork has been constructed as a masculine, heterosexual and 'heroic' activity that can exclude many students on the basis of their gender, sexuality, race, and levels of physical and intellectual ability. However, by the subversion of this construction by some staff (through course design) and students (through increased attendance on fieldtrips by a greater diversity of individuals) and through academic critique, we have shown that understandings of what fieldwork is and how we should interact with each other have (hopefully) progressed significantly over recent years. In fact the move towards student-led topic selection and research design means that for many students fieldwork can become (within limits!) what they want it to be.

CONCLUSION

When contemplating attending a fieldtrip students will often focus on the location of the field site and possibly on the types of assessment they will be asked to complete. Some individuals will experience anxieties about other people who will be going on the trip, especially if they don't already know any fellow fieldtripers. This is common, and also represents the significance of the social aspects of fieldwork. Given the intensity of spending several days with a group of people, more attention should be paid to how students can live and socialise together in mutually respectful ways and how they can work effectively in groups to achieve shared goals. This is not necessarily straightforward, but as this chapter demonstrates any investment of time and thought into ensuring good fieldtrip relations will be rewarded through the formation of new relationships and the completion of assessed work.

FURTHER READING/KEY TEXT(S)

- Levin, P. (2005) *Successful Teamwork*. Maidenhead: Oxford University Press. A short text aimed at students, which covers the challenges of group work in general.

- Rose, G. (1993) *Feminism and Geography: the Limits of Geographical Knowledge*. Cambridge: Polity. A punchy, ground-breaking critique of fieldwork as a masculinist tradition, set in the context of a broader feminist critique of Geography.

PART II

METHODS AND CONTEXTS

6

READING THE LANDSCAPE:DESCRIBING AND INTERPRETING FIELD SITES

OVERVIEW

This chapter addresses the following questions:

- How can you describe and interpret 'the field' – the places and landscapes that you encounter in fieldwork?
- How and why are notebooks, cameras, mobile phones, and other gadgets useful for describing and interpreting field sites?
- What is visual fieldwork and how can you interpret and manipulate visual images?
- How are other senses – including sound and smell – also important in landscape descriptions and interpretations?
- How can you explore field sites through the documentary sources you find there?

When you go on a fieldtrip, particularly one far from home, you won't need to be told to take a notebook and a camera, to look around at where you are, to take lots of pictures and notes to use in your field reports and also to share with friends and family, perhaps through the internet. But in order to get the most you can out of this new set of geographical experiences, and to ensure that where possible this supports your assessed work, you will need to think more deeply about how you structure, record, and interpret your observations alongside other representations of the places you encounter. This means paying attention to how others have described and interpreted places or what are sometimes called cultural landscapes: not simply copying their methods, but critically engaging with them and borrowing and adapting where it is meaningful and feasible to do so.

FIELD NOTES

Though you may enter the field equipped with gadgets such as digital cameras and sound recorders, camcorders and laptops, you should not forget their modest ancestors, beginning with the field notebook. A website promoting geographical curiosity, which is discussed in Chapter 9, makes the following suggestion:

> Whenever you go on [an expedition], always take a notebook. You'll end up having surprising thoughts, going off on a tangent - and forgetting them immediately. Any notes you get - descriptions of people, ideas about how your city is used, amazing graffiti you found - all these thoughts are your own, not taught you by anyone. So they're precious. Whether they're for song lyrics, an art project or just a bit of a self-journey ... you'll be glad you had them one day. (http://www.mookychick.co.uk/spirit/psychogeography.php last accessed 2 June 2010)

You are likely to go into the field with specific ideas about the sorts of data you wish to collect, but you would be well advised to leave some time and space for more open-ended observations and notes. These notes − including sketches, descriptions, photographs, and more − can be the first stage in a process of observation, interpretation, and presentation. By making notes on whatever interests you in the field, and the questions that these observations raise, you will begin to identify preoccupations and formulate questions. Rachel Silvey has reflected on the notes she took during some fieldwork in Indonesia:

> During this period of participant observation, I took extensive fieldnotes. While much of what I observed seemed inconsequential at the time, I had been advised to write everything down. This advice proved invaluable. At the time of fieldwork, and even for months afterwards, much of the material in my notes did not seem particularly useful. But ultimately it was essential to the interpretation of the interviews, and has proven useful many times since, as I have returned to the notes and the interview material and worked to make the findings publishable. (2003: 99)

In other words, our field notes can tell us what we are interested in, so reflection on these observations can help us to define and refine research questions and then to become more analytical and deliberate about the ways in which we describe places and landscapes. They can also help us to look back on how our ideas, thoughts, and experiences have evolved during our time in the field.

What might you include in your field notes? We have suggested that you try to keep an open mind about this, including some forms of observation you might be familiar with, and also experiment with others that might be new to you. You could begin with a technique that was commonplace among earlier generations of geographers but which has become quite rare: making a sketch. In the foreword to a book on landscape drawing for geography students, David Linton argued:

> It will be clear to anyone reading this book that there is no better way of becoming seized of the characteristic features of any landscape than by sitting down and making a drawing of it.

> The drawing is not merely a record. It is a means of enabling the geographer to see what he looks at and a step towards understanding what he sees. (1960: vii)

This is why, in an art gallery, you may have noticed art students sitting in front of paintings of sculptures making detailed sketches when they could just have taken a photograph. There is a simple reason for this: in drawing or describing the object in front of us we are forced to look more closely and carefully.

As Raymond Williams put it, 'we learn to see a thing by learning to describe it' (1961: 23). These descriptions can take many forms, beginning simply with words. Don Meinig argues that description is an intrinsically interpretive and creative act: as we describe geographies, 'we can never be describing something that is known, we are discovering it and investing it with meaning'(1983: 323). Of course, this is not easy. It is possible to give tips for getting started in the field, but no simple or comprehensive formulas.

Field notes can also be in an electronic form, of course, including photographs that have been taken with digital cameras and mobile phones. The architect David Adjaye (2010), who conducted an extensive survey of African cities (Figure 6.1), regards the digital photograph as a form of electronic sketch. 'The digital camera is like a sketch book', he says, 'but without the need to dwell on it for a long time. I collect the images and reflect on them later. For me it's a sketch diary of the urban environment'. For Adjaye, the digital photograph can be regarded as an initial response to a new environment:

> When I land in a place I jump in a local taxi and spend the whole day criss-crossing the entire city. I work out the scale of the city and its key criteria. It isn't about me trying to find buildings I like or find interesting ... because of the digital camera I shoot what there is, what I see.

Others will use photography – not only digital but also chemical, including conventional and disposable cameras, still and moving images – in different ways and given the significance of photography in geographical fieldwork these are reviewed in some depth in this chapter. One thing that geographical photographers in all their forms have in common is their specific use of the camera as an observational tool. Elizabeth Chaplin, a social researcher who keeps a photo diary, explains that 'the camera helps you to see actively, to pinpoint the taken for granted' (2004: 47). Whereas most people will take pictures of the remarkable and interesting she aims to do the opposite: to document the routine and the everyday. Students on fieldtrips, travelling as researchers rather than tourists, can learn from Chaplin's advice that keeping a daily photographic diary 'makes you look more closely' at the world around you, taking a second look as you discriminate between possible subjects, and it 'stops you from taking what you see for granted' (2004: 43).

Field 'notes' need not be limited to what you can see and can include other kinds of observations. You can make notes on the sounds, feels, smells, and tastes associated with places, as we discuss in more detail later in this chapter and also in Chapter 9.

Figure 6.1 David Adjaye, 'Urban Africa: A Photographic Survey', exhibition at Design Museum, London, 2010. Photograph by Richard Phillips

Before elaborating on some of the observational techniques that have briefly been introduced here, and before becoming too absorbed in technical details or particular empirical techniques, it is vital to locate these observations within the context of your developing fieldwork. Ideally observations will provoke reflections that will lead to further questions by which your fieldwork will find a focus and take shape. So the field notebook is also a 'reflective diary' – a term that was introduced in Chapter 2. We focused there on one form of reflection: identifying the skills you may be developing in the field. In this chapter we shall focus on another: the significance of what you have observed and described. This process of reflection runs throughout the fieldwork experience as a whole and cannot be contained within a notebook or a stage in the fieldtrip, but it will still help to use this document to focus your ideas. Here are some suggestions for how you can do this:

1   Read and then re-read your notes, the significance of which may not be immediately clear. Rachel Silvey, whose research in Indonesia is mentioned above, suggests that if your notes are extensive it can help to index them in some way, noting any recurring themes and patterns as you go along. She used a 'simple, alphabetical indexing system at the back of the field notebook' and found this saved 'hours of research time' (2003: 99).

2   Pay attention to what you have described. What drew you to it? Even the most appar-
    ently passive description – snapping whatever you see through the viewfinder of a
    camera – reveals a choice you have made; something you were drawn to. The picture is
    'taken' but also 'made' and this means that the taker/maker necessarily plays an active
    part (Chaplin 2004: 36).

3   Pay attention to the ways in which you are describing, including the things you find
    difficult to articulate (put into words). Raymond Williams (1961: 23–24) suggests that
    'we often literally feel ourselves creating as we struggle to describe certain new infor-
    mation for which conventional descriptions are inadequate'. This is because description
    can be 'vital' and creative, a way of opening our eyes and minds to 'new things and new
    relationships'.

4   Reflect on the significance of your observations both for your research questions and
    also for wider debates, which you may have read about in the academic literature. Ask
    yourself: 'Has your experience changed your perception of the research problem and
    the issues associated with it?' (Dummer et al. 2008: 477). The wider theoretical signifi-
    cance of what you have observed may only become apparent to you once you have had
    time to read your notes in the context of academic literature, perhaps after you have
    returned from the field.

VISUAL FIELDWORK

Having begun this chapter with a broad introduction to field notes – what and how you might
observe in the field, and how you might record and interpret your observations – it is now
time to take a closer look at methods that have been used to more systematically investigate
places and landscapes in the context of fieldwork. For better or worse the dominant traditions
in geographical fieldwork are visual, so it is appropriate to begin with visual approaches to
fieldwork. Visual methods, though deeply rooted within the discipline, have been invigorated
in recent years through technological changes that have opened up new possibilities for the
production and manipulation of visual images. The following paragraphs examine critical and
creative approaches to photographic fieldwork methods before turning to look at the limits of
these and explore non-visual and more-than-visual geographical fieldwork.

Photography

Photography has become an increasingly feasible medium for fieldwork in geography. Economic
and technical barriers have been eroded and students are becoming increasingly confident in
the production and manipulation of photographic images. Indeed you are likely to be more
competent than your professors in the use of emerging and rapidly developing visual technologies! But there is more to photography and other visual methods than technical mastery

and 'working with images is still a craft' (Grady 2004: 28). So we will not dwell on technological possibilities and details – which are always changing and developing, quickly rendering
obsolete any very specific discussions – but will instead use this section to explain how photography has been used by students in fieldwork: which questions it has answered, what other
students have learned from it, and what you can learn from their efforts and experiences.

Student photography on two fieldtrips – to Barcelona and Berlin – illustrates the ways in
which you might use cameras in your own fieldwork and the questions you could address in
doing so. This also illustrates that while digital photography has become affordable recently
there can still be a case for using other forms, including cameras that might initially appear to
be old fashioned or technically crude. James Sidaway (2002), leading a trip to Barcelona, provided students with disposable cameras and asked them to take photographs of the city. From
the many pictures they took, which were developed locally, students were asked to select the
four they felt best represented the city and then to explain their choice in an accompanying
text of up to 400 words. Alan Latham and Derek McCormack (2007: 243) set students in Berlin
a similar task. Equipped with digital cameras, they invited them to explore 'how different sites
were woven into the material and imaginative spaces of memory in Berlin' (2007: 246).
Compared with disposables, digital cameras promised a greater technical range, performing
much better in low light conditions and offering video clips as well as stills. In providing the
equipment, Latham and McCormack overcame the problem that students with better cameras
might have an unfair advantage over others without these.

What did these students get out of this photographic fieldwork? What, in other words, are
some of the things you might learn from similar work? First, they learned to use this observational technique to explore geographical concepts in particular places. Those in Berlin, for
example, were sent to 'sites of memory' such as the Soviet Memorial to the Second World War
and asked to visually document each of these. Wherever your fieldtrip takes you, and whatever
your interests are, you should also try to make connections between observations and ideas in
this way. According to Sidaway, the Barcelona exercise gave students 'an opportunity to think
about issues of representation in simple practical terms' and it 'helped them to understand and
practice reflexivity in research, and to reflect on geographical representation' (2002: 100). Their
loosely defined task forced them to address a number of questions:

- Why frame, photograph, and select particular scenes?

- In what ways do they typify the city? What criteria are being used when such typical
  examples are selected?

- How can these be justified?

- What would be the consequences of selecting other images? (2002: 100)

While on this trip students used photography to illustrate what they considered to be typical,
the same methodology can be applied to finding and identifying 'surprises' in the field.

Students on the Berlin fieldtrip felt that the photographic exercise had focused their observational skills. One student commented: 'I became more aware of what was around me and looked closely as opposed to solely wandering through' (Latham and McCormack 2007: 252). Another said that 'Seeing cities through the "eye" of the camera led to a new and enhanced feel of the city' (2007: 252). Photographic fieldwork had some other benefits too, not all of which had been anticipated. Latham and McCormack had encouraged students to ask permission if they were going to take photographs of individuals and this proved to be a conversation starter, leading to a series of interactions that might not otherwise have taken place. Some other researchers are more categorical in their guidance on photographing people and equally positive about the opportunities this creates for interaction. Elizabeth Chaplin's advice is 'always ask permission *before* photographing someone, and always get written permission *before* publishing the photograph' (2004: 45). Her experience has been that most people will gladly give their permission and many will engage the researcher in a conversation about the project.

Whereas the photographic projects on the Berlin and Barcelona fieldtrips concentrated upon a small number of pictures which were selected to explore broader themes, some other researchers have advocated a more systematic use of photography to produce broader sets of visual geographical data. Charles Suchar (2004: 162) used photography in studies of gentrification that adopted a formal sampling frame to direct the camera towards the ordinary and thus to build up a representative picture of selected areas: a 'photographic inventory'. 'The field research strategy', he explained, 'was to systematically photograph these former industrial areas, block by block, sampling/inventorying physical structures of the community in the hope of discerning comparable patterns of use, function and transformation' (2004: 151). This method has the advantage of imposing systematic discipline upon photographic fieldwork and revealing broader patterns that the human eye – drawn to the interesting and exceptional – might otherwise miss. It also assists in recording, observing, and reflecting upon chronological changes in environments and can be applied over different time periods. This could be charting change over years (and even decades if secondary photographic sources are available, as discussed in Chapter 5), days, or even over 24 hours (in order to observe the changes in how spaces are used and by whom, for example).

Auto-photography

Sometimes it can be productive to hand the camera over to someone else. The pictures they take may provide insights into their geographies, including intimate and private places that are off limits to you. A technique known as 'auto-photography' or 'self-directed photography' involves loaning cameras to research participants, providing some instructions on how to use them and what they should photograph, and then collecting the images as a form of data (Ziller 1990). Auto-photography has been used in a variety of geographical research projects: Sarah Johnsen, Jon May and Paul Cloke (2008) investigated geographies of homelessness while Lorraine Young and Hazel Barrett (2001) used this technique to explore the life-worlds of street children in the African city of Kampala, as did David Dodman (2003) in investigating the environmental perceptions of high school students in Kingston, Jamaica. Pictures are said to provide information about inaccessible or private spaces: such as parts of an African city and street children's lives there that are otherwise inaccessible to a western researcher. They are also said to provide information about how their occupants see and experience these places, private and public.

Another attraction of auto-photography is that this technique is said to engage research participants, challenging and inverting the unequal power relations between researcher and researched by allowing the latter to negotiate the research agenda in various ways: from choosing what to photograph to explaining its significance. Research participants generally say they enjoy the projects in which they are involved and are pleased to receive copies of the pictures: Johnsen, May and Cloke observed that the homeless people involved in their auto-photography project appreciated the photographs at a time of their life that was passing largely unrecorded.

In order to select potential participants you may wish to conduct screening interviews which can also be used to help structure your sample, perhaps according to gender, age, and other social categories. After that you will need to provide a camera and give some instructions on what to photograph and how to do this. Technical guidance will probably be minimal since you are likely to be using disposable cameras that you can afford to buy and, if necessary, lose. Instructions on what to photograph should be equally clear and simple. Sue Heath and Elizabeth Cleaver gave the following instructions in their study of the spaces of shared rental housing:

> Using as many of the photos on the camera as you wish, we would like you to make a visual record of what to you are the significant and meaningful aspects of living in a shared house and a shared household. Your photos may be related to any or none of the topics we have previously discussed with you. It's your camera and your record. If you don't use all of the shots on the film that's fine – just rewind when you've taken the photos you require. (2004: 70)

You may wish to follow up the photographic exercise with interviews in which you will use the pictures as 'interview probes' and ask participants to provide captions or explain their content and significance. Illustrating how this can be done, Johnsen et al. (2008: 197) invited participants to discuss each of the images they had taken, asking (among other things) about the places shown: where they were, what they were used for, by whom, and where.

Photographs and interview transcripts are usually analysed through qualitative means. In some cases, however, researchers have analysed the contents of photographs numerically, generally starting by coding images into types and then counting how frequently each of these appears. Pictures taken by Jamaican school children, for example, were coded into those depicting 'scenery/natural beauty', 'environmental problems', and 'environmental management', among other things. Dodman (2003: 297) acknowledges the limits of coding images in this way – as he puts it, 'no system of classification can do justice to the many levels of meaning present in the photographs' – but he also argues that this approach opens up new possibilities for interpretation including comparisons between sub-groups of respondents.

Students using auto-photography on fieldwork projects should be aware not only of the possibilities of content analysis but also of the barriers to this approach. Dodman's Jamaican project involved 45 cameras and over 800 photographs which is obviously beyond the scope of most undergraduate fieldwork. Similar constraints apply to forms of auto-photography involving advanced cameras for recording still and moving images which have been used by well-resourced professional researchers. For example, you are unlikely to be able to follow Sara Kindon's (2003) example in using participatory video. Still, we would encourage you to explore the technical means at your disposal and as always to be imaginative and innovative in what you do.

Other visual sources: found images

Whether you take pictures yourself, commission others to take them, or come across these in some other way, you will find you have a rich and complex data set. This is both an advantage and also a challenge. John Grady (2004: 19) observed that images could take many forms and express many impulses – 'ideology, personal statement or even accident' – and therefore they constitute a diverse and complex data set. However we should not be too overwhelmed by this. First, we can observe that geographical images contain two main types of information: about how people understand, use and experience places, and about the places themselves. This two-fold information reflects the double meaning of landscape as a way of seeing and as a material space. By interpreting geographical images in all their forms we can distinguish and draw out these two main types of information. This section broadens the discussion of photographs to take in a wider range of geographical images before providing guidance on interpreting this kind of data.

While photographs that are taken and commissioned in the course of fieldwork can give information about these material spaces and ways of seeing, so do photographs and other visual images that are produced by others which may be encountered and collected in the field, including paintings, maps, and visual images embedded in design, architecture, and the written word. The interpretation of landscape paintings as forms of geographical data was pioneered by Dennis Cosgrove (1984) and Stephen Daniels (1993) in their studies of the geographical images and imaginaries that accompanied and produced capitalism and nationalism in modern Europe and the United States. Contemporary cultural geographers, influenced by Cosgrove and Daniels, began to take all sorts of visual images seriously as forms of geographical data. These included historical and contemporary photographs. Joan Schwarz and James Ryan (2003: 1) argue that photography has been an 'ally' of geographical imagination and a 'powerful tool in our engagement with the world around us', revealing how people see their environments and shaping their ways of seeing. Photographs, they argue, are not simply documents about landscapes past and present, they are also used to actively shape peoples' relationship with the environment and this can range from mountains and valleys to domestic interiors.

As secondary sources – found rather than made by the researcher – visual images can take many different forms. Sourcing these images does not necessarily require 'fieldwork' as they can also be gathered via the internet, libraries, and archival and desk-based research, though visual images may also be collected in the field. These images are likely to include photographs that have been taken by other people and produced and consumed in context: for example, in travel and tourist promotions, real estate marketing, regional and local development and government, ethnography and family life. Images, some of which you might have been able to download individually from the internet, might therefore be encountered in the field in brochures and posters, in local newspapers, and on advertising hoardings. In these contexts the images acquire specific meanings and become part of the field itself (as Cheryl McEwan (2006) discusses in relation to fieldwork for development geographies).

Postcard 6.1 discusses some images that were found during the course of fieldwork in Paris. These illustrate how found images can be an intriguing source of information: about the places they depict, the places to which they were sent, and the places where these images can be found today.

Postcard 6.1: Postcards from Paris, by Richard Phillips (source: Richard Phillips)

(Continued)

(Continued)

A group of students from Wales was investigating traces of imperialism and colonialism in Paris. My guidebook to the French capital city gave us some useful tips, suggesting several sites in which imperialism was marked (Rough Guide 1995). These included the then-unreconstructed Musée des Arts Africains et Océaniens, which housed a collection of culture and creatures from the old French colonies, and the métro Bon Nouvelle, where police had brutally crushed a demonstration organised by the Algerian liberation front, the FLN, in 1961. The traces of imperialism and colonialism in Paris were not always easy to find, sometimes because they were and are ephemeral — museums being refurbished with more critical sensitivity than was once displayed and anti-colonial massacres unmarked — but these temporary traces can sometimes still be uncovered, particularly if you are prepared to use a little imagination. Visiting a street market, for example, and looking through some stalls selling books and old papers, we came across postcards that had been sent from Algeria. Some of these are reproduced here: one showing the modern-looking port and

(Continued)

(Continued)

European quarter, another the Arab quarter and some of its inhabitants. These interested us because they had survived as traces of the 'geographies of connection' that had once linked metropolitan France with Algeria. The postcards illustrated something of how the French saw – or wanted to see – this colony, suggesting pride in the European city they had built there and showing the smiling faces of apparently willing colonial subjects. These are also poignant images: the violence of the anti-colonial struggle in Algeria and also, as we had discovered, in Paris itself, undermined the postcards' optimistic suggestions about progress and social harmony. Their inscriptions – referring to family visits and social occasions – also stood in contrast to the tensions that erupted in Algiers, leading to the decolonisation of Algeria and the exile of hundreds of thousands of settlers, most of whom migrated to France where they were known as pieds noirs. Georges Perec, a French writer discussed in Chapter 9, explored the inscriptions on postcards – found or possibly invented objects – in more depth, in the poetic piece, 'Two Hundred and Forty-three Postcards in Real Colour'. These included the following messages, which once again speak of geographies of connection, in this case simply between home and holidays:

We're camping near Ajacco. Lovely weather. We eat well. I've got sunburnt. Fondest love.

We're at the Hotel Alcazar. Getting a tan. Really nice! We've made loads of friends. Back on the 7th.

We're sailing off L'Ile-Rousse. Getting ourselves a tan. Food admirable. I've gone and got sunburnt! Love etc.

We've just done Dahomey. Superb nights. Fantastic swimming. Excursions on camel-back. Will be in Paris on the 15th. (Perec 1997 [1978]: 218-235)

This scrapbook of postcards is not quite as random or eccentric as it might first appear. Perec echoes others before him who also collected and worked with 'found objects', in which he found humour, poetry, and visual interest. These postcards illustrate how the field is a good place to gather visual images and also to explore not only their content but also their contextual production and consumption, both of which produce cultural meanings that cannot necessarily be found in abstracted images that would have been downloaded from the internet or traced in picture libraries.

New visual media

Geography's visual tradition – conventionally associated with producing and interpreting maps and other two-dimensional representations – has been shaken up by new (and/or newly afford-able) media. Geographers are beginning to explore and experiment with moving images in particular. Though there is now a growing geographical literature on film – concerned with geographical representations in film (Shiel and Fitzmaurice 2001) and with economic geogra-phies of the film industry (see for example, Scott 2000; 2002) – geographers have only just begun to invest in making films. Matthew Gandy's documentary on landscapes of water in Bombay (discussed in Gandy 2008) set an exciting example of this but also illustrated some of the challenges of making films: his half-hour film drew upon research council funding, the technical expertise of a team of professionals, and an impressive creative input on the part of Gandy himself. This is inspiring but it might also be a little intimidating to undergraduates thinking of making their own films during short fieldtrips. Still, the barriers to aspiring film makers are diminishing, as technical advances bring film-making – sound and image recording and editing – within the scope of some students. Digital cameras and mobile phones increas-ingly record moving images complete with soundtracks, which can be downloaded onto lap-tops and manipulated or uploaded onto websites, and these advances look set to continue. So film, as a medium for undergraduate fieldwork, has at least reached an exploratory stage.

How might you produce and use moving images in fieldwork? Alan Latham and Derek McCormack (2007) have explored the use of video clips in a fieldwork exercise in Berlin, designed to explore and engage with the rhythms of that city. Their objective has been to exploit the possibilities of moving images specifically to investigate that which still images and descriptions had struggled or failed to capture, such as the temporal experience of travelling on the urban railway (the *U-Bahn*), and more generally dynamic geographies of movements and urban pathways. Students went to various sites around the city to explore site-specific rhythms, recording these through video clips, which some later uploaded onto websites and used in presentations. This project highlighted the challenges of learning and working with new tech-nology in a short space of time – many of the students needed to learn basic techniques such as keeping cameras still while recording movement. But this illustrated how technological advances are opening up new possibilities for fieldwork, specifically for reading landscapes, and how these work best when they are mobilised in the context of established questions and debates, rather than simply exploited as technological novelties.

Some other emerging technologies, uses of which have been explored in the context of environmental fieldwork, may have yet to prove themselves in the context of human geography. These include three-dimensional digital imaging, in which scanning devices and/or digital data sets are used in visualisation software to generate realistic perspective views from hypothetical station points: virtual camera images (Mitchell 2003). This technology has been used in 'ground truthing' exercises, in which computer-generated images are compared with actual landscapes to test the veracity of the former. It has also been used in the manipulation of observations: in the augmentation of 'real scenes' to include hidden and historical information such as geological and glacial data, and perhaps in plans, predictions, and scenarios for future landscape change (Priestnall 2009: S104).

Three-dimensional imaging also has applications in virtual fieldwork in which it is possible to move around field sites interactively and freely. Google Earth, which offers this facility, has been described as 'an exciting new teaching resource for geography' (Thorndycraft et al. 2009: 48), bringing 'benefits, such as the ability to "fly" around the study area, zoom in and out, and rotate and tilt images, which enable sophisticated interpretations of the landscape that may not be apparent through aerial photographs or a conventional field trip to the same locality' (Thorndycraft et al. 2009: 50). Digital mapping and 3-D visualisation have mainly been practised and pioneered in physical geography and other environmental sciences, where the visualisation of landscape is seen as relatively unproblematic and where conventional cartographic data is predominant (e.g. McCaffrey et al. 2003). It is not difficult to imagine how this technology might be useful in human geography and related disciplines such as urban planning and landscape design. But while we would encourage you to explore and enjoy these possibilities, we would also suggest that technology should be your servant and not your master. In other words, make sure your direction comes not from the latest gadget but from your own questions and ideas.

Interpreting and manipulating visual images

We have suggested that a visual image should be seen as a rich and complex data set, and now it is time to suggest how such data can be interpreted. Gillian Rose has proposed some questions that can help here. Some of these concern the production of the image (including when, where, by whom, and why it was produced) and its audiences (who consumed, stored, and circulated the image). Other questions concern the image itself and these are most likely to be relevant to you if on your fieldtrip you have either taken photographs or asked others to take these, or have collected visual material yourself and now want to interpret these images (Rose 2001: 188–190):

- What is being shown? What are the components of the image? How are they arranged?

- Where is the viewer's eye drawn to in the image, and why?

- What is the vantage point of the image?

- How has technology affected the text?

- To what extent does the image draw on the characteristics of its genre?

- What do the different components of the image signify?

- Whose knowledges are being excluded from this representation?

Recognition that photographs are made rather than taken by people, and that humans are equally active in the production of other visual and non-visual images, is reinforced by our understanding of how these images are produced and manipulated in the digital age. Images are made and remade through a series of events and processes, including production, reproduction, storage, processing, management, distribution, and consumption. So we must first abandon any thought of the photographic image as a mechanically produced reflection of nature. As a result we can then embrace the possibilities inherent in this more fluid conception of the visual image in actively manipulating and working with images. William Mitchell (2003: 290) argues that 'the technology of digital imaging, by comparison with that of chemical photography, creates a freshly re-enlarged space for ... intervention'. He suggests that while intervention can be 'arbitrary' and 'artistic' it still has the potential to be strategic and conceptually driven. This is not something with which geographers may feel intuitively comfortable. *National Geographic* magazine once sparked controversy by 'retroactively repositioning' a cluster of pyramids in a cover picture. This unsettled some readers who protested and got an apology, but the issue would not (and could not) go away so easily. Digital images are not only open to manipulation; they depend upon it. The production of digital images includes choices regarding 'colour palettes, contrast levels, resolutions' and 'there is nothing objective or inevitable' about any of these elements of the 'display generation processes'. As you will know if you have experimented with visual software such as Photoshop, it is possible to retouch and manipulate digital images much more freely than would have been the case with chemical photography. Mitchell warns that this can lead us down a 'disturbingly slippery slope' since there is no point at which 'a trivially retouched image becomes a fictional construction rather than a documentary record'. This makes explicit, in terms that are difficult to ignore, something that critics of conventional photography had been saying for years: photographs are made, not taken, and their realism is conventional and superficial (all quotations from Mitchell 2003: 289–290).

If we no longer see photographs simply as representations, we can begin to ask interesting questions about the form and limits of representation within visual and other descriptions. Eric Laurier and Chris Philo underlined the limits of words and maps to represent people and places, which they would argue are illuminated in 'the points at which language finds its limits: ... things, events, encounters, emotions and more that are unspeakable, unwriteable and, of course, unrepresentable' (2006: 353). While we should experiment with new forms of description, we should therefore acknowledge the limits of description. But Laurier and Philo make a further distinction: between the impossibility of representation on the one hand, and resisting representation on the other.

MORE-THAN-VISUAL DESCRIPTIONS

There are good reasons to be cautious about applying increasingly elaborate visual technologies to human geography fieldwork. Though it may be exciting to fly Harry Potter-style around a virtual field site, it is important to remember that people do not really do this and that disembodied virtual experiences miss much of what actually takes place in the field: embodied encounters that, in their messy ways, generate geographical knowledges. Virtual fieldwork is widely seen and modelled as a heightened form of visualisation, in which going to the field is equated with *seeing* the field. And yet the visual dominance of human geography is both limiting and problematic. Susan Smith (1994) gives three reasons for this: it encourages us to neglect our other senses in structuring and experiencing space and place; it excludes people who are blind or visually impaired; and more specifically, it distracts us from sounds such as traffic noise and music which play an important part in distinguishing places. In other words, there is more to geography than meets the eye. Cole Harris, the historical geographer, reflected on the limits of what can be seen in the field: 'I am an inveterate explorer of landscapes', he wrote, 'and I have found therein some of my moments of greatest pleasure and insight. Yet I am also aware of how much is hidden from my – from any geographer's – field gaze' (2001: 329–330). He concluded that visual impressions should be complemented with other forms of data such as

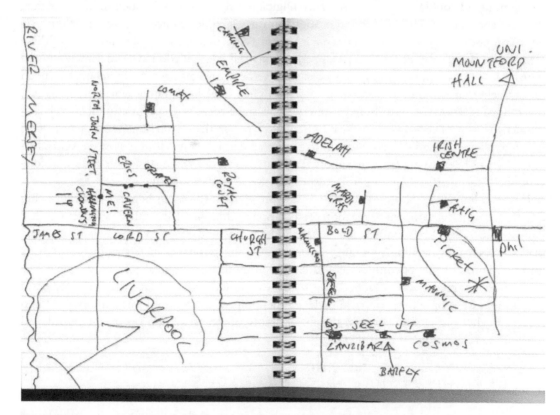

Figure 6.2 A singer-songwriter's hand-drawn map of Liverpool music venues, produced through research on landscapes of sound by Sara Cohen and Brett Lashua. *Source*: Brett Lashua.

archival records. Others, for similar reasons, have set visual sources alongside those associated with other senses, balancing the visible with that which can be heard, smelt, touched, and tasted.

These are good principles but how can you act on them? First, you could try to focus not just on what you see but also on what you perceive in other ways. Begin with what you hear. Susan Smith argues that sounds are important in defining places and geographical experiences and identities, while sound also 'has a social and political significance which, if it could be heard, might influence, change or enrich the interpretation of particular scenes' (1994: 234). She is particularly interested in music, which is important in shaping a variety of places – from elevators with background music to bars and restaurants with signature playlists (Leyshon et al. 1996; Anderson et al. 2005). To illustrate this, Sara Cohen, a professor of musicology, has investigated the geographies of music – sites for practising, recording, performing, and listening to music – and generated maps of musical landscapes such as the singer-songwriter's map of Liverpool shown in Figure 6.2 and a Liverpool hip-hop artist's hand-drawn map of his neighbourhood, in Figure 6.3 (see Lashua and Cohen 2010; Cohen and Lashua, 2010).

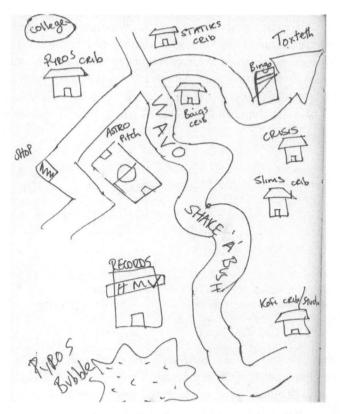

Figure 6.3 A Liverpool hip-hop artist's hand-drawn map of his Wavertree neighbourhood. *Source*: Brett Lashua.

A more radical soundscape might exchange the visual mapping shown in Figures 6.2–3 for representations ordered around sound itself and the content might also reference sounds and noises. There is no simple way of doing this. If you have attempted to record an interview in a public place such as a street cafe, and then listened to the recording, you are likely to have been struck by the volume and variety of background noises: sounds that your brain filtered out when listening to the speaker, but which the audio recorder picked up. Turning your attention to sounds you will need to open your ears to the sounds and noises around you, listening more carefully than you might normally do. Sociologist Les Back (2003) argues that, if we learn to listen as seriously as we have become accustomed to looking, we may have to find new ways of describing soundscapes: 'If we listen to it the landscape is not so much a static topography that can be mapped and drawn, rather it becomes a fluid and changing surface that is transformed as it is enveloped by different sounds' (2003: 272–273). Therefore, in order to become aware of soundscapes and to begin to describe them, you will need to be inventive, perhaps by experimenting with sound recording equipment which may be built into your digital camera or mobile phone. There are opportunities here for geography students to be creative and imaginative!

In contrast with visual geographies relatively little effort has been expended on researching and mapping soundscapes, smellscapes, and other sensory geographies. William Bunge, whose geographical expeditions are discussed in Chapter 9, mapped some of the smells of Toronto and Detroit in research conducted with local volunteers and students between 1972 and 1975. For Bunge, smells provided clues to social geographies, and this is illustrated in his descriptions of the 'unique smells' of a neighbourhood named Christie Pitts (Bordessa and Bunge 1975: 15–16):

> Part of this culture is expressed in the smells of the area, although in certain parts and at certain times, these smells are suppressed by machine-smells. At 7 p.m. on a summer evening, the cooking smells from kitchens waft out into the street. Onions and garlic are a strong feature in the tempting aroma from tomato sauces. In late September, when grapes, tomatoes and peppers are ripe and ready to use for wines and sauces, the smells from these become a part of life in Christie Pitts. Households make their yearly supplies at this time.
>
> Saturday is a busy day for residents and smells of cleaning, painting, gardening and garbage are present. Two foreign and strong smells intrude on the community daily: the smell of roasting oil from the near-by Planter's peanuts factory, and that of freshly-baked bread from the plant of Canada bread.

Though Bunge's radical brand of humanistic geography was influential, his initiatives on mapping smells have not been taken up in any sustained way.

More recently, the possibilities for researching and mapping soundscapes have been the subject of some creative research in geography and related disciplines such as musicology, as Postcard 6.2 illustrates.

Postcard 6.2: Soundscapes, by Brett Lashua

City soundscapes – clattering trains, announcements, street traffic, buskers, wind, construction, footfalls, machinery, the drone of voices and snippets of conversations – are noisy cacophonies. But what do soundscapes 'say' about urban inhabitants, social relations, and identities? Who belongs, where, and when? What can we learn by listening to urban space? When I taught music production at an alternative high school in Edmonton, we created soundscapes by first going on soundwalks. Soundwalks are journeys around the city centre with a portable recorder, paying attention to and 'collecting' sounds along the way. We'd traipse through urban passageways – like many Canadian cities, Edmonton has labyrinthine walkways (underground pedways, above-ground skyways) so pedestrians like us (but also not very much like 'us') may navigate the city without ever stepping into the bitter cold outside – capturing everything that passed by our microphones. Back at school, we'd edit and mix these 'found sounds' into sonic collages (soundscape compositions), sometimes adding in students' spoken-word poetry or rap lyrics (for mixing, free digital sound editor Audacity works well: http://audacity.sourceforge.net).

Removed from taken-for-granted contexts and with sounds oddly juxtaposed, soundscapes called my attention to the 'other' city that young people inhabited. (For example, one young woman roamed the city during lunch hour, saying hello to everyone she passed – no adults replied to her. Another recorded train station announcements and wrote rap lyrics that name-checked the stations; however, he stopped before University station because he 'would never go there'.) Like many North American cities, Edmonton was emptied of its office workers after 6 p.m. and largely deserted by adults. Come night time the city took on a different pace, hum, and rhythm. A 24-hour coffee shop populated with suited civil servants during the day overflowed at night with teenagers in hip-hop clothing. The bus shelters near the City Centre Mall – sites of arriving, departing, and simply meeting up – swam with young people at night. Shops were closed, food courts shuttered, but young people lingered, noisily, in passageways and in-between spaces: there were few acceptable places or times for teenagers to be in the city. Later there were those who didn't want to go home or didn't have homes to go to. Some were students I worked with at the alternative school. Labelled 'youth at-risk', most had failed or been

(Continued)

(Continued)

expelled from 'regular' high schools: poverty, addictions, gangs, violence (as perpetrators and victims), homelessness, and a lack of social support caused other difficulties. Most were First Nations (Aboriginal-Canadians) and racism and discrimination compounded the challenges of their lives. They often spoke of their treatment as second-class citizens, the daily abuse, and the verbal taunts of 'fucking Indians'.

I began to hear these social relations in the city soundscape. One young woman spoke of how different the underground pedways sounded during daytime, when full of voices, versus the quiet of night. During the day she felt out of place, as if young, First Nations people did not belong in the city of white, middle-class professionals. Similarly, familiar busy night-time spaces were deserted during the day, such as the gritty alleyways leading to 'after-hours' clubs where she would dance from 11 p.m. until 7 a.m. During our soundwalking tours she told me I was learning to see (and hear) things 'from a street kid's perspective'. That is, I learned that when struggling, impoverished, homeless, trying to stay high or simply stay alive, there were different movements and places to know – where to go, where and when to sleep or to stay awake, where to keep warm, where to find comfort and joy in spite of all other difficulties.

The sociologist Henri Lefebvre referred to the study of different spaces and paces of everyday urban life as 'rhythmanalysis' – considering comings and goings, patterns of movement, repetitions, schedules, gestures, traffic, speech, sudden noises, pauses and silences. My Edmonton rhythmanalysis alerted me to the persistence of what the author China Miéville (2009) called 'the city and the city', where citizens of one municipality are unable to see the inhabitants of the other, although – bizarrely – the cities share the same space. Edmonton is similarly two such cities, with spaces used differently at different times by inhabitants who do not interact. One is a city of power, privilege, affluence; one is a city of 'the Other', of poverty, discrimination, and disadvantage. Walking through Edmonton, I had been unaware of the city (the Other city) until young people taught me to listen to it.

If sounds and smells have been relatively neglected in student fieldwork and more generally in geographical research this is doubly true of the other senses, touch and taste, where empirical research falls behind theoretical assertions about the importance of this subject material (Rodaway 1994; Low 2005). Picking up on Mike Crang's point that qualitative methods 'often derided for being somehow soft and "touchy-feely" have in fact been rather limited in touching and feeling' (2003: 494), Robyn Longhurst advocates fundamentally embodied geographical research 'to examine what embodied senses such as smell and taste can add to our understandings of relationships between people and places' (Longhurst et al. 2008: 214-215). Once again, the question of how to do this research remains largely unanswered and open, and an invitation to imaginative geography fieldworkers!

DOCUMENTARY SOURCES

While you may read the field directly you can also collect documentary evidence about it, including written sources, images, and artefacts. As discussed in Chapter 3 you should see what secondary material you can compile before you begin your fieldwork through a variety of sources and media such as online newspapers and other resources, but you will also find some additional documentary sources within field sites. Some of these might seem to jump out at you, but you may have to actively search for others. The world is crammed full of geographical and sociological documents, as one critic has observed: 'People keep diaries, send letters, make quilts, take photos, dash off memos, compare auto/biographies, construct websites, scrawl graffiti, publish their memoirs, write letters, compose CVs, leave suicide notes, film video diaries, inscribe memorials on tombstones, shoot films, paint pictures, make tapes and try to record their personal dreams' (Plummer 2001: 17).

   Despite the range of information available over the internet, most secondary data remain in physical rather than electronic forms including archives, museums, media, and personal collections. Many archives and museums are actively seeking to digitise their collections, but it is a lengthy process with backlogs of items, and many other documentary sources – such as free local newspapers and personal items – are ephemeral, circulated and used for a short time in particular places before being lost or destroyed. For this reason, researchers can still benefit from visiting places and archives where documents and artefacts are held (see Figure 6.4). This section identifies some of the sites and sources that you may find useful for documentary research when you are in the field.

Libraries

It is a good idea to find out about libraries and archives before you travel to your field site and to research their holdings and visiting arrangements including their opening hours, charges, and access arrangements. Once in the field it will also be helpful to visit and review any resources that might assist you with your research, whether or not your project is explicitly documentary or archival. In a library you can browse through local collections and it is also worthwhile seeking advice from archivists and reference librarians who may be able to help you understand the context in which documents are held and provide background information to help explain their context. Reference collections will typically include directories, yearbooks, almanacs, registers and manuals, many of which are unlikely to be available over the internet. Local directories in particular can be utilised to obtain lists of organisations and companies that can form the basis of sampling for other research methods. Libraries also tend to hold national and local government

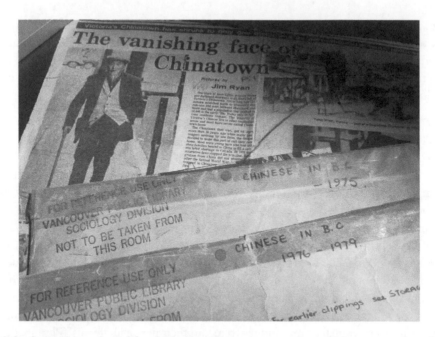

Figure 6.4 Selection of archived documentary sources on Chinese communities and geographies in British Columbia, available in Vancouver Public Library. Photograph by the authors

reports and filings of committee meetings. There may be a map library which could allow you to trace changes in the built environment in your field location or assist you in researching how the town or city has represented itself over time through maps. Public libraries also hold copies of local publications including newspapers and specialised trade publications. Finally, in addition to all the tangible sources they hold, libraries and archives themselves can be interesting places. You may be able to soak up the atmosphere of these local institutions, where you are surrounded by books and documents as well as the people who are using them.

Museums

Investigate what is happening at the local museums while you are in the field. You may get lucky and find an exhibition that is of relevance to your research topic, but in any case museums and the people who use them can tell you interesting things about a place. Most museums are only able to display a fraction of their holdings at any given time, so do pay attention to what may be held but not on display. The assistance of a knowledgeable and helpful museum curator may be a necessity in order to access and/or learn about all potential resources. Be open to non-written forms of data such as sound recordings and material artefacts and also consider the ways in which these holdings are presented. It is also worthwhile considering not only the collections themselves but also the spaces in which they are shown and housed.

Media Sources

In the field, you will come across images and sources of information from entertainment week-
lies to trade journals and locally broadcast television news that may not initially seem 'official'
enough to contribute to your research. In fact, all of these can provide fascinating insights into
geographical issues and tell you much about your field location and the people who inhabit it.
As Paul Cloke et al. (2004: 71) explain, 'newspapers articles and stories form a major part of
lives, alongside audio and visual news media' and these shape and inform our geographical
imaginations. You can use local media to familiarise yourself with the field location and the
people who live there – picking up local knowledge, understandings, and even ways of speaking that can help you become a better researcher and communicate more effectively – or you
can take this a step further and focus your field research on the media.

Figure 6.5   Selection of local newspapers held and available in Vancouver Public Library.
Photograph by the authors

Everyday documents

It is also possible to collect other informal and unofficial documents in the field, ranging from event programmes (for example for football matches or theatre performances) to flyers advertising local businesses, and from graffiti on walls to announcements broadcast in stations. You may also come across private documents which form an important part of many peoples' everyday lives: such as 'to do lists', emails to friends, left voice messages, post-it note reminders, home-made maps giving directions to friends, and personal diaries. Some of these may be archived, others simply lost or discarded and found or otherwise acquired, like the postcards illustrated earlier in this chapter (see Postcard 6.1).

You may decide to use one or more of the documentary sources introduced above to provide background material for other forms of empirical field research, perhaps to describe the historical context for contemporary observations or to devise a sampling frame through which to select areas, communities, or companies for closer investigation. Or, like the student fieldwork described in Postcard 6.3, you may choose to go further with your research in the libraries and archives and make this more central to your fieldwork. This can be challenging, forcing you to negotiate archives' and libraries' rules and regulations and plan your time around their opening hours. But archival research can prove rewarding and insightful, as Innes M. Keighren illustrates in his postcard from New York.

Postcard 6.3: Fieldwork in the Archive, by Innes M. Keighren

The New York Public Library on Manhattan's Fifth Avenue is the venue for a particular form of urban exploration. Here, a group of undergraduate human geographers, in the city for a week-long fieldtrip, will explore the history of New York through the archives of an organisation called the Committee of Fourteen – a citizen group that took an active interest in the city's moral geography. The Committee's archive comprises 96 boxes of material – including correspondence, minute books, financial records, and investigators' reports – accumulated between 1901 and 1932.

This archive was chosen to enable the students to explore certain issues they had encountered in the classroom. These included broader debates about the regulation of public space, the construction of racial and sexual identities, and the influence of surveillance practices. Time in the field was limited, so the students were required to prepare carefully. Before arriving in Manhattan, they completed a series of

(Continued)

(Continued)

staff-led tutorials during which they began to piece together, through secondary literature, the Committee's history, and to familiarise themselves with the archive's on-line finding aids. The students then selected and pre-ordered material, enabling them to start work as soon as they entered the reading room.

Through this archive, the students began to build up a picture of moral politics in early-twentieth-century New York. They traced how the Committee of Fourteen – which drew its membership from New York's elite and social reformers – dedicated itself to the elimination of prostitution, gambling, and alcohol. Its approach was two-pronged: lobbying politicians, lawmakers, and law enforcers; and conducting undercover surveillance of various public spaces where vice was suspected. The Committee's covert investigators visited bars, pool halls, dance halls, and hotels in black and immigrant neighbourhoods, seeking to map what they saw as a spreading and malignant geography of vice. All this has powerful resonances with contemporary New York, where moral campaigns extend to the 'Disneyfication' of Times Square and the elimination of smoking in certain public spaces.

From these fragments, the students address a number of contemporary concerns in human geography: one considers the politics of race through an examination of Greenwich Village's Black-and-Tan saloons; another attends to the representation of immigrant groups as pernicious threat through attention to the Committee's reports and contemporary newspaper coverage; a third examines the link between surveillance and the political and judicial regulation of behaviour. In this sense, the archive is not the ossified remnant of a city now vanished, but a lively resource which allows the students to understand how Manhattan came to be what it is now through a series of ongoing social processes. Dogged digging in the archive offers up a valuable context to the contemporary cultural, political, economic, and social issues which they encounter elsewhere in the geography curriculum.

Stepping beyond the archive and the library, the students emerge into the modern city, keen to trace what has become of the spaces they have read about: the Women's Night Court, where suspected prostitutes were tried in front of morbidly-enthralled crowds; the Golden Swan saloon, where Eugene O'Neill once drank and where he based his famous play, The Iceman Cometh; the Green Cup Café where the Committee's investigators reported the morally-troubling mixing of

(Continued)

> *(Continued)*
>
> *black prostitutes and white patrons. One building has become a branch of the New York Public Library; one, a quiet and leafy park; another, a pizzeria. Although the students are disappointed that the edgy and unpredictable city they have been exploring by proxy has apparently been washed away, they conclude that the history of New York is a continuing story of its population's vices and its attempts to banish them. They end their urban exploration with a taste of modern Manhattan – a slice of cheese pizza from what was once the Green Cup Café.*

Field Landscape Interpretation

There are almost as many reasons to describe places and landscapes as there are lines of geographical enquiry, so this chapter has been primarily concerned with the ways in which we describe rather than with what we describe and why. So it would have been too narrow to frame the interpretation of places through geography's landscape tradition. Still, it is helpful to acknowledge the main ways in which geographers have approached landscapes, since this helps to set out some of the things you can look for when describing and interpreting field sites.

There are two main ways in which places and landscapes – as material spaces and as representations – have been interpreted in geography. First, as evidence about the people and/or culture that produced them. A tradition of landscape studies spans the work of Carl Sauer, who concentrated on rural and historical geographies, through to John Brinckerhoff Jackson, who shifted the focus to suburban, domestic, and other 'ordinary' landscapes. This tradition concentrates on describing material vernacular landscapes and asking about the sorts of peoples and cultures that fashioned them (Jackson 1984; Wilson and Groth 2003). Studies of ordinary landscapes include, for example, urban graffiti (Ley and Cybriwsky 1974), fast food restaurants and coffee shops (Fishwick 1995; Smith 1996; Winchester et al. 2003: 37). American geographer Peirce Lewis identified a number 'axioms' for reading landscapes such as these, designed to help students 'make cultural sense of ordinary things that constitute the workaday world of things we see' (1979: 11). These axioms revolve around the claim that the human landscape 'provides strong evidence of the kind of people we are, and were, and are in process of becoming' (1979: 16). Lewis stressed that these places do not always speak to us very clearly, meaning that we may have to work hard at uncovering their secrets, interrogating their silences, and uncovering their hidden histories if we are to get beneath the surface. Don Mitchell politicises this approach to landscape interpretation, focusing attention on the production of spaces and the conflicts that take place within and through them. This means 'searching below the surface of material landscapes like city blocks or national parks, "ethnic" neighbourhoods and monumental buildings, as well as of paintings, photographs, gardens, and other more representational landscapes, to uncover the conditions under which a landscape is made' and the 'culture wars through which landscapes are made' (2000: 114). He compares the landscape to a 'vortex' in which 'swirl all manner of contests – between classes, over gender structures, around issues of race and ethnicity, over meaning and representation'(2000: 139). Secondly, then, landscapes are interpreted as indicators of the social relations and struggles of the people who not only made them but who also contest their meanings. James Duncan has recast landscape interpretation, reading the landscape less as material artefact and more as 'signifying system', proposing 'a methodology for interpreting landscapes' that re-reads landscape as a system of 'cultural production' that 'may be integral to both the production and contestation of political power' (1990: 3). He suggests a series of questions that students of landscape would do well to ask:

- What does a landscape representation mean to those who produce, reproduce, or transform it?

- What differences exist between insiders' and outsiders' readings of landscape?

These questions shift the focus from the landscape itself to relationships between people that are channelled and expressed through this representational and material space (see Mitchell 2000).

SUMMARY

This chapter has discussed how and why the description and interpretation of landscape can be a significant and exciting part of the fieldwork. The key points were:

- We need to think creatively and critically about places and landscapes we encounter in the course of fieldwork.

- Field notebooks can be an invaluable tool for recording observations, experiences, and thoughts.

- Technological advances have widened the possibilities for recording and manipulating visual images in fieldwork.

- Geographers are beginning to explore and interpret non-visual and more-than-visual landscapes, and there are many opportunities for creative undergraduate fieldwork in this area.

- Technologies and gadgets are helpful but not essential. More important here is your own enthusiasm, creative spirit, and critical imagination.

CONCLUSION

Sometimes we will go out into the field with an open mind, sometimes with specific questions; a mixture of the two is probably advisable, bringing out the best of both worlds: curiosity and purpose. In any case, field experiences will often unsettle very specific questions, leading the researcher to reformulate them in the light of experience. Meanwhile, open-ended curiosity usually leads to more specific lines of enquiry, once the fieldworker decides what is most interesting and decides to follow this up. Explorations tend to lead towards more specific descriptions, and descriptions tend to lead to interpretations, which in turn will engage with broader theoretical debates.

FURTHER READING/KEY TEXT(S)

- Mitchell, D. (2000) *Cultural Geography: A Critical Introduction*. Oxford: Blackwell. This book provides a critical overview of cultural geography, setting field methods such as landscape interpretations within their wider theoretical context.

- Rose, G. (2001) *Visual Methodologies: An Introduction to the Interpretation of Visual Materials*. London: SAGE. This book, written by a geographer but for a wider audience, provides a wide-ranging, conceptually rich, and practically useful discussion of visual sources and methods

7

INTERVIEWING FOR FIELDWORK

OVERVIEW

This chapter addresses the following questions:

- What is an 'interview' and when is it an appropriate method for fieldwork?
- How can you select, seek and gain access to interviewees?
- What should you consider when preparing for and conducting interviews?
- How can you learn to be 'reflexive' in interview-based fieldwork?

This chapter focuses on interviewing as a research method but also discusses areas of overlap with other methods including questionnaires and focus groups. It explains how we select knowledgeable individuals or institutions to interview, approach our potential interviewees, and subsequently conduct interviews.

When you start to think about fieldwork and consider which methods are appropriate to answer your research questions, a natural instinct is to 'find people who know the answers and can give you the answers'. The assumption that there are others in the field who can be sources of information for us and our research is often a valid one and this search for knowledgeable research participants underpins many research methods, including interviewing, focus groups, and participant observation (see Chapter 8). However, interviewing is not simply about entering the field and passively seeking 'answers' from others. Interviewing has become one of the most popular methods for research in the social sciences (Atkinson and Silverman 1997) including human geography (Cloke et al. 2004), but paradoxically this has served to 'dumb down' the method. In this chapter we encourage you to move away from assumptions that interviewing is 'easy' (it is, after all, just chatting?) towards more sophisticated understandings of the interviewing process. We explain that interviewing can be a critical and challenging method which requires thought, planning, and the investment of time.

Academic research articles, based on data collected through interviews, will rarely provide a full and rigorous justification of this methodology and this sets a poor example for students to follow. More usefully, for students wondering whether and how to conduct interviews in the field, there are some excellent textbooks on geographical research methods which contain chapters on interviewing and discuss interviewing in theoretical and practical terms (see, for example, Flowerdew and Martin 2005; Clifford et al. 2010). Rather than replicating this generic literature on interviewing, this chapter has a more specific objective: to offer guidance on how students can design and conduct interviews *in the field*. It provides practical advice, supplemented with real examples from students and academics in different research environments.

If you use interviews imaginatively, rigorously, and effectively you will find yourself meeting people you would otherwise almost certainly never have cause to spend time with, and in locations that can take you away from the 'normal' spaces tourists inhabit in your field location (such as business premises, government buildings, and people's homes). There is nothing quite like finding yourself meeting – and connecting with – someone from a very different background and set of experiences: interviewing fifty-year-old award-winning female business owner whilst being served jasmine tea in the board room of a 40th floor office in the Shibuya district of Tokyo; or sitting in a simple cafe, while a homeless person tells you about his or her life on the streets; or listening to an elderly farmer, who has invited you to sit with him outside his home in Buenos Aires, Honduras (see Figure 7.1). Interviewing is a recipe for some highly memorable fieldwork experiences!

Figure 7.1 Tony (a student) interviewing a resident of Buenos Aires, Honduras, outside his home. Photograph by Richard Phillips

WHAT IS AN 'INTERVIEW' AND IS IT AN APPROPRIATE METHOD FOR YOUR RESEARCH?

To those who are unfamiliar with qualitative research methodologies and their application in the field, there may appear to be little difference between meeting to speak to people and stopping individuals on the street to ask them questions. However, there can be significant differences based on the content of the questions and the methods used to obtain the answers. The definitions of and distinctions between interviews, focus groups, and questionnaires are summarised in Table 7.1. This should help you to understand how these methods differ and also to determine which is most appropriate for your research. You should pay particular attention to the variances between questionnaires and interviews, since it is common for less experienced researchers to conflate these.

The term 'qualitative interviewing' refers to in-depth, semi-structured, or loosely structured forms of interviewing (Mason 2002). Interviews have been defined as 'conversations with a purpose' (Burgess 1984: 102). This means that interviews involve interaction or dialogue between the researcher or interviewer and the interviewee. Put simply, interviewing is the process of finding, contacting, and meeting with research participants with the purpose of asking questions about their experiences and knowledge, and then listening – in open and non-judgemental ways – to what they say.

The use of interviewing spans many sub-disciplines of human geography, including historical, cultural, political, and economic geographies. In our experience undergraduate fieldwork using interviewing has covered topics such as: transnational firm entry methods into foreign markets; environmental policy-making prior to a large sporting event; the provision of childcare and its impact on household relationships in an underprivileged area; and the origins of produce sold in a 'local' farm shop.

Interviewing (like all research methods) is by no means a perfect science so there is always room here for innovations and improvements. There is no reason why students themselves cannot also seek to contribute to the development of interviewing as a method. So while this chapter provides specific advice and guidance on how to conduct and plan interviews, we would also encourage you to think critically and imaginatively about interviewing in the field.

WHO TO INTERVIEW AND HOW TO GAIN ACCESS?

Having decided to conduct interviews in the course of your fieldwork, the next stage is to think more carefully about exactly who it is you intend to speak to, how you will make contact with them, and how you will convince them to devote an hour or so of their time to your research. Rarely is the process of sampling, determining target interview respondents, and gaining access a straightforward one. A number of challenges and barriers may have to be overcome, often demanding serious commitment in terms of time and dedication. One of the frustrations

Table 7.1 Summarising the central characteristics of questionnaires, interviews and focus groups

	Definition	Purpose and forms	Limitations
Questionnaires	Often categorised as quantitative due to their emphasis on factual and/or numerical data. The questionnaire survey represents 'an indispensable tool when primary data are required about people their behaviour, attitudes and opinions and their awareness of specific issues' (Parfitt 1997: 76).	Purpose is to collect data that are representative of a population and to assess the statistical significance of the results. Can take a variety of forms including telephone surveys, postal surveys, face-to-face interviews, drop and pick-up questionnaires and internet surveys. The distanced relationship between interviewer and respondent reduces the influence of the researcher.	Questionnaires will not yield information on the processes that have caused events to happen, the individuals and decision making behind events, nor the underlying policies. In-depth discussions about the viewpoints of individuals are not possible. To produce statistically significant results a large number (hundreds) of questionnaires must be conducted.
Interviews	Aim is not to be representative of a particular population, rather to 'understand how individuals experience and make sense of their own lives' (Valentine 2005: 111). Based on the understanding that all knowledges are situational and contextual, interviews seek to 'ensure that relevant contexts are brought into focus so that situated knowledge can be produced' (Mason 2002: 62).	Encourages immersion in the field in order to interact with the social actors whose accounts are privileged as data sources. Interviews can be structured, semi-structured or structured depending on the research context. They can use thematic, topic-centred, biographical or narrative approaches. All seek to achieve a fluid and flexible structure.	Data collected, and results revealed, are not representative of a whole population. It is often difficult to make generalised statements. Interviewing can be a time-consuming process.
Focus groups	A group of people, usually between 6 and 12, who meet in an informal setting to respond to questions set by the researcher. Interaction between researcher and respondents can differ to that of interviews. The term 'discussion group' or 'group interview' may also be used.	Effective in 'capturing tacit or experiential knowledge, seeing understandings and feelings as socially constructed rather than independent' (Hoggart et al. 2002: 214). Can be used to examine new or existing government policies, or environmental issues, for example.	Recruitment of participants is often time-consuming and it may be difficult to coordinate up to a dozen people. Topics for discussion can be limited i.e. personal and/or sensitive issues are rarely discussed in groups. Can be used in fieldwork as a method of validation or presentation of research findings.

experienced by human geographers is the perception (often from 'harder' scientists) that all we do is 'go out and chat to people and write about it'! In fact, interviewing is a challenging and time-consuming process that when done well will require a certain degree of skill and tenacity on the part of the researcher. This section will outline the process of sampling to determine potential interviewees and distinguish the two main 'types' – broadly defined as 'professional' and 'personal'. It will then offer some practical advice about how to gain access to interviewees, relating this specifically to undergraduate fieldwork and emphasising the sort of work that can be conducted before entering the field.

As explained above, one of the key ways in which interviewing differs from questionnaires is that the former does not seek to be fully representative. However, do not interpret this as meaning that researchers do not have to consider whom they should speak to and how potential interviewees should be sampled. Although interviewing is not used to prove or disprove a set hypothesis and rather to find, interpret, and discuss qualitative findings, the researcher is still required to develop a reliable and valid method that includes identifying a sample population and sampling from this. For example, if your research project focuses on the activities of Japanese electronics firms in your field location, the first stage will be to find/construct a list of all such firms. If this list is extensive you may wish to differentiate between the firms by categorising them (for example according to size or length of presence in the field location). You can then select (or 'sample') from this list, making sure you include a number of firms from each category. If you do not do this the interviews you conduct may be skewed towards a particular type of firm and your results will tell only a partial story. Be aware that you are not trying to answer everything about your topic – you are trying to answer your research questions comprehensively – so your sampling strategy should reflect this. Identifying a list of potential interviewees is an important step in the research process and should be done methodically. The discussion of documentary sources accessed through archives and libraries in Chapter 6 may help you to compile lists of individuals and organisations. Further advice on sampling strategies can be found in all of the core qualitative methodology textbooks.

You should also take into account who you are including in your research (and hence giving a 'voice' to) and who you are excluding. Historically social science research has marginalised, inadequately represented, and even completely excluded the experiences of many sections of the population, including women, the young, ethnic minorities, and the gay and bisexual community. Linda McDowell (1992) highlights several seminal research contributions that totally excluded women in their analysis, citing an infamous study by William Whyte (1955) entitled *Street Corner Society* in which the author seems to have been completely unaware that he had interviewed only men. While many geographers have worked hard to represent previously unheard voices, interviews continue to be structured around power dynamics and differentials, not all of which are understood or addressed. McDowell (1992: 405) argues that 'conventional research methods in human geography' – especially interviewing – have suffered from 'gender blindness'. She pointed out that 'male researchers may privilege male respondents without considering whether the information so obtained is systematically biased'. You should therefore take time to properly consider who you wish to interview – and thereby represent – in your research and if you are affected by any research blindness.

When narrowing down your list of potential interviewees to approach in the field, be aware that your list needs to be much longer than the number of interviews you plan to conduct. Not all the approaches you make will be successful. One question frequently asked by students is 'How many interviews do we need to do?'. There are no set amounts for this as much depends on the type of interview, its potential, the nature of the topic, and the sample size. 'How long is a piece of string?' is a favoured staff response that is often not satisfactory for those students who crave a set number here. To gain a more comprehensive answer your best strategy would be to sit down with a member of staff and talk them through your topic, sampling strategy, and interview plans.

Depending on the nature of your research topic, and therefore the type of social actor you are seeking information from by interviewing them, you may not be able to establish a target list of potential interviewees. For example, where your research focuses on organisations such as firms or public organisations, directories and lists can be used. In contrast, if your research requires that you speak to individuals on a private basis (i.e. asking them about their personal lives, circumstances, and feelings), such lists are not publically available. As such recruitment strategies will often be required that use different (or variations in the combination of) methods of approach.

Traditionally each interview respondent would be approached via a formal letter, often written on university headed paper, sent to them in the post. This would have had the advantage of seeming 'official' and important, but today could seem slow and expensive in comparison with an instant (and free) email communication. A letter can also get lost and/or be placed straight in the wastepaper basket! Email approaches have the advantage of being faster, but are just as easily ignored or 'junked'. Therefore, as researchers have increasingly begun to adopt email as a form of interview approach, the use of a formal letter has not necessarily been lost. It is advisable that in order to retain an 'official' air to your research, you should compose a letter of introduction that you can attach to your email. You should include details of your research project and make sure you are clear about what you expect from the respondent (i.e. a sentence along the lines of 'should you wish to participate in this research your contribution would take the form of an interview lasting around one hour at a place and time of your convenience'). The letter should also detail some ethical aspects of the research, such as a reassurance that the interview would be confidential, that data would not be distributed beyond the project team, that no individuals would be named in the report, and that the final report would not be publically available. A difficult issue – which all researchers face – is how we can convince potential interviewees to give an hour of their time when often there is little that we can offer in return! You should try to develop an approach that suits the type of interviewee you are approaching. For example, in the case of large corporations (or indeed, government officials) a little flattery can go a long way, so letters can begin with a statement that lets the individual (and the firm or organisation they work for) know that they have been selected on the basis of their importance in the sector and that the research will be incomplete without their contribution.

Approaching potential interviewees by telephone is daunting and will demand a certain set of skills from one or more of your group members, but it can be worth the effort. In certain geographical contexts (for example, the USA, Canada or Australia) it is feasible to find the name of a respondent in a directory or from the internet and contact them to introduce yourself and arrange an interview. In other places (such as Japan or Central and Eastern Europe) it is expected that you will participate in a more formal and lengthy process of introduction. Regardless of the context, you may find that you need to combine phone and email. In the context of corporate interviewing it can be most effective to first phone a company to find out the name and email address of the most appropriate person to interview; second, to email a letter of introduction to that person; and third, to leave a period of time (anything from a few days to a week, but never more than a fortnight) before phoning that individual (or their personal assistant) to ask if they wish to participate in the research. Step three may have to be repeated several times before you are able to secure an interview and your success will often depend on how willing you are to make a slight nuisance of yourself with repeated phone calls (repeated emails are likely to be ignored). It is also advisable to 'make friends' with the personal assistants of senior executives as they act as 'gatekeepers' (see below) and can make sure their bosses have read your email and letter and also control their diaries.

Gaining access to interviewees is a complex process of negotiation that is sometimes refreshingly easy but at other times can be frustratingly slow and indeed sometimes impossible. Are you able to pick up the phone and cold call potential interviewees? This isn't an easy task for everyone and doesn't necessarily get any easier the more calls you make, but it may become a valuable skill in your life post-graduation. How much do you want or need a particular interview? Your group needs to plan the amount of time you spend chasing specific people and prioritise according to their potential importance to your research project. It is advisable to start approaching research participants before you enter the field. The process of securing an interview can take several weeks, so if you wait until you arrive at your field location you may well fail to arrange a sufficient number of interviews. It is also psychologically valuable to have some interviews arranged before you leave for the field – this can be encouraging and help to keep you focused on your research project.

If your research topic requires you to interview individuals on a more personal basis (i.e. asking about their thoughts, feelings, and experiences) different strategies for recruitment will have to be used. You may wish to use 'on-site' recruitment as discussed above whereby you would visit a location when your potential interviewees may be present. One downside to this approach is that the sample would be self-selecting. For example, if you were conducting a research project on criminal activities in an area you could visit the police station to find some criminals to interview. However, your sample would only consist of unsuccessful criminals (i.e. people who have been caught). To find successful criminals you would have to infiltrate the criminal community (which is potentially very dangerous and unlikely to receive ethical approval!). Therefore, in order to find interviewees it may first be necessary to investigate any organisations that work in the area of your research, such as trade associations, government departments, and/or non-governmental organisations or charities. Information on these organisations is publically available and often makes an excellent first port of call for research. Individuals who work for such organisations are often highly networked and will be able to act as 'gatekeepers' for your research. A gatekeeper is a contact who can provide access to key people in a specific setting or they can be an individual who exercises control over physical access and provides or withholds information. For example, for those conducting research on primary education headteachers are often the gatekeepers: '[they determined] when we visited the school, where we visited the school, whom we talked with, and for how long' (Burgess 1991: 47). If you are able to identify any individuals or organisations whom you feel may become important gatekeepers for your research, you should endeavour to contact them as soon as you can, and certainly before arriving in the field.

While you are in the field conducting your research you may well find that you begin to deviate from your original list of potential interviewees and/or initial expectations of where your research would lead you. In many instances this will be a positive process as you are 'snowballing' in your research. 'Snowballing' is the term used to refer to the process of obtaining more information and access to additional interviewees through previous research respondents. During an interview a respondent may ask 'Have you spoken to so-and-so? ... you must, she knows everyone in this industry'. Gaining this contact, and being able to approach them using the interview respondent's name, can often make the process of securing an interview easier (as you are demonstrating that you are 'connected' and therefore worth investing time in). Snowballing is also often used to find and recruit 'hidden populations' – groups who are not easily accessible to researchers via traditional sampling strategies. Whichever methods you use to find your interviewees, each will require an investment in terms of time and organisational skills. It is very important to keep detailed records of who you contacted and when you did so in order to avoid getting mixed up. You should try to interview an appropriate selection of people, but also leave sufficient flexibility in your research methodology to allow for unexpected avenues to be followed and/or snowball interviews to take place.

PREPARING FOR AND CONDUCTING THE INTERVIEW

Much of this chapter focuses on the interview with the expectation that you will be conducting face-to-face interviews. While there are other forms of interview available to the researcher (such as email, telephone or Skype interviews) this book specifically addresses research that is conducted *in the field*. It may be that a small proportion of your interviews will be conducted remotely (for example, short follow-up emails upon your return home), but when you are in the field you should expect to conduct your interviews face-to-face. This section will address some of the practical issues surrounding interviewing in the field before we turn to discuss issues of reflexivity in research.

How will you structure the interview?

While you are arranging your interviews there will be a number of decisions that will need to be made regarding the interviews themselves. You will need an interview schedule – a pre-prepared document that contains a list of topic areas and/or questions that you wish to ask. As outlined above, your interview can be highly structured (set questions followed in a set order – although this rarely happens in reality), semi-structured (allowing flexibility in the order in which questions are answered and leaving the interview open to unanticipated avenues of discussion), and unstructured (few questions, allowing the interview to take its own direction). Most undergraduate fieldwork interviews are semi-structured, but take some time here to think through which approach will best suit your research topic (for an example of a schedule see Figure 7.2).

Example Interview Schedule: Apple Supply Chains

1 Interviewee:
   - What is your role at the organisation?
   - How do you envisage your role changing in future years?

2 Supply chain dynamics:
   - How do you envisage the supply chain industry as a whole changing in future years?
   - What are the company's goals or targets to achieve efficient supply chain management and how will you attain this?

3 Supply chain management:
   - Do you directly transport apples from the producers or are regional distribution hubs used?
   - Which countries do you import from?
   - What percentage of apples come from outside the USA?
   - What percentage of apples are from the EU?

4 Regulation:
   - Do any regulating bodies govern your industry?
   - If so, who are these? How do they impact on your business?

5 Consumers:
   - How have consumer demands changed over the last decade?
   - How do you factor consumer taste into your business model?
   - Do your consumers care how far their apples have travelled to reach the store?
   - How do you anticipate customer consumption patterns changing with regard to apples?
   - How do you anticipate customer consumption patterns changing in general with regard to environmental concerns around food miles?

Figure 7.2   Example of a semi-structured interview schedule. This group of students decided to examine the supply chains of food retailers in their field location: a city in North America. They wanted to investigate the degree to which environmental factors were important in determining where produce came from and how large retailers sourced their produce. The group focused their research on examining one particular commodity: apples.

Figure 7.2 identifies five key areas of questioning/topics that the interviews should cover. The first asks general questions about the interviewee and these are designed as ice-breakers to get the interview going rather than questions that are fundamentally important to the research. It is, however, vital that you understand who you are speaking to and what their background is in relation to your research area. Interviewees may admit that they are new to a job or role and will therefore emphasise that their knowledge is not quite as vast as you may have hoped! The interview schedule should list some specific research questions (making it semi-structured) that can be asked in any order. Interview schedules can be flexible and you will need to expect to jump from topic to topic as natural conversations do not follow predicable patterns. When you are designing your own interview schedules you must first decide how structured you want them to be. Listing specific questions is useful for ensuring similar questions are asked in each interview and as a prompt during interviews (you may 'lose your place'!). After this try to consider the number of questions you wish to include and endeavour to achieve a concise summary that you can quickly scan through during the interview (also remember that seeing pages and pages of questions will intimidate the interviewee).

How many group members will attend the interview?

Much depends on the size of your group. If you are a group of three or more it is possible to split into two and you can therefore conduct more than one interview at a time. You also need to consider how the dynamics of interviews will be affected by the number of people present. How will a lone interviewee feel if confronted by six interviewers? Is it possible for all the group members to contribute if everyone is present? We would advise that you think about the roles that are required. You might find that two is an ideal number as you can take it in turns asking questions (and help each other to fill any awkward silences that may appear!). Whatever you decide, it is customary to inform interviewees of how many people will be attending the interview. This is especially important in some cultural contexts: for example, in Japan it is preferable if the number of interviewees and interviewers is the same. A Japanese company will therefore send two representatives to be interviewed if there are two interviewees. In addition, where you are asking people about potentially sensitive issues, or visiting them in their own home, it may be inappropriate for more than one or two interviewers to be present.

How will you record the interview?

Many qualitative researchers will record their interviews using a Dictaphone and then transcribe the interviews verbatim (word for word, together with silences, gestures, and interruptions). You may wish to do this as it provides a definitive recording of the interview. If you do so, it is still advisable to make notes during the interview in order to make sure you have the key points and if possible some good quotes. Dictaphones can fail, batteries can run out, and sometimes the location of the interview can make the recording unintelligible. We would advise that you take notes and discuss the interview immediately afterwards so you may make further notes. Remember also that some universities will require that you obtain written permission to conduct the interview and also to record it. It may be that your interviewee does not wish to be recorded. Ask just once about this and do not press individuals about recording interviews – your interviewees are well within their rights to say no and you should not create a difficult and tense atmosphere before the interview begins by trying to convince them otherwise. Just be prepared to make copious notes instead!

Where should the interview take place?

This may be something over which you have very little control, or you may be asked where you would like to meet. In either event, the location will have an impact on the interview. For corporate and institutional interviews you will often be expected to hold the interview at their offices. This may be in order to save time for the interviewee, but it also sends a message about the status of the interviewee as you are shown to his/her office or meeting room. Occasionally a corporate interview can take place outside the office when the interviewee suggests getting out of the office and having a coffee in a café. These more neutral settings can result in a more relaxed atmosphere and sometimes the interviewee will divulge more information and/or personal opinions than he or she necessarily would while in their office. One downside to such meeting places is that they are often noisy and the quality of any tape recordings will be poor (espresso machines are particularly loud on Dictaphone recordings!). Unlike when interviewing people in a professional capacity, when conducting research on the personal circumstances and opinions of individuals it is more likely that you will be able to suggest a meeting place. If you used 'on-site' recruitment, that site may also provide a space that you can use and is familiar to both you and the interviewee. Again, meeting in cafés or restaurants may be possible, but if the topic is particularly sensitive you may require a more private space. It is also possible that you will be visiting interviewees at home which will put them more at ease and offer you insights into the everyday lives of your research respondents. However, an interview at home must only be offered by the interviewee and should not be suggested by the interviewer.

Sarah Elwood and Deborah Martin (2000) suggest that the physical location of an interview will directly affect the discussion that takes place. This is therefore not a trivial matter and a consideration of the interview location should therefore be included (and justified) in our research methodologies. Robyn Longhurst recalls that she 'once made the mistake of helping to facilitate a focus group about the quality of service offered by a local council at the council offices. The discussion did not flow freely and it soon became apparent that the participants felt hesitant (understandably) about criticising the council while in one of their rooms' (2010: 109). Similarly, a corporate executive is unlike to criticise their company's strategy if interviewed at his or her workplace. If we are seeking critical insight and honest opinions from our interviewees, interview location is an important facilitator. As Elwood and Martin conclude, 'Reflection on the microgeographies of interviews is a process that starts before the actual interviewing begins, and continues throughout the research and analysis. Understanding the ethical implications and analytical significance of interview sites may help researchers to navigate the process of selecting and analyzing interview sites, while they try to balance the needs of research with the interests of participants' (2000: 656). Above all we should heed Gill Valentine's valuable advice: 'for your own safety never arrange interviews with people you do not feel comfortable with or agree to meet strangers in places where you feel vulnerable' (2005: 118).

How else can you prepare for interviews?

First, it is very important that you arrive at interviews fully prepared and informed. It is crucial that you make sure you have done your homework and researched the person, organisation, or company that you are interviewing. Make sure that all available information has been found and read (one of the strengths of working in a group is that you can split this between you). You will want to avoid wasting time in the interview collecting data that are already in the public domain. For example, if you are interviewing a representative from a firm you should read their website and, if available, their press releases and annual report (see Chapter 6 for more details on such documentary sources). If you do not do so you will waste time asking questions to which you should already have the answers (e.g. number of employees, company history, turnover, etc.). You need to be asking questions that are pertinent to your research. Similarly, if you are interviewing an academic make sure you have read any of their latest publications that relate to your research topic, otherwise the interview will be dominated by the academic providing an outline of their research findings. A more profitable exchange would arise from you critically engaging with their work, asking questions, and talking to them about your own research and how it relates to theirs. Second, make sure that you dress appropriately for the context in which you are interviewing. Smart clothes are expected for corporate or government interviews although some industries are more concerned with suits and ties than others. If in doubt wear smart clothes as you won't regret it (whereas you may if you are underdressed). If you are visiting people in their homes or in informal contexts, you should still make an effort to be presentable and not wear any inappropriate clothes (too short, too tight, etc.). Do not forget that you are not just representing yourself and your group, but also your institution.

REFLEXIVE RESEARCH: CROSS-CULTURAL INTERVIEWING AND POSITIONALITIES

Researchers using qualitative interviewing have increasingly paid attention to calls to consider 'reflexivity' in research, recognising the need to give due regard to the interpretive, political, and rhetorical nature of empirical research. Reflexivity is about 'ways of seeing which act back on and reflect existing ways of seeing' (Clegg and Hardy 1996: 4). As such, being reflexive turns the attention 'inwards' towards the researcher(s) and the research context. In other words, it is necessary for you to reflect on how you are conducting your research and to acknowledge that you are part of the research rather than independent of it. This section will discuss two elements of interviewing that require reflexive consideration. First, conducting research outside our home country and how the culture can affect our data collection, and second, our own 'positionalities' in research.

When conducting cross-cultural research in a bounded timeframe, there will be some challenges that will need to be overcome and some limitations on the data we will be able to collect. While qualitative methodologies are now the most commonly used approach in cross-cultural studies, there is a general lack of specific focus on cross-cultural interviewing and its implications for data collection and data interpretation (Shah 2004). An interview 'displays cultural particulars' (Silverman 1985: 174); it is determined by discursive relations and situatedness. As Shah (2004) suggests, our own understandings of interaction between the interviewee and interviewer may not be similarly interpreted by cultures that are outside western capitalist societies. Therefore conducting interviews of all kinds outside our home countries necessitates reflection and a re-evaluation of our previous understandings of our research practices and interpretation of meanings. Postcard 7.1 details student fieldwork in Malaysia, highlighting some of the issues that will be discussed further below.

Postcard 7.1: Interviewing in Cross-cultural Contexts: Student Fieldwork in Sabah, Malaysia, by Kate Lloyd

Conducting fieldwork and interviews in the cross-cultural context of Sabah, Malaysia, has been highlighted by students as one of the most difficult yet rewarding aspects of their fieldwork experience. Throughout their three week stay in Kipouvo village just outside of Kota Kinabalu, the capital of Sabah, the students experienced a range of interview scenarios which included group interviews with government officials, individual interviews with indigenous village members, and community-based focus groups. The challenges they faced included language barriers, cross-cultural misunderstandings, and trying to undertake complex fieldwork in very short time periods.

Prior to leaving for the fieldwork, there was a significant part of the unit devoted to cross-cultural understanding and issues such as language which could impact on the collection of data in a cross-cultural context. Students spent time reflecting on their own 'maps of consciousness', how they are influenced by their positionality and the perspectives that are shaped by their own unique mix of race, class,

(Continued)

(Continued)

gender, nationality, sexuality, and other identifiers which influence how the world is viewed and interpreted (Mullings 1999). Emphasis was placed on the importance of the process over the outcomes in an effort to manage the high expectations students often have about being able to collect data in a new cross-cultural context.

PACOS focus groups

For the majority of the three weeks the students were divided into groups and worked on a range of community projects with a local NGO called the PACOS Trust, a community-based voluntary organisation that has been working to raise the quality of life in indigenous communities in Sabah, Malaysia. In the first week they worked with PACOS staff to prepare the guides, activities, and data collection tools that would be used during a programme evaluation community workshop. Throughout the fieldwork, language barriers were considered to be the biggest challenge for the students. For example, of the four PACOS staff members working with the groups, only the coordinator spoke limited English, resulting in difficulties on both sides – e.g. questions and answers were not understood and this made it difficult for the students to understand the project and for PACOS to explain their objectives. Language barriers also may have led to different answers (from the coordinator) to the same question on various occasions – and the 'goalposts being continually shifted'. Focus groups were used as the key data collection tool and the students ran three of these in total: one with the men of the village, one with the women, and the third with the children. Similar language barriers existed when working with the communities, however instead of focusing on the limitations students were encouraged to build a rapport with the community members and communicate using photos they had brought with them, maps, songs and dance in order to engage and exchange information. They also worked with a PACOS staff member who translated questions and responses.

Homestay interviews

In the second week the students spent 2-3 days in a homestay outside of Kota Kinabalu, Sabah, where they had the opportunity to interview their host family and community about socio-economic issues related to

(Continued)

(Continued)

the impact of homestay tourism on their families and communities. Again language barriers were significant as little English was spoken in the homestay community. To help overcome language barriers students were paired up with the local University of Malaya, Sabah (UMS) students who accompanied them to the homestay. Students were encouraged to learn as much as possible with, through, and about their local peers and to reflect on the diversity and their experiences throughout their three-day-long homestay. The UMS students were also tasked with collecting data for the same project and with help from their 'buddies' the students were able to work through their structured interview questions which had also been translated into Bahasa Malay. While the majority of students found the experience positive, those who were very frustrated by the process felt they were unable to really engage in the interview process because of their buddies' lack of experience in interpreting. For example, some students who were cited reported that a lengthy response would be translated into one or two words. This resulted in frustration from many students who were reliant on their buddies for data. This experience reveals the importance of setting expectations prior to the fieldtrip and despite the many years we have run the fieldtrip there remains a need to emphasise the importance of the process rather than the outcome. Participant observation and participation was also used as a way of overcoming language barriers and students collected data through personal impressions recorded in their diaries and participating in village activities like rubber tapping, fruit picking, rice pounding, traditional music and dance, cooking, and simple everyday tasks.

Group interviews

Negotiating access to government officials to interview required that students follow the appropriate protocols. Official letters of introduction were needed to request each interview and we recognised that our relatively privileged position as staff and students from an Australian university helped to facilitate this access. These group interviews would usually begin with a presentation to the students by the official, often on current government policy, followed by a question-and-answer session. While language wasn't so much of a problem here as many officials spoke English or had professional interpreters, it

(Continued)

(Continued)

was getting beyond the government policy rhetoric that frustrated the students and often inadequate responses to politically or culturally sensitive topics such as land rights and related legal issues were common. An essential part of the data collection process was scheduled time to reflect on the interview experience as soon as possible after the event. This would take place over dinner and on the bus on the way home, where students could fill in the gaps in interviews, clarify their interpretations, and discuss the responses. Upon reflection students reported finding the cross-cultural issues and language differences to be the hardest barrier to deal with, despite these also being the key reasons for wanting to participate in the experience.

When interviewing we should be prepared for our own expectations to be challenged. It is rare to enter any interview (whether at home or abroad) and be able to extract the exact data we require – to expect to do so is to deny the agency of individuals and the societal embeddedness of knowledge and how information is shared. An entire text could be written to explain how and why culture matters in the exchange of information, but for the purposes of this chapter a few illustrative examples will be provided make this point. In Jennifer Johns' experience of corporate interviewing across the globe, there are variations in the kinds of data interviews yield depending on the context in which these have been conducted. For example, British and American executives are often quick to offer their personal opinions on their company's strategies and to participate in discussions about how the company is operating and its future plans. These executives are rarely formally prepared for the interview and do not bring any supporting documentation with them. They do become more hesitant, however, when their company's financial performance is raised. Obtaining information on profitability is particularly problematic and once this is asked about the interview will invariably become less open for a while before the conversation returns to more amenable topics. In contrast, interviewees from South East Asia tend to request the interview questions before the interview and come to the meeting loaded with documentation. They are keen to impart quantitative data (and appear more open about financial data than their Anglo-Saxon counterparts) and will have concise answers to the questions prepared in advance. It is, however, far more difficult to instigate any discussion about corporate decision making (even when interviewing the Chief Executive Officer or Managing Director). The rich, discursive data that qualitative interviewing seeks are more difficult to obtain. To illustrate, Japan has been described as 'fact-rich but data-poor' (Bestor et al. 2003: 234). This situation is not due to any reluctance on behalf of the interviewees, it is purely a result of the cultural context in which the interview is conducted and the culturally-specific expectations of the researchers that cannot be fully met, as Mark Wang highlights in Postcard 7.2.

Postcard 7.2: China Field Class: Meeting the Real People and Getting Real Answers, by Mark Wang

For the past twelve years, the University of Melbourne has run a fieldtrip to China that has included sites in the Yellow River basin and the Yangzi River valley. Conducting a fieldtrip in China raises some challenges about how to engage with the local population and how students can collect their data. Based on our experiences in China, the followings tips will help you to conduct interviews in a foreign country:

- *Think carefully about how to access local populations. This can be difficult in some countries and we had particular problems in China. We found that organised interviews with government officials were not successful. It did not matter what level of government the officials worked in or if they were pure politicians or had formerly worked as professors or experts. Government propaganda and opinions were frequently quoted with rarely any critical views given. Similarly asking officials to arrange interviews and visits for us was difficult. When visits with ordinary Chinese citizens were organised, the individuals were unable to speak freely about their views.*
- *If official channels fail try other potential contacts and gatekeepers. We started to arrange all visits and interviews through local contacts such as Chinese professors. Given the difficulties of arranging 'genuine' interviews through official channels, if students want to speak to local people they have to rely on staff to help them or seekout their own ways of approaching people.*
- *Plan in advance how you will manage translation. The main barrier to interviewing ordinary Chinese people is language. Apart from my Chinese background and ability to speak Mandarin, about five to seven students each year will also be native Mandarin speakers. We also sometimes take graduate students as translators. When we conduct interviews with urban Chinese people or peasants we usually divide into three groups with at least one native Chinese*

(Continued)

(Continued)

speaker in each of these. We also arranged it so that at least one Mandarin speaker is allocated to project groups that require semi-structured interviews.

- Establish what the role of the interpreter is. Interpreters are reminded that their role is to interpret exactly what each side says, irrespective of whether students like or agree with it as it is not the interpreter's views that are being sought. The interpreter is a conduit. Our students are asked to speak in short sentences that can be easily translated; if they have a complex question they must break it down into small bits; if a respondent gives a long answer and the interpreter does not, enquire as to what is going on.
- Think about where you can conduct interviews so that interviewees are at ease. We try to interview Chinese peasants in their houses, either in sitting areas or in front yards.
- Remember your purpose. Keep in mind what sort of information you need from interviewees and try to avoid questions that are too long and complicated. Build up a picture of a complicated issue with a series of small questions.
- Ask people about what they know – about themselves, about what they do, about what they think. Do not ever ask people about 'other people', or 'people in China', or 'farmers', or 'people in Beijing'.
- Develop a standard set of questions and ask them in the same way in each household. Of course this does depend on the household composition and its answers, but try to get similar information about each household. Keep probing until you get the information you need in the form in which you want it. But don't turn interviewees off.

Finally, the use of local contacts for informational and translatory services can be very significant in cross-cultural contexts where the researchers do not speak the language. The relationships between researcher, translator/interpreter, and interviewee adds another layer of complexity to the research experience. Their use is not necessarily straightforward and, as with other aspects of interviewing, some time and preparation should go into making sure that the translator is used as efficiently as possible. Academics will often use local translators (usually postgraduate students found through contacts at local universities) with highly varied results. In most cases, students will be a good source of local knowledge and will offer highly valuable assistance. This is not, however, always the case. Postcard 7.3 discusses how the positionality of a researcher can influence the relationship with local contacts.

Postcard 7.3: Local Contacts in Cross-cultural Contexts: Experiences of Interviewing in Hungary, by Jennifer Johns

Working in the field can present challenges beyond academic, organisational or practical concerns. The context in which we are researching and our own positionalities can interact in sometimes unpredictable and difficult ways. Often we do not need to travel far to face particular dilemmas in the field. I faced a specific set of challenges when working on a large project as a research assistant in Central and Eastern Europe. While in Hungary I struggled to communicate and work effectively with my local translator. This was partly due to my gender – although the translator was also female – but was primarily as consequence of my age (in my early twenties, I was younger than her).

Early on in our working relationship, it became apparent to me that the translator was not impressed with my age and had seemed to have been expecting to work 'for' a more senior (and older) academic. I did not appear to fit the bill! My initial response was to meet regularly with my translator and seek to get on with the job of arranging and conducting interviews as best I could. Few sources of advice were available and none of my methodological training or reading had addressed the issue of age from the perspective of young researchers in the field (apart from some implicit references to seniority in interview power relations). Our relationship was strained and research progress was slow.

A breakthrough came unexpectedly and gave me pause to think about how I was managing the situation. We were walking to attend an interview with a small video games company in a suburb of Budapest when we passed a dog that was sitting outside its house. I went over to the dog and spoke to it but then turned to my translator and said 'Silly me, he speaks Hungarian not English!'. She thought this was hilarious and we both had a shared moment of seeing my communication with the dog as a metaphor for our situation. I used this as an opportunity to talk through the issues with the translator and communicated that I wanted her to work 'with' me and not 'for' me. She expressed concern that my research would be unsuccessful as my corporate interviews were with older men. As it turned out my age was not a barrier to completing the research successfully, I just had to work harder to negotiate access to respondents and during

(Continued)

> *(Continued)*
>
> *interviews relied upon my knowledge of the industries being studied to come across as intelligent and informed. In a short time, the translator and I had a much more productive working relationship and the experience highlighted how the assistance of local contacts is often essential to our research and these relationships need to be fostered regardless of our own positionalities.*

As researchers it is important we recognise that we are not objective, impartial robots entering the field without past experiences and our own viewpoints. Who we are will directly impact on how we collect data, particularly in relation to interviewing where our dialogue and questioning will influence the answers we receive: 'Whether we like it or not, researchers remain human beings complete with all the usual assembly of feelings, failings and moods ... there is no method or technique of doing research other than through the medium of the researcher' (Stanley and Wise 1993: 157). Clare Madge (1993: 296) argues that it is crucial to consider 'the role of the (multiple) 'self', showing how a researcher's positionality (in terms of race, nationality, age, gender, social and economic status, sexuality) may influence the 'data' collected and thus the information that becomes coded as 'knowledge'' (see also Rose 1997). So you should think about your own background, circumstances, and characteristics and reflect upon how this will impact on your research.

One of the most pronounced ways that positionality is articulated in interviews is through the power relations that exist between researchers and their informants. Power imbalances between interviewees and interviewers exist on two levels: real differences associated with access to money, education, knowledge, and other resources, and perceived differences which exist in the minds of the participants (whereby they feel inferior or superior) (Scheyvens et al. 2003). As a relatively inexperienced researcher entering the field for the first time, it may seem as if the balance of power is weighed against you in interview situations. This may seem particularly acute when approaching and interviewing what have been termed 'elites' (this chapter has preferred to distinguish between professional and personal interviews). Certainly, when faced with individuals who consider themselves to be in powerful positions (such as management or politics) the researcher can feel inferior. You should ask yourself, however, if there is anything that you are able to do about this? How will it impact on the data you collect? If you demonstrate yourself to be articulate and informed on the research topic the interviewee is likely to respond with his or her own insights. Research participants can also 'gain' power by failing to respond to the interview process as the interviewer intends. For example, Rajni Palriwala explains how her fieldwork in Pakistan was 'subverted' by her research participants:

Despite their good intentions, the villagers' perceptions and mine regarding data collection did not always coincide. The villagers, especially the women, would get bored and tired of what appeared to them as repetitious questioning. They saw no need for me to interview so many people and the same people repeatedly ... All through the period I was collecting data for my research I was also being thoroughly researched. I was questioned about my life, my hopes and future prospects and my reactions to their lifestyle. (1991: 32)

Perhaps more ethically problematic are interactions where the researcher assumes themselves to be superior to their research subjects, or where participants feel themselves to be inferior (due to conscious or unconscious acts by the researcher). This is discussed in more detail in Chapter 4, but in relation to interviewing we can see such power imbalances impacting on the levels and abilities of respondents to engage with the research (fear and insecurity can accompany feelings of inferiority) and this can result in participants telling the researcher what they think they want to hear, thereby compromising the research findings.

Qualitative interviewing relies upon an honest and open engagement between researchers and the researched. Being reflexive should be part of the research experience and each researcher should think about their positionality and how it may have affected their research. In group situations this may appear more difficult as you will have to consider the positionalities of all group members. But this can also be a good opportunity to learn: you may begin to notice how your age, gender, appearance and other characteristics shape the ways in which different people respond to you, and you might be able to contrast the ways in which interviews, conducted by different individuals, yield different kinds of data. Were the interviews different in terms of the types of discussion or information provided? Can you attribute this to any of the particular personal characteristics of the interviewers? Where you able to observe power relations between yourselves and research participants? Did these seem unbalanced? If so, how can you seek to achieve greater balance and is this necessary? These are all factors that you should bear in mind when you are reading through your interviews and preparing your research findings.

SUMMARY

This chapter outlined interviewing as a research methodology. As with many aspects of fieldwork, the process of planning and conducting interviews can be time-consuming and pressured. However, the types of data that are produced and the social interactions experienced are well worth the investment. The key points of the chapter were:

- Interviewing seeks to generate data that are insightful without being statistically significant or formally representative of a known population. The method should be regarded as distinct from questionnaires, although there is no reason why both cannot be combined in a multi-method approach.

- While there are different forms of interviewing, it is anticipated that interviewing in the field will mainly consist of face-to-face meetings. The process of arranging interviews can be lengthy and sometimes frustrating, so some practical advice was offered on how to successfully gain access to interview respondents. It has been stressed that much of the planning as well as approaching interviewees can be done before entering the field.

- Careful planning is necessary in order to conduct effective data collection and ensure that you get the most from your interviews. You should be well prepared for these, think about where the most appropriate places to conduct the interview are, and behave and dress in ways that are appropriate to the field context.

- The social and cultural embeddedness of knowledge demands that researchers themselves become immersed in the local context and, as such, cannot view themselves as detached and independent. Similarly, each researcher will bring their own influences to the field that will affect the interviewing process. This chapter recommends that you adopt a reflexive research strategy and reflect upon your own positionalities.

CONCLUSION

Due in part to the continuing popularity of interviewing in human geography and the social sciences generally, this method can be perceived as straightforward and rather simple. In fact, interviewing is far from easy and as this chapter has demonstrated there are a number of aspects to conducting interviewing that require planning, careful execution, and reflection. Should you choose to use interviewing in your fieldwork – either as a sole method or as part of a multi-method approach – you should be prepared to meet some challenges, particularly in the initial stages of identifying and approaching potential interviewees. Do not be too disheartened by rejections because if you persist you will eventually manage to arrange some interviews (and hopefully some before you enter the field). Conducting interviews can be intense and tiring and this chapter emphasises the responsibility that each researcher has to conduct themselves ethically while interviewing in the field. In addition to the richness and insight of the data generated by interviewing (when conducted thoroughly and thoughtfully), there is another reason why interviewing is so popular – researchers will find themselves enjoying the experience of meeting and connecting with individuals whom they would probably never have had cause to otherwise.

FURTHER READING/KEY TEXT(S)

- A key source for advice on 'conversational interviews' is Gill Valentine's (2005) chapter 'Tell me about ... using interviews as a research methodology' (in Flowerdew, R. and

Martin, D. (eds) *Methods in Human Geography: A Guide for Students Doing a Research Project* (2nd edn). Edinburgh Gate: Addison Wesley Longman). It offers guidance on who to talk to, how to ask questions, and how to practise interviewing skills.

- For a concise review of practical issues related to interviewing see Robyn Longhurst's (2010) chapter on 'Semi-structured Interviews and Focus Groups' (in Clifford, N., French, S. and Valentine, G. (eds), *Key Methods in Geography* (2nd edn). London: SAGE). The author uses her own interviewing experiences as illustrations.

8
PARTICIPANT OBSERVATION AND PARTICIPATORY GEOGRAPHIES

OVERVIEW

This chapter addresses the following questions:

- What is participant observation and how is this useful in fieldwork?
- How should you analyse and write up the findings of participant observation?
- What is participatory action research and what is its relevance to fieldwork?

The chapter introduces the various ways in which we can use our observations and engagements with people as a research method. These include eating, clubbing, and wandering. We discuss how other researchers have used participant observation and participatory research, highlighting the ways in which these methods can be used in fieldwork.

A picture of Brooklyn Bridge by David Hockney includes a telling detail: the photographer's feet (Figure 8.1). This illustrates how people are always part of our pictures of the world, whether these take the form of artistic images or more formal geographic representations such as maps, websites, or research reports. To put this another way and introduce a term that will be explained in the course of this chapter, 'all observation is participant observation' (Kearns 2005: 192). Our choice is not about *whether* we want to be present in these pictures – we always are – but about *how* we want to be present: how to participate in the field and how to understand the difference this makes. This chapter explains two related but distinct approaches to participation in fieldwork: participant observation and participatory action research.

Figure 8.1   David Hockney 'The Brooklyn Bridge, Nov. 28th, 1982' Photographic collage edition of 20 109 × 58" © David Hockney

PARTICIPANT OBSERVATION

Participant observation (hereafter PO) dispenses with some of the formality and structure associated with survey research methods such as questionnaires and with the detachment associated with some forms of observation and landscape description, in order to pursue a deeper involvement in and understanding of a place, community, or situation. Its aim is to understand human geographies from the perspectives of those who inhabit them. In other words, 'outsiders' attempt to see the world from the perspectives of various 'insiders'.

As its name suggests, participant observation has two components: observing *and participating*. Geography students may feel more comfortable and familiar with the former: describing and mapping the world 'out there' as accurately as possible. Participation can be more challenging.

Eric Laurier, a geographer who has used the technique in a study of café culture, explains that 'Participant observation involves spending time being, living or working with people or communities in order to understand them' (2003: 133). This is a form of ethnography: a more generic and eclectic set of research methods that geographers have borrowed from other disciplines including Anthropology and Urban Sociology. Anthropologists traditionally immerse themselves in the field: 'living, eating and sleeping with the investigated population' (Hoggart et al. 2002: 253). In practice though not all participant observers get quite so close to the people they are researching, so PO can take many different forms with different degrees of participation and observation. Human geographers have adopted and adapted these methods selectively and creatively, according to new times, places, and research imperatives. Exponents of participant observation all agree that, like swimming or dancing, this methodology is difficult but not impossible to explain and is best learned through trial and error. Ultimately the experience you will learn most from is your own, but the advice and experiences of others suggest a series of steps which will help you to decide whether and how to use participant observation in your own fieldwork and then how to use it better and more productively. As this chapter shows, the potential rewards of PO as a research methodology merit the investment of thought and time in developing an approach that suits your fieldwork aims.

To explain participant observation, and perhaps to inspire you to have a go at it yourself, it may help you to learn about some examples of how others have used this technique. These come from detailed research projects, carried out over longer periods of time and with more resources than you will be likely to muster on your fieldtrip, but they nevertheless illustrate the sorts of things you might imagine doing yourself – suitably scaled and adapted to fit your own resources and time in the field.

Eating

Eating is an important part of any fieldtrip, and one that can be turned from a mere necessity to a form of participant observation. We explore places not only by looking at them but also by using our other senses, as a result becoming conscious of the sounds and smells (as discussed in Chapters 6 and 9) and also the tastes associated with a place. Whether this means going out to local *cafés* and restaurants in search of 'authentic' experiences, eating in national and global chain restaurants, or buying food in shops and markets to cook in your hotel or hostel, eating and drinking can tell you a lot about a place and the people who live there. David Bell and Gill Valentine explain that food, and the way people eat it, speaks of 'a whole set of contemporary social and cultural issues, from health to nationalism, from ethics to aesthetics, from local politics to the role of transnational corporations in global regimes of accumulation'(1997: 3). An interest in food is something that fieldworkers can share with other travellers. Whereas a typical tourist may be interested in 'sampling other cultures through their food' (1997: 4), the fieldworker is encouraged to think more critically and analytically about the meanings of food, in the context of debates about issues such as consumption, gender and national identity,

Figure 8.2 Eating and drinking can be valuable and insightful ways of forging relationships with people in the field, including other researchers and locals. In this photograph, student Richard George (left) and fieldtrip leader Sara Parker share a meal with villagers in Sikles, Nepal. Photograph by Gehendra Gurung

culture and multiculturalism, body image and nutrition (Zelinsky 1985;Cook 1995). So, as a fieldworker, you may not only want to find food you like to eat, but also food that may be interesting and significant in other ways (see Figure 8.2).

Eating, as a form of participant observation, may be open-ended and broadly directed at understanding a place and the people who live there. Or it might be more focused, brought to a particular question which you may be investigating in your field project work. An example of fieldwork involving participation, at a lunch attended by migrants in New Zealand, illustrates the sort of research that you might imagine doing on your own fieldtrip (students we have supervised in the field have done similar things). To investigate 'the roles played by food in women's domestic lives and spaces', Robyn Longhurst and a research assistant attended a 'shared lunch' at the Waikato Migrant Resource Centre (WMRC) in Hamilton, New Zealand (Longhurst et al. 2008: 210–211). The two researchers *participated* by bringing food, eating with the others who were seated on a long table, and joining in the conversation. They also *observed* how others approached their food: which food they chose; how they combined different dishes; how they divided their meal into courses; how they interacted with each other. Longhurst and the research assistant also recorded their own experiences: how they behaved, the emotions and sensations they experienced, and finally how they interpreted all this.

Notes on this event, unlike those that might be drawn from an interview or focus group, were concerned less with what people said and more with what they did , in other words, with actions and body language. For example, Longhurst described the ways in which others were eating, noticing in particular that some people combined on their plates spicy dishes such as *kimch'i* (fermented vegetables) with sweet dishes such as pavlova (a dessert). She also observed a 'crinkling of the nose' and 'screwing up of the face' when someone tasted something they did not seem to like or expect (Longhurst et al. 2008: 211). As well as this she recorded her own feelings, noting that she was not keen to eat some dishes such as spicy sheep stomach, but still felt somewhat obliged to move beyond her 'food comfort zone' (2008: 211). Writing up these findings, the researchers and their co-authors worked towards some broader conclusions about the significance of the shared lunch for understanding experiences of migration and embodied research methodologies.

PUBBING AND CLUBBING

Whereas eating is something you must do on a fieldtrip, going out to bars and clubs is something you may choose to do, particularly if yours is an urban fieldtrip. As discussed in Chapters 4 and 5, this fieldwork 'tradition' can be problematic and its associations with alcohol and in some cases soft drugs can be alienating to other students for personal or religious reasons. Still, for many students evenings and nights out will provide some of the strongest impressions of the field and can be understood as another form of participant observation. An understanding of clubbing might, for example, speak to broader debates about experiences of space, sound-scapes and geographies of music, spaces of identity, the night-time economy, geographies of consumption, and moral geographies. This was illustrated in an ethnography of clubbing by Ben Malbon. Though not a template for you to copy directly, this provides an example from which you can learn and some techniques you can borrow, selectively and critically. Malbon's research – beginning with drinks and followed by clubbing and eventually a night bus home – was not simply an extension of his own social life: he set up nights-out with club-bers whom he had selected for academic reasons and these were followed up with interviews and documented in research diaries.

Similarly, pubs and bars can provide environments in which it is possible to engage with research participants in less formal ways than may be afforded by other methods such as inter-viewing. It might be possible to observe people and their interactions and even overhear con-versations. The sociable atmosphere may also encourage ice-breaking conversations and present opportunities to find, and engage with, research participants. This could be facilitated by shared experiences such as watching a sports event in a pub (see Postcard 8.1). However, the relaxed atmosphere of pubs and bars should not translate into a sloppy approach to data collection. The same rigours of research planning, site selection, sampling, structuring the data collection and recording notes should be applied regardless of the location in which PO is being conducted.

Ben Malbon wrote up his participant observation by making notes during and immediately after nights out, which he fleshed out in more detail the morning after. For example:

> 2 a.m. – main dance floor, chaos: The music dominated the dance floor. Everyone was dancing – on the balcony, on the little stages that projected out onto the dance floor like catwalks (look at me, 'cos I'm looking at you!), in the bar, behind the bar, *on* the bar. I really enjoyed dancing. I felt myself slipping in and out of submission to the music. No sooner had I forgotten what I was doing, and my dancing had become almost automatic, than I was suddenly aware of myself again, conscious of moving my feet, looking at what my arms were doing. I looked at people dancing and noticed how overtly they were looking at everyone else. I don't just mean glancing either. I mean really *looking* at someone, as though that was completely normal. I could feel myself being scanned, but wasn't affronted or anything by this. We all seemed to want the music to take us over; to *become* us in some way. Okay, so we each stamped our individuality on it in our own way – a neat little step here, an arm movement there – but the clubbers were essentially doing the same thing as each other and in the same place and at the same time. (Malbon 1999: xii)

Wandering

Another thing you will find yourself doing in the course of your fieldtrip is simply wandering around. Jane Jacobs, the author of a pioneering critique of modern city planning, illustrates how it is possible to learn from wandering around and engaging with people and places (see Figure 8.3). Enchanted by a neighbourhood she had wandered into in Boston, Jacobs recalls the spontaneous desire to participate in some way:

> The general street atmosphere of buoyancy, friendliness and good health was so infectious that I began asking directions of people just for the fun of getting in on some talk. I had seen a lot of Boston in the past couple of days, most of it sorely distressing, and it struck me, with relief, as the healthiest place in the city. (1962[1961]: 9)

Here, Jacobs experimented with and practised a form of participant observation (though she did not call it that) and she drew conclusions about what this could show which other methodologies could not. She suggested that by being in this part of the city, by walking around and participating in it as best she could, she had learned things that official statistics and formal social science surveys often concealed or missed. So she phoned a city planner and told him: 'You ought to be down here learning as much as you can from it' (1962[1961]: 9). She drew broader conclusions from what she had seen that day, and from what she learned as a resident of Hudson Street in New York, where she observed and described the daily rituals of a 'sidewalk ballet' involving all sorts of people and practices. Once again Jacobs did not just observe; she participated, making her entrance on the sidewalk around eight in the morning: 'I put out the garbage can, surely a prosaic occupation, but I enjoy my part, my little clang, as the droves of junior high school students walk by the centre of the stage dropping candy wrappers'. This description is focused around an interpretation of urban life:

Under the seeming disorder of the old city, wherever the old city is working successfully, is a marvellous order for maintaining the safety of the streets and the freedom of the city. It is a complex order. Its essence is intricacy of sidewalk use, bringing with it a constant succession of eyes. (1962[1961]: 50)

Figure 8.3 Getting involved: Jane Jacobs in 1961

Source: http://www.janeswalk.net/about/jane_jacobs (last accessed 17 August 2010).

WHAT YOU CAN DO

These extracts from research involving participant observation illustrate some of the things that students might imagine doing on fieldtrips. On the surface these might seem 'easy', but this participant observation is actually as difficult as it is enjoyable and rewarding. To do it well you will need to approach this as carefully and industriously as you would any other research method. If you have not used participant observation before, it is important that you try this out before your fieldtrip. Or if you want to use a fieldtrip to learn and practise this technique, you should not expect too much from this first attempt in terms of findings. You can do this somewhere nearby and accessible such as a street, market, or café, or even a student residence. Getting started is largely about gaining confidence and finding ways to interact that feel natural and are also insightful. You can begin, like Jacobs did in Boston, by trying to engage with people in ways that seem appropriate and comfortable, not forcing yourself on anyone but simply asking directions or the time. Tim Bunnell, describing his own fieldwork in Kuala Lumpur, illustrates some of the ways in which you might do this (see Postcard 8.1). You may choose to follow Bunnell's specific examples, but his more general point is that participant observation means responding to particular places in appropriate ways by improvising and using your imagination.

Postcard 8.1: Breakfast, Football and Haircuts: An English student in Kuala Lumpur, by Tim Bunnell

In 1997, I travelled to Kuala Lumpur (KL) as a young doctoral student to carry out research on state-led urban megaprojects in and around the Malaysian national capital. My interests included the lifeworlds of ordinary people in the city.

One day when I had a morning interview scheduled, I decided to get up very early and try to reach Kuala Lumpur City Centre (KLCC) before what KL-ites called simply 'The Jam'. I succeeded and decided to kill the several hours of time before my interview by updating my checklist of topics and questions over breakfast. The eating options in the vicinity were polarised between upmarket hotels – which I knew that I could not afford – and a covered section of stalls catering to construction workers around the perimeter of the KLCC site. I took a deep breath and headed in to order roti canai (a kind of unleavened bread that is served with dhal or curry) and teh tarik (a sweet, frothy tea). When I came to find a seat at a table, space opened up with none of the eaters wanting to get too close to the lone white guy in the smart trousers and shirt. It soon occurred to me that they all probably thought – sadly, from my skin colour as much as from the clothes I was wearing – that I was one of the expat 'bosses' on the site. In retrospect I could have exploited this case of mistaken authority, but instead I tried to strike up a conversation with the men nearest to me.

It turned out that many of the men at that worksite canteen were from Indonesia. One thing I'd learned – from a gap year backpacking around the region – was that a good way to get young men talking was to mention English football! Indonesians will habitually ask people whom they meet 'dari mana?' (literally 'from where?'), a phrase to which one could use replies ranging from, 'I have just come over here from my apartment in Brickfields [another part of the city]' to 'I'm from England'. With a slight distortion of geographical fact, I got into the habit of saying that I was from Liverpool (in fact, my family is

(Continued)

(Continued)

from the northwest of England, but from Chester, not Liverpool). Liverpool was somewhere that all of the Indonesian workers had heard of, and most went on to dredge up lists of LFC's players, past and present. English football and Liverpool in particular became my main ice-breaker, the way in for talking to urban megaproject workers – the people who were literally performing the labour of Malaysian nation building – and so for gaining grounded perspectives on city lives.

Football was not the only ice-breaker, of course. In another part of KL which was being affected by the construction of a major new rail terminal, my way in to local gossip was to have my hair cut in the vicinity. This meant that I spent a lot of time in barbers' chairs but even ethnic Indian barbers who didn't like English football were happy to chatter away in English about local issues.

What can students learn from this? Whether you already have or are prepared to acquire language skills or work through translators, it is important to find ways in which to establish meaningful human contact with those whose insights or experiences will inform your research. So my advice is to try to learn languages, think of suitable ice-breakers and, if that fails, go and have your hair cut.

To conduct a sustained participant observation you would need to go through a series of stages which are explained and illustrated in the following paragraphs (for a more detailed introductory exercise, see Bennett 2002: 145). Not all of these stages may be relevant to you, and you may not necessarily want to approach them in the order shown here, but it is still helpful to identify each of these stages as the majority will apply to most forms of PO. You will need to apply these broad principles selectively and critically.

- *Select a research site.* Since participant observation 'involves strategically placing oneself in situations in which systematic understandings of place are most likely to arise' (Kearns 2005: 196), it is first necessary to decide what kind of place you would like to understand. Like Malbon, whose research was motivated by a passion for clubbing, you may start out with a clear idea about the places you are interested in. Or, like Longhurst et al. you may begin with theoretical interests and general questions, and need specific places in which to explore these. Many students, preparing to conduct fieldwork somewhere they have never been to before, may feel ignorant about the place they are going to, or the themes and questions they can explore through that place. If this describes you, don't worry too much, for there are advantages to being something of an outsider. As such you can be more open-minded than a local, according to Jaquelin Burgess and Peter Jackson (1992: 153), who explain that: 'Your perceptions may be more acute than an insider's less focussed curiosity, dulled by routine observation and habitual experience'. This means that it can be a good idea to conduct PO in a place that you are not already familiar with. It is better not to take this too far however, for example by placing yourself somewhere so different or challenging that you feel out of your depth. Hester Parr's (1998) study of mental health communities, though exemplary for academics, was extremely challenging and required a major investment of time and emotional energy which would be beyond the scope of most undergraduate dissertations or fieldwork. So, while it is good to reach outside your comfort zone, it is also a good idea not to reach too far. A compromise suggested by Kearns (2005) is to select a location in which you are a stranger but not completely out of place. To do this you will have to decide what kind of place you are interested in and then conduct your groundwork (perhaps through the internet or other secondary sources) in order to identify and find out a bit about specific sites which you may then decide to visit.

- *Make ethical choices.* Unlike some other research methods such as interviews, it is not always possible to explain the purposes of participant observation studies to everyone who is potentially involved in them, or to explicitly negotiate the terms in which participation may take place (see Chapter 4). Imagine Jane Jacobs walking along the street in Boston, explaining herself to everyone she chatted to or passed; this simply would not have worked. This forces you to make ethical judgements, not all of which can be passed on to ethics committees or determined through the application of ethical guidelines. One choice you may need to make is whether to conduct your research overtly or covertly. As we have already explained it can be difficult or impossible to be entirely overt, though you might be able to get round this by explaining yourself to key figures such as community leaders or gatekeepers. Sometimes researchers will choose to act covertly, whether for practical reasons or because not doing so might undermine their research. Covert research can sometimes be justified but it can also be uncomfortable and ethically problematic. For example, a doctoral student who conducted his research covertly while working as a car mechanic later reflected that he felt he was betraying and deceiving the people he met, who became friends during the course of the project (Rose 1987). In contrast, other social science disciplines such as management studies will routinely use covert participation observation – for example researchers taking paid employment in the firms they are studying – and regard this as an ethically valid and valuable research method. When conducting your own participant observation you too will need to decide whether you will tell people what you are doing; whether to show them your notes and/or provide feedback in any way; whether such feedback would be feasible; and whether you feel comfortable with representing other people in this way.

- *Assess the risks to yourself and others.* Participant Observation brings its own share of risks, including variations of the more general risks explained in Chapter 2. If you are conducting research covertly and your unwitting participants find out, there is a risk that you may find yourself in some kind of danger, but overt research also involves risks that more detached forms of observation do not. Risks such as these may be greater when you are away from home, perhaps in a foreign country, and where you may not be so familiar with local medical resources (in the event of a problem) or with the laws or ways in which the police deal with issues such as this. Hoggart et al. (2002: 274) identified a series of risks associated with participant observation, including legal danger (continuing the example of clubbing, this might include taking illegal drugs), ethical danger (taking drugs if doing so is against your principles, or if it incriminates or influences fellow students), and physical danger (taking drugs that may be harmful). It is not our place tell you what you should or should not do in the field, but we would suggest that you think through the legal, ethical and physical risks associated with possible forms of participant observation, discuss these with each other and with your fieldtrip leaders, and then come to your own conclusions.

- *Gain access to a setting.* Some places, such as the street scenes described by Jane Jacobs, will be easy to access. Others, including semi-public spaces such as shopping malls and train stations and semi-private spaces such as community centres and churches, may be policed by security staff and by the use of CCTV cameras, and might also have written or unwritten rules of conduct. To gain access to these places you may need permission, possibly from formal authorities or perhaps from informal 'gate-keepers'. Gatekeepers are influential figures who may be able to welcome you and introduce you to others, as well as perhaps giving you tips on how to participate when you are there. Sometimes gaining access to a setting can mean showing you can fit in – for Malbon, getting into a club meant dressing in a particular way and chatting to the host at the door. Or it could mean writing polite letters of introduction and patiently waiting for invitations, as for example when Longhurst secured an invitation to the shared lunch. Or, as with Phil Crang's research in a Mexican restaurant, it can mean applying for a job, being hired and trained up, and then working for a sustained period of time (Crang 1994). Some of these techniques will prove more practical than others for students on short fieldtrips and it will be up to you to decide which if any are right for you.

- *Decide how to present yourself.* As discussed above, the way you dress and present yourself physically can determine whether or not you are admitted to a place or event, but it can then influence your ability to participate and interact with people within that environment. Waiters, as Crang found, are required to dress and groom themselves in particular ways while they are working. And bodily presentation is not all about clothing.

Hester Parr (1998), researching people with mental illness, became conscious of the non-visual aspects of her presence. Feeling that perfumed deodorant and shampoo was setting her apart, she decided to hold back on personal grooming before attending the mental health centre. There are, of course, limits to how far one can dress in order to blend into a situation. You may not be able to afford to dress for certain events – Ladies' Day at Royal Ascot for example! And you might also decide that it would not be ethical or convincing if you were to adopt cross-cultural clothing or dress as a member of the opposite sex.

- *Decide on how to participate and by how much*. Participant observation takes many different forms and involves different degrees of participation. Distinctions have been drawn between the participant-as-observer, who gets more involved, and the observer-as-participant, who tends to stand back from situations and play a less active role. Different forms of participation and relationships with participants are illustrated in the contrast between Parr's effort to blend in and really participate in mental health centres and Robin Kearns' attempt to observe medical clinics without getting too involved. Kearns 'blended into the small crowd of clinic attendees, inconspicuously observing events under the guise of reading a newspaper' (Kearns 2005: 202). Another decision you need to make, regarding participation, is whether to work individually or in groups and, if the latter, how large these should be. It can help to involve more than one person, whether for safety reasons or in order to get a broader perspective, but too many students can undermine participation – sometimes it is easier to shy away from engaging with the unknown when surrounded by others – and make you look conspicuous. You will need to make your own judgements about this, considering the places and events you are participating in and the ways in which others behave there, whether alone or in groups.

- *Observe and take notes*. Observe the setting, the people around you, and yourself, and describe all of these in some way. For this you will probably want to use a discrete field notebook rather than a conspicuous laptop or clipboard and you may also want to make notes in private moments when doing so will not disrupt the flow of activities. Your observations and notes are likely to revolve around a series of simple questions, which can help you to observe more carefully. These may include: 'What is happening? When is it happening? Where is it happening? Who is (and is not) engaging in what kinds of activities? How are people responding to what is happening?' (Hoggart et al. 2002: 276). Try to make your notes straightforward and detailed, describing what you see and what happens rather than what you think these things mean: there will be time for this kind of interpretation later. Your notes will often be in the first person, describing what *you* are seeing, doing, and feeling. Written in the moment, they may be in the present or past tense. These notes will also be wide-ranging because when you make them you will not be sure what is important or why, though much of this will come into focus later on (Silvey 2003).

- *Analyse field notes.* The analysis of field notes will often begin with transcription, something you may wish to do as soon as possible – not only because some of your notes may be cryptic and perhaps scribbled down in haste, but also because you may be able to add to and develop them while the field experience is still fresh in your mind. Some researchers suggest that it can be helpful to use qualitative data analysis programmes (Hoggart et al. 2002) or card indexing systems (Silvey 2003), but the quantity of data generated through PO on undergraduate fieldtrips will rarely justify the investment that would be required by either of these. Better simply to transcribe notes onto your laptop and, other than through key word searches, analyse the data by hand. At this stage you may begin to interpret your findings, asking what they mean. It can be a good idea to use a different colour or font to distinguish your observations from your interpretations and judgements (Schensul et al. 1999).

- *Write up findings.* Many students find that the most difficult thing about participant observation is the writing-up. A generation ago students struggled with the idea of writing in the first person – using 'I' or 'we' – and 'striking the right balance between offering their own interpretation and acknowledging their sources' (Burgess and Jackson 1992: 155). Today students are generally more familiar and comfortable with the principle of writing in the first person, but many still find this difficult in practice. Unfortunately there is no easy way round this: ethnographic writing is difficult! In the absence of a simple formula we would suggest you learn from others who have practised this form of research and try writing in the styles illustrated by the three studies discussed above, on eating, clubbing, and wandering. You may wish to write something approaching a conventional field report which incorporates field notes, perhaps using text boxes to set these apart. These quoted sections may have the immediacy – probably the first person, present tense and rough edges – of a diary and they will contrast with the more polished form of the report as a whole. There is no formula for writing up participant observation and there are many ways of doing this. To find your own style there is no alternative to wide reading and practice, which will help you to determine the form that is most suited to your own project and abilities.

The many steps involved in PO, each introducing a series of challenges and constraints, illustrate how this is not only a powerful form of research but also a difficult and slippery one. For these reasons, Katy Bennett (2002: 148) argues that 'participant observation is not the method to use for a short-term research project', where there may not be time to develop skills, negotiate access, form and manage relationships, and so on. She acknowledges, however, that PO is still possible for student projects, and Ian Cook (2005) reinforces this point by describing a series of dissertations that students have completed in this way. One worked at a fast food restaurant, for example, while another participated in a music festival. The key is to be realistic about what can be done in the time available by considering the investments that are necessary at each of the stages identified above and making appropriate choices. PO is more feasible when you are relatively close to a community or practice and can easily gain access and begin participating. For example, you may find it easier to gain access to, blend in and participate with a student community in your field location, rather than attempting to get into a hospital, prison, or yacht club in the same area. And PO is more feasible in field-work when it involves easy-come easy-go relationships, steering clear of people who may be vulnerable or who might perhaps expect you to follow through the relationship in some way. This is why we have focused this chapter on examples of PO that a typical student *could* imagine doing on a fieldtrip – clubbing, eating, and wandering round a city, for example – and the intention has been that you should learn from these and borrow from them both critically and selectively.

But even if you have successfully negotiated all the hurdles identified above, and found a project that is academically meaningful, logistically practical, and ethically defensible, you may still feel that something is missing. You might feel that you have been too busy asking what your research participants can do for you rather than what you can do for them. As explained in Chapter 4 you would not be the first person to think along these lines, or to consider research that gives something back, or is redesigned to engage with the participants' needs, interests, and ideas from the outset. This ethical agenda has led some geographers to move away from PO and towards a related but distinct methodology known as Participatory and/or Action Research. This approach, explained in the next section, radically rethinks the purpose and structure of research projects, building impacts into the heart of the project rather than (possibly) tacking them on at the end, and involving participants at every stage.

PARTICIPATORY GEOGRAPHIES

Participatory Action Research (PAR) is an eclectic term, encompassing a number of participatory and/or action (impact-oriented) research forms which have collectively 'been defined as a collaborative process of research, education and action, explicitly oriented toward social transformation' (Kindon et al. 2007: 9). Conceived as 'research "with" rather than "on" people' (Heron and Reason 2006: 144), PAR unsettles the power relations between researchers and participants, flattening out the hierarchies in which researchers traditionally call the shots: deciding what to research, how, where, when, and why. Research questions and agendas are determined by participants rather than by academic theorists or policy makers, or the research-er's own curiosity. If everything works well the research will gain a practical ethos and demo-cratic spirit (Reason and Bradbury 2006: 7). More specifically, PAR is often suited to research involving participants who are 'excluded' and 'oppressed' in some way (Kindon et al. 2007: 9). This includes communities and groups experiencing some form of disadvantage or problem, such as people with disabilities (McFarlane and Hansen 2007), migrants (Pratt 2007), and indig-enous peoples (Hume-Cook et al. 2007).

Though diverse, PAR tends to involve a number of common steps, identified by Sarah Kindon (2005) as follows:

- Identify potential stakeholders/participants.

- Make contact with selected stakeholders/participants.

- Begin to establish relationships with stakeholders/participants.

- Collaboratively explore issues and gather information.

- Reflect on ethics and establish a Memorandum of Understanding.

- Collaboratively design research process and methods.

- Discuss and identify desired action outcomes.

- Work together to implement research and collect data.Collaboratively analyse data.

- Plan research-informed action with feedback to participants and others.

- Evaluate process and action as a whole.

Here the stages of conventional research design are effectively expanded to involve participants at every stage, in what Caitlin Cahill calls a 'cyclical analytic-reflective process' (2007: 184).

In practice, however, PAR encompasses a spectrum ranging from research that engages participants at every level to projects that include more modest forms of interaction: consulting and informing participants where possible and adapting conventional research techniques where practical. This continuum is illustrated through examples of actual research, which explain what this approach is about and provide some methods and ideas that students can learn from and apply. First, a study involving people with disabilities illustrates how participatory research can involve conventional methods that are being deployed in innovative and sometimes revolutionary ways. Interviews, a conventional methodology in human geography fieldwork (Chapter 7), were applied within a participatory framework by Hazel McFarlane and Nancy Hansen. These researchers, who identify as academics and activists, wanted to conduct 'emancipatory research' that would involve and empower people with disabilities (McFarlane and Hansen 2007: 88). This project illustrates some things that are realistic in undergraduate fieldwork and also throws some critical light on conventional methods conducted outside a participatory framework. Unlike some PAR researchers, McFarlane and Hansen did not involve the participants in designing the project – which would have been time-consuming and complex – but they did provide a list of topics in advance and invited participants to determine the times and places in which they would like to be interviewed. They felt these things would unsettle the power hierarchies associated with conventional interview research. They also worked, if not within their existing networks then within their positions as disabled women, who might more easily gain the confidence of potential participants and understand their needs and experiences. As they explain, 'we introduced ourselves as life-long disabled women and briefly outlined our research interests and commitment to a participatory research, emphasising our willingness to facilitate participation on their terms' (2007: 91).

Two other examples illustrate innovative methods that go beyond traditional social science methods and embrace participation within the research process as a whole. Both of these adapt visual methods. Divya Tolia-Kelly explains that: 'Visual methods have long been used by those wanting to engage with the experiences of those marginalised within society, for example children, women, and people with mental illness, and by researchers of rural development policy in the majority world' (2007: 132). In the first of these examples, Lorraine Young and Hazel Barrett (2001) used participatory methods to explore street children's perceptions and experiences of Kampala. For this research, which is discussed in Chapter 6, they gave disposable cameras to the children and asked them to take pictures of the places that were important to them. These open-ended instructions allowed the children to help decide what the project was about and therefore also involved them in shaping the research. One reason the researchers chose participatory research was that PO was not feasible under the circumstances: foreign white women knew they could not convincingly, ethically, or safely hope to enter the lives of African street children as participant observers (see also Kindon 2003; McEwan 2006).

Figure 8.4   Tanka Gurung, a youth group member in Sikles, Nepal, with Richard George, a student from the UK, discussing photographs that were taken by local people during a participatory photographic project. Photograph by Sara Parker

Methods such as these can sometimes be feasible in undergraduate fieldwork. For example, students from Liverpool conducted a participatory photographic project in Nepal, working with local children to generate and interpret images (Figures 8.4–5; see also Figure 1.3).

Another example of PAR that may be accessible to student fieldworkers was illustrated by Tolia-Kelly's project involving South Asian women in London. She explains that visual methods are particularly appropriate to participatory research because they are inclusive, side-stepping the limitations of written and oral practices. Participants completed the following exercise: 'Describe below, in writing, or a drawing, or however you like, the landscape that best represents your idea of home'. (Tolia-Kelly 2007: 138). Though other elements of this project – such as the involvement of a professional artist – would be beyond the means of most student fieldworkers, this participatory method may still be feasible for you.

Some other examples of PAR in the academic literature illustrate how the ideals of this form of research are particularly difficult to achieve in undergraduate fieldtrips, which tend to be too brief for meaningful and sustained investments in participant communities. In the previous section, we suggested it could be wise to steer clear of participant observation projects that required the cultivation of relationships with vulnerable or oppressed communities in which it

Figure 8.5 Participants in a photographic project in Nepal share their stories with student researchers. Photograph by Sushil Gurung and Sara Parker

was particularly crucial to get these relationships right and follow them through – to not forget them when you are back in your home country, perhaps jetlagged and preoccupied with other things. This comment applies equally to PAR, particularly where oppressed and vulnerable groups are involved. PAR should not be attempted lightly because the participants will live with the consequences. Consider some of the impacts that PAR researchers have made. Through their research involving people with disabilities, McFarlane and Hansen (2007: 92) helped some women take control of their 'emotional and experiential archive' and, as a result, one woman recognised that she was in an 'abusive relationship' and left her partner. Other examples of PAR illustrate forms of intervention that are simply beyond the scope of under-graduate research and also underline the point that interventions are only wise where deep levels of understanding have been developed and relationships cultivated over periods of time. Brinton Lykes led a PAR project designed to 're-thread' a community in post-war Guatemala: 'to tell a story of war and its effects while facilitating personal and community change, thereby improving the quality of community life in a post-war context of persistent poverty' (2006: 269). These interventions illustrate the sensitive issues in which PAR researchers have been prepared to engage.

A good rule of thumb for students is that it is better not to make any promises or plans that you won't be able to keep to and not to rush into anyone's life or community trying to make a difference that you may not fully understand! Indeed, experienced PAR researchers are critical of others who attempt to fast-track this approach. Geraldine Pratt contrasts her own successful collaboration with a Canadian Filipino centre with other researchers' failure to do the same, and one of the major reasons she gives is her own team's commitment to 'building trust and community ownership' over the long term: i.e. 'eleven years of collaboration' (2007: 98). The danger of attempting PAR in abbreviated fieldtrips is that you may give the impression of attempting another form of extractive research which is fundamentally incapable of following through the objectives espoused by many PAR researchers: 'collaborative research, education and action oriented towards social change' (Kindon et al. 2007: see inside cover; Monk 2007: xxiii).

Reasons for why it is not wise to attempt a more radical form of PAR on a fieldtrip include the following: first, Cooke and Kothari (2001) argue that this technique, effectively the new orthodoxy in development geographies, can often be a cover for schemes that remain top-down and extractive, and in which power relations between researcher and researched remain asymmetrical; second, innovative forms of PAR demand investments in skills development that may be expensive and time-consuming – participatory video, for example, requires equipment and the skills to use it, including video, production and editing skills, some of which may have to be bought in from consultants and freelancers (Kindon 2003; Hume-Cook et al. 2007); third, and most obviously, not all research is concerned with 'ordinary people' (Kindon et al. 2007: 1) or with oppressed or vulnerable groups, which PAR will set out to engage and empower. If you are researching elite groups such as managers or professional migrants, for example, there is no obvious way in which you would use PAR, and the question of what kind of impact you might wish to have will be more difficult to answer, but it is likely that you will not simply be looking to empower your research participants or the groups they seem to represent (Staeheli and Mitchell 2005; Phillips 2010).

There are, however, some ways in which forms of participatory research can be used in student fieldwork. Though not strictly PAR, the fieldwork described by William Gould in Postcard 4.1 illustrates how participatory principles can be put into practice in the field. Gould's account of a fieldtrip involving British and African students who were working together and supporting and learning from each other illustrates the ways in which fieldwork can be empowering and engaging for the students who instigate projects and fieldtrips, as well as for others whom they encounter and work with in the field, by interrogating and breaking down hierarchies and power relations among researchers (students and fieldtrip leaders) in addition to those between researchers and researched communities (Nelson et al. 2009). Peter Hopkins' postcard in this chapter, likewise, describes fieldwork that uses participatory approaches where possible, and this pragmatic example provides a useful example for under-graduates who are seeking to build participatory elements into fieldwork in practical ways (see, for example, Kesby 2000; Pain and Francis 2003; Hopkins 2006; Hopkins and Hill 2006; Alexander et al. 2007).

Postcard 8.2: Using Participatory Diagramming to Explore Young Peoples' Geographies, by Peter Hopkins

During fieldwork for a Scottish Refugee Council project about the needs and experiences of unaccompanied asylum-seeking children in Scotland, I conducted over 100 interviews with service providers and unaccompanied children. Working alongside Malcolm Hill, I also met a group of unaccompanied minors who had created a youth-group called 'Young Survivors Step to the Future'. During this meeting, we employed participatory diagramming as a method for finding out what the children felt were the 'good' and 'bad' things about Scotland and the 'good' and 'bad' things about their countries of origin.

In this project participatory diagramming sessions involved the use of large sheets of flip-chart paper, pens and post-it notes. With each exercise, the flip-chart paper was divided into two sections (such as 'good' and 'bad'). Post-it notes were then used by the young people to record their ideas in response to each issue, with one post-it note being used for each point. Having placed these on the flip-chart, the participants were then asked to collect together similar post-it notes

(Continued)

(Continued)

and to produce a ranking of the top three issues on each side of the flip-chart paper. This process therefore produced a useful set of prioritised issues about, for example, three 'good things about Scotland' and 'three bad things about Scotland' according to the views of unaccompanied asylum-seeking children. Rachel Pain and Peter Francis (2003) have outlined a number of other ways in which participatory diagramming might be employed depending on the specific focus and angle of the issue being ideas, the construction of a timeline, and the use of cause/impact diagrams or ranking exercises.

Since participatory diagramming can be used in combination with other qualitative methods, and since these were designed by the researcher rather than the participants, this project does not illustrate an exclusively participatory methodology. It is necessary to acknowledge these differences: i.e. between research with participatory elements and research which is fully participatory. However this project still demonstrated some of the more general benefits of participatory diagramming:

- It enabled the young asylum seekers to express a range of views and perceptions of Scotland and their countries of origin, some of which we had not anticipated.
- Some of these points might have been particularly difficult to verbalise within the group but proved easier to express in writing.
- This method was successful in involving quiet young people who would not normally contribute verbally in a traditional classroom setting, but who were happy to write their ideas on post-it notes and contribute to the diagram.
- The participants chose their level of involvement and adapted the tools to suit them.
- This proved a quick method and provided an efficient snapshot of young people's perspectives and experiences.
- The group work setting proved inclusive and engaging, helping the participants to define problems and suggest solutions (Pain and Francis 2003). This demonstrated the potential of participatory diagramming to change and challenge power relations within research.

Participatory diagramming does have its limitations and problems though. In this project I was conscious of my powerful position relative to the

(Continued)

(Continued)

participants and the diverse ways in which they may have viewed me – as an adult, male, white, researcher, university lecturer, and so on. Another issue is that, although many young people may be accustomed to participating in activities similar to this, participatory diagramming may be novel to some of them and thus it would require a more extensive introduction. Some of the unaccompanied asylum-seeking children did need me to explain in detail the purpose and processes associated with the exercise, but I found that these problems could be ameliorated. I convened group discussions to explore key issues emerging from the exercises described above. These enabled the participants to clarify their various points and proved useful in identifying areas of disagreement or a lack of consensus. Participants were asked if they would be interested in taking part in an individual interview. For those who accepted this invitation, the diagramming exercise provided a useful context for this and was often referred to during the interview by way of illustration by both the young person and the researcher.

SUMMARY

This chapter introduced participant observation and participatory research methods and discussed the variety of ways in which these could be conducted during fieldwork. These methods can be enjoyable and rewarding for both researchers and research participants. The key points of the chapter were:

- Participant observation and participatory research can be distinguished from more formal methods such as interviewing or secondary sources.

- Participant observation can be conducted in many different environments and ways. These include, but are not limited to, the examples discussed in this chapter – eating, pubbing and clubbing, and wandering.

- Participant observation and participatory methods are challenging but potentially rewarding.

CONCLUSIONS

Participant observation and participatory research methods overlap with some other field methods and they can also benefit from being used in association with them. Since PO and

PAR are difficult techniques to conduct and write up it can be wise to back them up with other methods that are more predictable and, frankly, easier. It can also be insightful to triangulate your methods by using different approaches to explore the same issues and compare findings. Moreover, PO and PAR can be used to complement other forms of fieldwork. For example, Longhurst et al. (2008: 213) felt that it was not appropriate to explicitly discuss certain issues at the shared lunch in which they participated; instead they saved these for more formal and private interviews. Similarly, in her study of the film and television industry in Manchester, Jennifer Johns (2004; 2010) combined corporate interviews with participant observation conducted in bars and clubs where members of the industry congregated and socialised. This participant observation helped Johns to plan and interpret her interviews. Like these researchers, you do not need to decide between participant/participatory and more formal research methods. On the contrary we would encourage you to put these together by using a range of methods in your engagement with the field. This chapter can then be read alongside others – including those on interviewing – as part of a broad and inclusive approach to fieldwork.

Participant observation and participatory approaches require you to make choices about the kinds of relationships you are looking for in the field. Deeper (but not necessarily better) relationships (associated with PAR) include participation in every stage of the research process and possibly actual initiation of the research itself. Shallower (but not necessarily worse) forms (associated with more conventional PO) include participation in the form of consulting and informing participants who may then play more passive roles in the research process. The latter may be more appropriate and feasible for your fieldwork given the constraints on most undergraduate field research. The judgements you make about the kinds of participant or participatory fieldwork you conduct, and the depth and form of relationships these entail, are likely to defined by the choices you make about which relationships will be most productive and ethical in the context of your particular fieldwork (see Chapter 4). Once again, this comes down to your own judgement.

FURTHER READING/KEY TEXT(S)

- Bennett, K. (2002) 'Participant observation'. In P. Shurmer-Smith (ed.), *Doing Cultural Geography*. London: SAGE, 139–149. This accessible and practical chapter includes a useful exercise in participant observation.

- Cahill, C. (2007) 'Participatory data analysis'. In S. Kingdon, R. Pain and M. Kesby (eds), *Participatory Action Research Approaches and Methods*. London: Routledge, 181–187. This project – involving a group called the Fed Up Honeys – explains better than an abstract methodological formula can what a thorough PAR project might look like.

9

HOW TO BE AN EXPLORER: REDISCOVERING YOUR CURIOSITY

OVERVIEW

This chapter addresses the following questions:

- How can you be curious and open-minded in your fieldwork? Why is this important?
- How can you start to see yourself as an explorer who is ready and willing to see the world afresh?

This chapter builds upon a central message of earlier chapters – that good fieldwork research benefits from openness, imagination, and flexibility. It then extends this further to look at how and why curiosity and exploration are valuable and how we can foster and develop creative approaches to fieldwork.

If you have signed up for a fieldtrip, there is a good chance you have done so out of curiosity about a place you do not yet know. Your challenge will be to nurture your geographical curiosity – an excellent point of departure – through a mixture of structured and open-ended research. This book has concentrated on the former: carefully planned and closely targeted field methods, which you can use to gain useful skills and good grades. But structured fieldwork has its limitations too: though capable of generating reliable and high-quality findings, it can also close down the possibilities for discovery and experience and distract you from the reason you wanted to do fieldwork in the first place: your more open-ended curiosity. This chapter invites you to open your mind to the world around you, engaging with the field as creatively and openly as possible. This is variously a counterpoint to and a continuation of the chapters that have come before. It provides suggestions for how you may 'observe the world around you as if you've never seen it before' (Smith 2008: 1). It does this by highlighting some experimental approaches to fieldwork which emphasise openness, spontaneity, creativity, and playfulness.

CURIOSITY-DRIVEN FIELDWORK

Undergraduate study is often very prescriptive. Course handbooks explain that 'By the end of this module, students will know this and/or be able to do that', and students will be assessed accordingly with coursework and exams to measure the learning outcomes. This is the case with fieldwork as with other forms of learning. An advantage of prescriptive fieldwork is that students will know where they are and what is expected of them. And it is important for them to also know how to design and execute goal-oriented projects, as we explained in Chapters 2 and 3. There is a danger, however, that too much of this can lead to 'instrumental learning' – knowing what is asked of you and performing accordingly – which can constrain your learning experience. In a pamphlet for teachers published by the Geographical Association it is stated that 'A leader ought first to decide carefully the purpose of any proposed fieldwork or visit and question whether the out of class activity is the most desirable way of achieving that end' (Geographical Association 1995: 1). This is a top-down approach to fieldwork, which puts the onus on field leaders to decide what will happen and why. Still, most universities would recognise that too much structure can make teaching and learning rather wooden and they would try to leave open some opportunities for flexibility and freedom. The leader of the University and College Union, which represents lecturers in British universities, has recently argued that adventure, freedom, and curiosity are fundamental academic values. As she put it, 'Universities must continue to be spaces in which the spirit of adventure thrives and where researchers enjoy academic freedom', with space for 'curiosity-driven research' (Phillips 2010). What is true for lecturers in their own research should also be true for students. And where better to find adventure, to explore places and ideas, than in the field?

Fieldtrips do vary and students will find different degrees of latitude and freedom built into these, which means that some will be encouraged and supported as they take chances and explore a bit whereas others will feel more constrained. If you are on a more prescriptive and tightly choreographed fieldtrip, in which you feel that curiosity and adventure are not encouraged, you could of course devote some of your spare time to exploring, perhaps by trying out some of the techniques for curiosity-driven research that are outlined in this chapter. Clare Herrick, who has taken fieldtrips to Santa Cruz, California, has noticed that students tend to insist on 'the freedom to enjoy and experience a new place in their own time'. She observes that 'students may actively reject the necessarily "over-organised" nature of some fieldtrips, calling for more free time in a schedule dictated by the need to conduct relevant and pedagogically valuable research projects in a limited time period' (Herrick 2010: 111).

You may feel more comfortable with prescriptive fieldwork, in which the aims and methods are clearly set out. Indeed some studies have shown that certain students will prefer to learn strategically, seeking the paths of least resistance to success in exams and assessments, or will simply seek to 'be educated' in return for their sizeable fees (Bradbeer et al. 2004). These are understandable feelings, but there are a number of personal, political and practical reasons why we would encourage you to experiment with some less structured approaches to learning, particularly in the field. First, curiosity-driven projects and activities can be more fulfilling because they are capable of bringing the world to life for you. This can be described as a form of 'enchantment': 'a sense of having one's nerves or circulation or concentration powers turned up or recharged – a shot in the arm, a fleeting return to childlike excitement about life' (Bennett 2001: 5): 'You notice new colours, discern details previously ignored, hear extraordinary sounds, as familiar landscapes of sense sharpen and intensify' (2001: 5). Enchantment and wonder are positive additions to the emotional rollercoaster associated with fieldwork, a high to set alongside lower and more stressful experiences. As discussed elsewhere in this book, some students do struggle emotionally with the 24/7 social experience of fieldwork while others will do the same with the physical activities involved, or the travel, or the work itself. Kwok Chan Lai argues that emotional experiences are not a by-product of fieldwork, they are 'inseparable parts of fieldwork learning' (2000: 167). This resonates with Liz Bondi's (2005) observation that geographical research is already driven by human emotions and feelings and her argument that we should embrace, interrogate, and direct this. Lai advises field leaders and students alike to embrace the possibilities of 'affective-focussed fieldwork', both by reflecting on and learning from emotions and also by being open to the emotional possibilities of fieldwork. These possibilities can be particularly rich if you open yourself up to encounters with people and places and do not hide behind too formal a fieldwork methodology.

Second, curiosity-driven fieldwork can take on a political and intellectual significance, forms of which are explained and illustrated in this chapter. Remember though that as discussed in Chapters 4 and 5, while geographical fieldwork has been criticised as a 'masculinist' and exclusionary tradition these practices are much more open-ended, with all sorts of radical and subversive possibilities, some of which are illustrated in this chapter. Curiosity-driven fieldwork has the potential to open up new ideas and lines of enquiry which more structured and heavily planned forms of learning might restrict. Historically, curiosity has been regarded as 'the impulse to improper inquiry' (Lee 2007: 109): 'Just as the church frowned upon "curiosity" as being contrary to a proper inquiry into God's universe, I fear one risks institutional excommunication in truly following one's curiosity as artist or academic' (2007: 112). Curiosity-driven exploration threatens and offers to get you into trouble! In a book about the history and culture of science, Sander Bais observes that 'All children run into self-proclaimed authorities like parents who keep telling them in solemn voices that it is strictly forbidden to go through this or that door, because something horrible could happen' (2010: 21). Finally, if you have not been persuaded by these personal, political, and intellectual arguments for curiosity-driven fieldwork – arguments that will be fleshed out in the course of this chapter – you might be persuaded by the more practical point that open-ended fieldwork can help you to develop skills that can be important to your degree and your job prospects. As discussed in Chapter 2, even seemingly dour academic regulators such as the UK's QAA do sometimes acknowledge the value of curiosity:

Geographers develop their geographical understanding through fieldwork and other forms of experiential learning, which helps to promote curiosity about the social and physical environments. (QAA 2007)

So, beware of professors who keep you too busy on fieldtrips! While you may not feel entirely comfortable with unstructured and open-ended fieldwork, we would encourage you to follow your curiosity and set your own agenda at least some of the time. This could be the most exciting and productive part of your trip.

BEING AN EXPLORER

Being an explorer can mean departing from formal, at-worst mechanistic research methods. This is easier said than done. Though a critic of formally structured fieldwork, humanistic geographer Yi Fu Tuan was equally sceptical about 'unstructured' fieldwork, conducted 'just to see what's out there, with no prior questions in mind' (Tuan 2001: 40): 'An undertaking of this sort is believed to stimulate the imagination, leading one to ideas inspired by objects in the field rather than by words in a book'. This, he argued, was impossible because human eyes and minds are never simply open to experience, and that however receptive we may try to be, we are always anticipating, filtering, focusing, structuring, and interpreting our experiences. Tuan's dour conclusion was that 'casual outings' had never made him 'wiser, or even more knowledgeable' (2001: 42). But exploratory fieldwork need not be entirely 'casual' for there are ways of cultivating an open mind and a curious condition. Matt Baillie-Smith illustrates below how students conducting fieldwork in India have adopted some open-ended methods, seeking to cultivate curiosities and avoid the blinkers associated with prematurely focused research.

Postcard 9.1 Open-ended Fieldwork in South India, by Matt Baillie-Smith

Having collected our baggage, the silence of student participants on the minibus as it pulls out of Thiruvananthapuram airport in South India and onto the highway always seems in sharp contrast to my excitement at arriving. Curious about what has or hasn't changed since last time (from the conditions of the road surface to the latest contracts for mobile phones being advertised), wondering when we will stop for a dosa (a South Indian pancake), considering whether it is going to be a particularly hot day for the journey, I sense I am spared

(Continued)

(Continued)

some of the students' anxiety about whether the whole of India will be like the chaotic seeming road, whether the food will be okay or the heat survivable. In developing an approach to a field visit which is open-ended and fluid, these often bewildering early experiences are not the bit before the field visit starts, but the very stuff of the fieldwork.

Our approach works to encourage a curiosity that works through, and against, powerful imaginaries of place, space, and identity that mediate understandings of India and the global South more particularly. It might seem easier to enable people, on what is usually a first visit to India, to observe the world as if they have never seen it before. But, particularly in India, there is a lot more baggage to be dealt with than the endlessly debated rucksack contents collected at the airport. Ideas of 'development', 'poverty', and 'need' can generate Orientalising imaginaries of India which will mediate participants' perspectives with their curiosity shaped by ideas of what India lacks and tempered by the instrumentality of 'helping' or 'charity'. Popular spatial imaginaries of the extremes of the Himalayas and the steam of the tropical jungle may privilege particular ideas of environmental spaces, thereby erasing the social. Colonial and post-colonial histories of exploration and 'adventure' alongside ideas of 'helping', 'volunteering', and charity can shape a curiosity that is as much about the researcher, with the risk of assumed 'rights' to mobility and fantasies of 'discovery', 'bravery', and 'making a difference'.

Our fluid approach is centred on allowing significant time for reflection, exploring emotional reactions, re-imagining project ideas and possibilities, and changing minds. This is the central 'cultural work' that is essential to the fieldwork, the 'open-endedness' helping to widen some horizons and foster new curiosities. We work closely with Indian academics, NGO colleagues, and students not only to make the familiarity of popular imaginaries 'strange' but also to make the strangeness first encountered as we leave the airport seem more 'familiar'. In some ways 'difference' is our guiding problematic and theme, with the field visit empowering participants to engage with difference in creative and curious ways, as well as to think beyond difference in exploring the settings they find themselves in. Sometimes students are sent off around the city in an auto-rickshaw for an hour with no planned itinerary and on their return will share reflections

(Continued)

(Continued)

with Indian partners, asking questions and reflecting on why particular things are 'noticed'. These can then begin connections to, amongst others, urban geographies, geographies of religion, of youth, and of gender, as well as the more obvious geographies of development.

Students' self identity, and the ways this develops and is negotiated whilst in India, are critical. For some, this will prove a significant challenge when it deviates from the imaginaries of the 'helper' mentioned above. In many respects, our fluid approach is as much about understanding the significance of positionality in shaping the creation of particular geographies as it is about enhancing understanding of the geographies of South India; without the former, the latter is impossible. Through this, students can begin to see the contours, contradictions, and nuances of the places and spaces they are in. They can also begin to think more critically and reflexively about the caste system or about child labour, for example, mindful of the baggage they might have brought but now able to understand where they might be asking from.

In this approach, the construction of student projects can produce unexpected outcomes. One participant chose, as their 'field project', to keep a reflexive diary and to narrate their experiences as well as take on the role of describing the group's processes of change. Another individual, when in India, began to see commonalities with their Christianity and the experiences of young Christians in South India and went on to construct their project around exploring those experiences. Others have returned to more conventional 'development' themes, such as writing around issues of organic and sustainable agriculture and analysing the impact of NGO education projects. For some, a project may emerge on their return home, when learning around positionality and difference provides a new lens on what was previously just 'familiar'. Key to this is providing a way for participants to not simply explore South India, but to also be curious about themselves as they do so.

As Tuan warned, there is nothing straightforward about open-ended research, which can be like trying to 'get lost'. In a book entitled *A Field Guide to Getting Lost*, Rebecca Solnit articulated the disruption necessary here in shedding banal and routine ways of seeing:

> To lose yourself: a voluptuous surrender, lost in your arms, lost to the world, utterly immersed in what is present so that its surroundings fade away ... And one does not get lost but loses oneself, with the implication that it is a conscious choice, a chosen surrender, a psychic state achievable through geography. (2006: 6)

So learning to see the world with fresh eyes and writing about or otherwise representing this can be just as challenging as any other fieldwork. One way of getting started is to learn from others who have done this previously – some of whom have written manuals and suggested missions, while others have simply taught by example. Joanne Lee, the art historian introduced above, explains that curiosity-driven research lends itself to a 'free-ranging method of inquiry', which is 'not easily regulated' and is therefore unconventional, eccentric, and even 'improper' in tone (2007: 109). It is therefore no surprise that we find some of the most creative and exciting geographical fieldwork taking place outside the formal context of universities and among communities of what radical geographer Bill Bunge once termed 'folk geographers', whose research and interventions are proliferating and being shared and communicated via the internet and various other forms of popular culture. Geography students, seeking inspiration for their own fieldwork, have much to learn from these free-ranging and variously open, spontaneous, creative, and playful geographical inquiries which are introduced in the following paragraphs.

'Folk geographers' can take credit for some of the most exciting and unconstrained geographical research. Bunge was a champion of this group. He forged an inclusive collective geographical project involving people of all ages and many different backgrounds: 'taxi-cab drivers, Italian and working class Anglo community leaders [and] blacks' (Bordessa and Bunge 1975: iii). These teams of researchers conducted large-scale urban expeditions which employed a wide variety of methods, variously established and innovative, ranging from mental mapping to sensory and emotional mappings, to detailed observations of peoples' uses of urban space – how verandas were used for example, and where children played in the street. These projects were in some cases playful and exploratory, in others much more conventional. They ranged from first-person descriptions of sound and smellscapes to quantitative geographical descriptions, for example maps of the city showing rents per square mile. So this research was eclectic rather than eccentric, and never wacky for the sake of it, but concerned primarily with building up a meticulous, alternative, democratically compiled picture of life in the city, which could then be used to substantiate specific arguments about how space should be used.

Whereas Bunge's project involved large numbers of 'folk geographers' but was coordinated through a university, other lively and exploratory geographical research has originated entirely outside the academy and this can be particularly innovative and inspiring to students seeking to broaden their approaches to fieldwork. In *How to be an Explorer of the World,* Keri Smith suggests a series of exercises, experiments that have been designed to reawaken and cultivate curiosity: 'Start with whatever makes you feel a twinge of excitement'(2008: 2), she advises, offering practical suggestions, many of which 'have been pilfered, borrowed, altered, and stolen from great thinkers and artists'. For example, 'Grocery shopping with John Cage':

> Collect things in your basket based on one variable of your choosing (such as colour, shape, size, packaging, foods you've never eaten, things you don't understand, food that are flat, etc.) You do not have to purchase them unless you want to. Document them somehow. (2008: 105)

This is a lively book, not only in its suggestions but also in its visual style, which uses a creative design to spark the reader's geographical imagination (see Figure 9.1). This is equally true of a similar book entitled *Mission:Explore* (Geography Collective 2010), which is aimed at children and is illustrated and presented accordingly (see Figure 9.2). Its suggestions or 'missions' propose geographical investigation through forms of play: for example, 'Play hide in shop. Go to a shopping centre and play hide-and-seek. Which are the best three shops to hide in?' (2010: 145). This book was compiled by a group calling itself 'The Geography Collective', which introduces itself as 'a bunch of Guerilla Geographers' including 'geography explorers, doctors, artists, teachers, activists, adventurers' who 'think it's really fun and important to get exploring and questioning the world' (2010: 196).

These exploratory geographies have more formal counterparts and influences too. Influences, some of which are mentioned if not formally cited in *How to be an Explorer*, include books that may be familiar to geography students, including Gaston Bachelard's *Poetics of Space* (1964) and Georges Perec's *Species of Space and Other Pieces* (1997[1978]). Perec's book includes aphorisms,

Figure 9.1 *How to be an Explorer of the World* by Keri Smith (2008) Exploration #35: 'invisible city'.

Source: Smith (2008).

Figure 9.2 'Blindfold yourself'. Source: *Mission: Explore* (Geography Collective, 2010). This book comes with a tongue-in-cheek 'WARNING' on the front – 'This book is dangerous' – while the back cover issues an invitation: 'Become a guerrilla explorer and extreme missioner with missions that defy gravity, see the invisible and test your mental agility'

sketches and exercises, some of which may seem familiar to geographers: for example, 'The street: try to describe the street, what it's made of, what it's used for. The people in the street. The cars. What sort of cars?' (1997 [1978]: 50). Perec pushes this exercise, which initially seems rather banal, to a point at which it becomes illuminating. Instructing the reader-explorer to

'Carry on/ Until the scene becomes improbable', he is inviting us to look so closely, and describe in such detail, that we begin to see the world afresh.

Exercises such as these, which encourage individuals to conduct geographical research independently, resonate with more collective projects, in which geographical explorers converge through meetings and festivals. A high profile example of this is *Conflux*, a free festival held in New York every year, which bills itself as 'a platform for artists, urban geographers, technologists and others to organize and produce innovative activities dedicated to the examination, celebration and (re)construction of everyday urban life' (http://confluxfestival.org last accessed 2 June 2010). Conflux events are free and open to the public and include 'walks and tours; lectures, workshops, and panels; street games and tech-enabled expeditions; interactive performance; social/environmental research; public art installations; audio/video/film programs'. The broad aim of all this is to find, in cities, 'a laboratory for creative experimentation and civic action' and it recognises the need to continually experiment with how to do this: 'Through public interventions, artist-facilitated walks and tours, interactive performances and installations, bike and subway expeditions, and more, Conflux artists will confront and rewrite the rules of urban public space'.

Though Conflux is a tangible festival, which takes place in and engages with specific geographical areas, its own documentation hints at its double life, marked by a strong presence on the internet and engagement with other communications technologies – the precise mix and form of which changes from year to year. At the time we were writing this book, the Conflux website was advising participants to promote their projects on their own websites or blogs and through social networking tools such as Facebook and MySpace: 'For example, use Twitter to post updates on the production of your project, post works-in-progress pictures on Flickr'. Much the same is true of projects such as *Mission:Explore*, which invites those who have completed missions to report their experiences and findings on Twitter and through the project website (www.missionexplore.co.uk), which also serves as a forum for new and bonus missions.

Other forums for geographical exploration are *primarily* web-based. Specific websites, like technologies, will change from year to year as some are neglected or closed down while others are launched, but there remains a lively web-based culture of geographical exploration. Mookychick, for example, is a website set up by the writer and artist Magdalena Knight. As with the other projects illustrated above, this website makes suggestions about how to carry out geographical research: 'Try to find patterns where there aren't any. Look out for graffiti, words on shop-signs and posters. Talk to local people, and take plenty of photos'. These general suggestions are followed up with more sustained exercise plans (detailed illustrations of which are provided later in this chapter). In addition to their suggestions for conducting experiments and exploring, websites such as this include space for projects, both for communication between collaborators and commentators on ongoing projects, and also for posting findings. The Mookychick homepage invites the reader to ask questions about his or her environment as well as explore:

Ever felt drawn to strange old warehouses or puzzled over why everyone looks like a robot on their way to work? With the aid of a few helpful exercises Mookychick shows you the semi-occult art of psychogeography – finding out how the environment you live in shapes the way you think. Becoming a psychogeographer is as easy as studying graffiti and poking your nose where it doesn't belong ... (http://www.mookychick.co.uk/spirit/psychogeography.php last accessed 2 June 2010)

Some of the geographical research techniques advocated and explained by the sorts of manuals, festivals, websites, and writers illustrated above can simply be borrowed and applied to exploratory fieldwork. Indeed some should be, since they are not only lively, engaging, and helpfully specific but are also close to the sorts of questions that are already being asked by many geography students. Some of these missions explore new ways to describe and map geographical environments, for example:

Blind observation. Go around your room in the dark and identify all the objects in it by touch. Describe them. (Smith 2008: 85)

Structure. Document part of a building(s) that most people ignore (examples including the ceilings, bathrooms, corners, closets, and the insides of drawers). Pay attention to the hidden places. (Smith 2008: 64)

Memorise a place. Using only your memory and a pencil, draw a map of somewhere. Now explore that place using only your map. What did you include and exclude, enlarge and shrink? (Geography Collective 2010: 142)

Rubbish map. Look at litter from your local area and see where it has come from. Draw a map to show which countries the rubbish has come from. Can you calculate how many miles it has come before being dumped? Warning: wear gloves or use a grabber and don't go picking up filthy sharp stuff. (Geography Collective 2010: 106)

Missions are outlined in more detail in some cases, for example on the Mookychick website, which outlines a detailed project and its rationale:

Set aside an afternoon and go somewhere safe and consumerist, like the hippest part of town wherever you live. But remember, you're not there to do shopping. You can do exercises like this alone or with an interested friend. But with two of you the desire for shopping will automatically increase - so no shopping until the dérive is over!

Your task for this adventure is to set yourself a time limit then spend the next couple of hours wandering around, noting down any graffiti you find, both by writing it in a notepad and taking photographs of it. This means that you're not looking where consumerist society wants you to look - you know, at shops or billboards, the usual suspects. Screw that. Find yourself exploring bus stops, public toilets and side streets. Go to the places that are invisible when you're purely focused on shopping. Notice all the things you're not meant to see as a good little citizen - the cctv cameras, the drunks, the strange little hang-outs and alleyways.

When you've finished, treat yourself by going and buying something tiny and pointless and pretty, or even the pair of shoes you've had your eye on for so long, or buying a drink and sitting down outside in a cafe or little park, and really enjoy your consumerist moment - you've poked into the inner workings of the invisible city, so you've earned your Coke! Collect all your photographs and stick them in a scrapbook labelled Soho/Times Square/Blah/whatever your hip shopping district is called. You'll be surprised at how much satisfaction and meaning you getting from collecting such unglamorous photos. (http://www.mookychick.co.uk/spirit/psychogeography.php last accessed 2 June 2010)

Websites such as these also provide useful practical advice, including tips that may be useful to fieldworkers who are interested in designing their own creative geographical research projects. The Conflux website fleshes out the practicalities associated with conducting and developing the sorts of exercises and experiments illustrated here. For example: 'Be resourceful: recruit your friends to help you and use this website as a tool to post further questions and suggestions for the event production, as this can help all participants; consider your connections with school or community groups that might be able to assist you with your event' (http://confluxfestival. org last accessed 2 June 1010).

Once you start looking – and a good way to do this is to try googling terms such as psychogeography – you will find many different websites, publications and projects, indicating the creativity and range of geographical imaginations and explorations taking place. One final example of these illustrates the ways in which these exploratory techniques connect with some more formal academic field methods. An example of participant observation in Chapter 8 referred to the urban activist Jane Jacobs, who regularly wandered around neighbourhoods in New York and Boston and built her observations into her commentaries on urban dynamics and city planning. Jacobs has been an inspiration for many and one of the ways in which she is currently being remembered is through urban walks called 'Jane's Walks', which are promoted on the internet and which promise to promote 'walkable neighbourhoods, urban literacy, cities planned for and by people' (http://www.janeswalk.net/about last accessed 17 August 2010). Once again, geographical explorations and wanderings are linked to broader political and intellectual projects with open-ended possibilities.

MEANINGFUL EXPLORATION

Referring to psychogeography, Mookychick makes it clear that it is not proposing 'purposeless play' – the phrase Keri Smith self-deprecatingly applies to *How to be an Explorer* (2008: 104) – but is instead attempting something meaningful. This website claims that readers who take its suggestions will merit the 'new sexy-hot title – Psychogeographer!' It explains this term with a brief review of psychogeography, a field of critical urban geography that has been most closely associated with the Situationist International, a political and artistic movement that emerged in Paris in the 1950s. Situationists, according to this website, pioneered a playful form of geographical research: 'this is called going on a *dérive*, or urban drifting' and involves 'a gentle walk with the aim to discover something new about your area'.

This website's suggestions for further reading on 'notable psychogeographers' identify another strand of contemporary geographical research which is flourishing outside universities and from which academic geographers have much to learn: the wanderings and writings of relatively high profile writers such as Iain Sinclair, Will Self and J.G. Ballard. Sinclair identifies as a psychogeographer and writes books about places he has traversed on foot and, occasionally, on local buses. He also writes about slow and deliberately unspectacular journeys: walks through the forgotten edges of cities and local bus journeys, each with a twist that goes against the grain dictated by the planners and property developers – agents, in his view, of neoliberal capitalism – and each seeking out disruptive and creative geographies. Similarly, journalist and broadcaster Will Self has brought a version of Situationist practice to his column in the London *Independent* and to a book about a journey (partly on foot) from London to New York. Like Sinclair, Self's project involves re-awakening the imagination, unsettling the banal and the routine, and bringing geographical experience back to life. This draws upon the work and rhetoric of Situationist, led by Guy Debord, who advocated new and disruptive engagements with cities. The '*dérive*', a key term in the Situationist vocabulary, was conceived as 'an experimental and critical drift through urban terrain' (Pinder 2005b: 24, quoting Guy Debord). The *dériveur* walks against the grain of the modern city. Walking – in cities that were being reorganised around motor vehicles – took on a new significance. To walk was to contest the technocratic power of city planners and managers and to walk off the map was to contest the terms of the modern city.

> Everyone unthinkingly followed the paths learned once and for all, to their work and their homes, to their predictable future. For them duty had already become a habit, and habit a duty. They did not see the deficiency of their city. They thought the deficiency of their life was natural. We wanted to break out of this conditioning, in quest of another use of the urban landscape, in quest of new passions. (Guy Debord 1959, quoted in Blazwick 1989: 40)

This struggle against the utilitarian, rational functionality of the modern city explains the significance, for the Situationists, of attributes one might not normally expect to find in a critique of urban geography: humour, polemic, poetry, play, provocation, and trickery.

Situationist rhetoric can be esoteric and slippery, but its currency among popular writers and bloggers shows that it can also be inspiring. Geographers, too, take inspiration from the ideas and methods pioneered by the Situationists. Keith Bassett, who leads human geography field projects in Paris, has explored ways in which students can apply Situationist concepts and methods to their fieldwork. He typically sends groups of five or six students out into the city armed with tape recorders and cameras and tasked with 'exploring the psychoge-ography' of an area 'using a variety of different approaches in combinations that the group members could decide for themselves' (Bassett 2004: 404). He also makes some useful suggestions for students who are thinking of borrowing psychogeographical techniques. First, he sets these techniques in an academic context and in so doing he speculates on what if anything is distinctive about the psychogeography practised by students rather than, say, artists. The students in Bassett's group are 'urged to experiment with the Situationist vocabulary of *unites, d'ambiences, plaques tournantes, pentes,* passages, axes, borders and defences, paths of attraction and repulsion etc., perhaps extending them with suggestions of their own' (2004: 404). Whereas some of the artists, performers, and explorers illustrated above tend to cite the Situationists rather emblematically and implicitly, the students in his group are asked to apply and interrogate these terms in a more sustained and explicit manner in order to establish a dialogue with these concepts. Though some of the general ends of this project are shared with other aspiring psychogeographers – for example, participants learning 'to open their eyes and ears to what is often taken for granted or ignored in negotiating urban space' – some aspects of the project are more clearly academic, concerned with exploring the theoretical through practical experiments and strategies (2004: 408).

Postcard 9.2: Just Drifting, by Alastair Bonnett

A group of students files uncertainly through the doors of a care home for the mentally ill in Gateshead. They stop in the middle of the packed dining hall and, after a brief consultation amongst themselves, decide they have arrived at Rathaus Steglitz on the Berlin U-Bahn. These are pyschogeographers, mixing up the map and getting as lost and disoriented as possible in order to see the city in new and unexpected ways. Or less grandly, these are students not sure what they have got themselves into. Discomforted, embarrassed, trespassing, they blunder out into the fresh air.

I arrived at this pyschogeographical 'drift' with a lot of political baggage. It had been organised by an architecture student at Newcastle University. I was the only lecturer to come along but I certainly wasn't in charge. It was entirely extra-curricula. In my slightly over-heated political imagination such undisciplined forays into the unknown were part of a transgressive revolutionary current that was trying to identify spaces of release and transformation in a routinised and closed-up city. It certainly felt a bit edgy. We ended up anywhere: aisles in Tesco's, gloomy walkways behind shops, places that had once been normal but had become odd, and odd non-places that had become destinations.

But were we doing something genuinely exciting or behaving like a bunch of arrogant radical dandies? Maybe both. The other 18 students that turned up for these drifts (there were five in all) were bemused

(Continued)

(Continued)

but happy to waste an afternoon re-wiring cartography. What would happen? The possibility that we would be bored, that participants would decide the whole thing was silly and leave, that we would be challenged verbally or physically ... such thoughts created a permanent atmosphere of anxiety, an anxiety which led to a kind of relieved excitement when we ended up enjoying ourselves and realised that we were, indeed, thinking about and using the city in ways we had never thought about before.

James Burch, who organised these events in 1994, asked us all to fill out a questionnaire at various 'U-Bahn stops' (he also wrote up our adventures for a magazine about 'urban exploration' that I edited; see Burch 1995). The questions probed our emotional state. Filling in the blanks we were asked to 'Describe where you are ... I am ... I feel ... I want to ... Describe who you see ...They are ... They feel ... I want them to ...' and so on; questions that deepened the awkwardness, the humour, and the possibilities.

This sounds pretentious because it was pretentious. But that is sometimes a risk worth taking. A decade and a half later I still remember my drift with a mixture of disquiet and exhilaration. I learnt that my routines are fragile, easily thrown off course. For once, years ago, I walked along streets I had no reason to be walking along, walked into places where I was not supposed to be, not knowing where I was headed or what my destination would be. I'm not sure anymore that my 'drift' did have a political meaning, at least not in the kind of libertarian, flag-waving way I had once imagined. But it stays with me as something thrilling and oddly disturbing. Perhaps it reminded me of how much, actually, I need and enjoy my spatial routines ... the same roads, the same places, the same faces. You have to be truly disorientated, at least once, to know the value of not being lost.

BORROWING TECHNIQUES AND TAKING INSPIRATION

However, for all this practical advice it is not always possible or a good idea for geography students to directly *borrow* ideas from the sources listed and illustrated here. Some of the techniques outlined above – in particular the travel and other geographical writing associated with figures such as Iain Sinclair and Will Self – are anything but straightforward and are more easily admired and interpreted than directly emulated by students. These accomplished and inspiring writers do not provide any shortcuts or simple formulae. Students can learn from them, but mainly by example, and their lessons in methodology are variously general and implicit. Though critical readings of travel writing are now an established subfield of geographical research, less attention has been paid to setting out how geography students can 'do travel writing' themselves. Nor do we have any easy answers to this question – a full response here would be the remit of a creative writing class – though a few pointers for doing so can be found in travel writing itself.

Some of the other methods illustrated in this chapter are simply impractical in the context of student fieldwork: Bill Bunge describes 50 million person hours of fieldwork, conducted over several years in two cities, and research on this scale is obviously not feasible for small groups of students. More importantly innovations can appear to lose their critical edge once they have been tried and tested, systematised and mainstreamed, so it may be necessary to learn from the spirit rather than the letter of some of the material covered in this chapter. Many of the techniques pioneered by Bill Bunge, for example, have since been brought to the heart of the discipline and refined, such that it would be meaningless to replicate them. His research on soundscapes and children's geographies has in each case been superseded and this has helped spawn various new journals and even subfields with the result that it is no longer wise to look directly to Bunge for methodological points of departure.

How, then, can you learn from and reinterpret (rather than simply attempt to replicate) those expeditions? There are many things that you can potentially learn from Bunge but I will highlight only two here. First, Bunge was methodologically eclectic and pragmatic, using whatever methods and sources he could to advance the broader project. In other words, for all the creativity of some of his techniques and the originality of some of his mappings, Bunge was not dismissive towards more conventional methods and sources such as interviews and quantitative data and he kept methods in place by always remembering the purposes they were intended to serve. Second, he recognised and cultivated the collective nature of research, involving 'folk geographers' as well as their professional counterparts, and acknowledged the importance of all those who were involved in data collection, analysis, and use. This is pertinent to fieldwork where students must rely upon each other for travelling as safely and happily as possible and will generally have to work together in groups (see Chapter 5 on group work). This fieldwork shares many characteristics with that of psychogeographers and urban explorers of one kind and another and also shows that students need not cultivate Situationist chic in order to pursue many of the same, shared objectives and values, including collective, democratic, curiosity-driven learning.

In other cases, there is more ambiguity about how to relate to the methodological innovators of previous generations. As illustrated above, Keith Bassett asks challenging questions about academic engagements with psychogeography: 'Can one use Situationist tools for an academic exercise in this kind of way without effectively de-radicalizing them to the extent that they become lifeless and un-illuminating?' (2004: 408). And does it defeat the purpose to instruct students to conduct psychogeographic missions, even when they have the latitude to interpret these in their own terms? In other words, should these methods always remain outside the remit of assessed student work? Bassett also raises questions about the meaningfulness of replicating these techniques today, over half a century since the movement flourished in its original form. Mere replication of these techniques is particularly problematic since (a) the movement was committed to spontaneity and play, and this precludes canonising and simply repeating techniques, something that smacks of the mechanistic approach that alienates most students from methodology modules; and (b) Situationists responded to a particular set of historical and political circumstances. While some of the issues they addressed remain unchanged, others have been addressed to a point, while others still have arisen which demand we address them in new ways. Rather than simply replicating Situationist practices, Bassett suggests that we must reinterpret them. This poses questions for students who may be considering some form of psychogeographical projects in the field: not simply offering the reader answers, but asking questions, how to learn from previous innovators, and how to follow the spirit – not necessarily the letter – of their work. This precludes simply prescriptive or didactic conclusions – telling students what to do – and it ends, instead, by setting out questions for students to answer themselves.

SERIOUS PLAY: EXPLORATORY FIELDWORK

Keri Smith's assertion of 'purposeless play' is self-deprecating and perhaps even disingenuous, though it does seem to be in a good cause: Smith is steering clear of pomposity and intellectual pretension. Others are a little more explicit about the reasons for their playfulness. The Geography Collective state the obvious – that they 'think it's really fun and important to get exploring and questioning the world' (2010: 196) – though of course they are writing for children. Others attempt more challenging explanations. Georges Perec claimed never to feel 'comfortable talking about [his] work in abstract, theoretical terms' (Perec 1997 [1978]: 138), but his translator was more forthcoming, describing *Species of Space and Other Pieces* as a book about 'urban and domestic space and how, these days, we are made to occupy it' (Sturrock, in Perec 1997 [1978]: vii). Perec's interest in relationships between writing and space – in the use of words to mark, define, and remember spaces – is evident not only in the content of his writing but also in its organisation and presentation on the page: 'This is how space begins', he explains, 'with words only, signs traced on the blank page' (Perec 1997 [1978]: 13). His broader project, as discussed above, was to reanimate and defamiliarise everyday geographies by looking at them very closely and describing them to the point at which they begin to seem strange.

The inclusiveness and sense of fun inherent in many of the projects illustrated in this chapter can be traced to a field tradition that reaches back through the twentieth century to include a variety of local surveys, represented in books such as *The School Looks Around* (1948):

> Boys and girls are naturally interested in their immediate surroundings, in the behaviour of those who live about them and their work, in the physical features of their houses and streets, and in the machinery of everyday events. Their natural inquisitiveness is too often discouraged by adults who get tired of answering questions, and the youngsters soon cease to ask and to look round them curiously. They acquire the adult lack of interest in immediate things all too soon.

> The local survey method is an attempt to reverse this process; to use the boys' and girls' immediate interests to examine things they can understand, to look at the neighbourhood with open eyes, to feel at home in different sections of the community in which they live as school children, as future workers, and as young citizens ... (Layton and White 1948: 1)

This tradition can also be traced further back, through geography fieldwork that encouraged children to adopt the 'spirit of explorers' (Ploszajska 1998: 764) and brought imagination and humour to the learning process.

This brief historical detour speaks to the 'why' question – the reason for exploratory geographies – because some historical figures, and those who identify with them, have been explicit about their reasons for approaching geography in this way. David Stoddart (1986), whose history of Geography celebrates the excitement of learning, communicates the message that to study geography in the field is a vital activity in a way that book learning is not: it makes you feel alive. Stoddart's 'heroes' are not theorists but practical figures such as Thomas Henry Huxley, author of *Physiography* (1877), who communicated and promoted a form of geography that 'was to be learned in the village and the countryside, not read about in books. The field trip and the specimen were means to knowledge', he added (Stoddart 1986: 47). For others, including some of the historical figures cited here, the field tradition is closely linked with political projects: not the anti-establishment politics hinted at by some of the more contemporary exploratory geographers, nor the radical projects claimed by those who identity with the Situationists and psychogeography, but the mainstream politics of promoting forms of imperial citizenship. Local surveys and school fieldwork were promoted by the Royal Geographical Society and endorsed by the School Inspectors, who 'placed increasing emphasis on the value of a school's grounds and locality as resources for geography lessons' and 'suggested that geography, if taught by personal observation and active experience, became a fascinating and relevant school subject, rather than a tiresome mnemonic exercise' (Ploszajska 1998: 759). Continuing in this tradition, *The School Looks Around* (1948) was 'issued under the auspices of the Association for Education in Citizenship' (Layton and White 1948: i) and its values were made explicit:

> The local survey can help to bring the individual into sympathy with his surroundings, not passively, but as an active unit. By giving him some understanding of his immediate environment, it can build a better approach to the larger world, and develop a technique for acquiring further knowledge and for judging events beyond personal experience. Our object in this book is to discuss local surveys as a method of education, and especially of education for citizenship. (1948: 1)

Geographical surveys have therefore been deployed for a variety of reasons and in a variety of contexts: from citizenship projects to state education to community projects with more radical political programmes.

SUMMARY

This chapter examined notions of curiosity and exploration in fieldwork and argued that by opening ourselves to possibilities and new ways of thinking and doing we can engage with our field environments in more exciting and fulfilling ways. The key points were:

- Curiosity-driven fieldwork is about spontaneity, creativity and playfulness. We advise against always taking highly structured approaches to fieldwork and encourage all students to find time to free themselves from the restrictions of your own and others' expectations.

- Being explorers in the field means exposing ourselves to new experiences, getting lost, and finding ways to see the world afresh.

- There are many sources of inspiration from within, and beyond, geography that suggest new ways of describing and mapping geographical environments. Examples of how we conduct meaningful exploration are drawn from psychogeography and the Situationists which offer radical counterpoints to the more formalised and routine research methods outlined in previous chapters.

- We should reinterpret existing ideas rather than replicate them as each fieldwork situation and the group of individuals conducting the research will be unique. Nor should we dismiss more conventional methods and sources – it is important to balance innovative ideas with the practicalities of fieldwork.

CONCLUSION

By asking not only how exploratory research has been and can be conducted, but also *why*, it is possible to begin to put these techniques into context and see that they should not be adopted mechanistically or simply through a desire for novelty. Some advocates of exploratory fieldwork, echoing figures and groups as diverse as Stoddart and the Geography Collective, have suggested that first-hand experience and outdoor learning can make you feel alive and engaged. Others have applied exploratory methods for quite different reasons, ranging from the patriotic and pedagogical agenda pursued by Her Majesty's Inspectors and the Association for Education in Citizenship, to the radical projects of Bill Bunge. So both in field practices and also in the reasons that are given for them there is continuity and change, tradition, and innovation. When you go into the field you are at once inheriting and renewing a tradition and – if you get it right – also doing something entirely original.

FURTHER READING/KEY TEXT(S)

- Perec, G. (1997) *Species of Space and Other Pieces* (trans. J. Sturrock) Harmondsworth: Penguin. Perec is an imaginative writer, whose attention to buildings and street scenes is inspiring and innovative.

- Smith, K. (2008) *How to be an Explorer of the World*. London: Perigee/Penguin. This is a lively and inspiring book with some useful suggestions for further reading, and many ideas for 'explorations' you can try out yourself.

BIBLIOGRAPHY

Abbott, D. (2006) 'Disrupting the "whiteness" of fieldwork in geography', *Singapore Journal of Tropical Geography, 27*: 326–341.

Adjaye, A. (2010) 'Urban Africa: A Photographic Survey', exhibition, Design Museum London, available at http://designmuseum.org/exhibitions/2010/urban-africa-a-photographic-journey-by-david-adjaye (last accessed 28 October 2010).

Alexander, C., Beale, N., Kesby, M., Kindon, S., McMillan, J., Pain, R. and Ziegler, F. (2007) 'Participatory diagramming: a critical view from North East England'. In S. Kindon, R. Pain and M. Kesby (eds), *Participatory Action Research Approaches and Methods: Connecting People, Participation and Place.* London: Routledge.

Anderson, B., Morton, F. and Revill, G. (eds) (2005) 'Geographies of music and sound'. Special Issue of *Social and Cultural Geography, 6*(5).

Ash, A., Bellew, J., Davies, M., Newman, T. and Richardson, L. (1997) ' Everybody in? The experience of disabled students in Further Education', *Disability and Society, 12*(4): 605–621.

Atkinson, P. and Silverman, D. (1997) 'Kundera's Immortality: the interview society and the invention of the self', *Qualitative Inquiry, 3*: 304–325.

Attwood, R. (2009) 'Glamour, not strategy, drives students abroad', *Times Higher Education, 17* September. Available at http://www.timeshighereducation.co.uk/story.asp?storyCode=408205&sectioncode=26

Bachelard, G. (1964) *Poetics of Space* (trans. Maria Jolas). New York: Orion.

Back, L. (2003) 'Deep listening: researching music and the cartographies of sound'. In A. Blunt, P. Gruffudd, J. May, M. Ogborn and D. Pinder (eds), *Cultural Geography in Practice.* London: Arnold.

Bais, S. (2010) *In Praise of Science: Curiosity, Understanding and Progress.* Cambridge, MA: MIT Press.

Bassett, K. (2004) 'Walking as an aesthetic practice and a critical tool: some psychogeographical experiments', *Journal of Geography in Higher Education, 28*(3): 397–410.

Belbin, M.R. (1981) *Management Teams: Why They Succeed or Fail.* Oxford: Heinemann.

Bell, D. and Valentine, G. (1997) *Consuming Geographies: We Are Where We Eat.* London: Routledge.

Bennett, J. (2001) *The Enchantment of Modern Life: Attachments, Crossings and Ethics.* Princeton: Princeton UP.

Bennett, K. (2002) 'Participant observation'. In P. Shurmer-Smith (ed.), *Doing Cultural Geography.* London: SAGE.

Bestor, T.C., Steinhoff, P.G. and Bestor, V.L. (eds) (2003) *Doing Fieldwork in Japan.* Honolulu: University of Hawaii Press.

Blazwick, I. (ed.) (1989) *A Situationist Scrapbook.* London: ICA/Verso.

Blunt, A. and Dowling, R. (1996) *Home (Key Ideas in Geography).* London: Routledge.

Bondi, L. (2005) 'The place of emotions in research'. In J. Davidson, L. Bondi and M. Smith (eds), *Emotional Geographies.* Aldershot: Ashgate.

Bordessa, R. and Bunge, W. (eds) (1975) *The Canadian Alternative: Survival, Expeditions and Urban Change* (Geographical Monographs No. 2). Toronto: York University.

Bottomley, A. (2001) 'It's not what you study, it's how you benefit from your study that interests us'. *PLANET*, Special Edition 1, July: 24–25.

Bouma, G.D. (1993) *The Research Process.* Melbourne: Oxford University Press Australia.

Bradbeer, J., Healey, M. and Kneale, P. (2004) 'Undergraduate geographers' understandings of geography, learning and teaching', *Journal of Geography in Higher Education, 28*(1): 17–34.

Bracken, L. and Mawdsley, E. (2004) '"Muddy glee": rounding out the picture of women and physical geography fieldwork', *Area, 36*: 280–286.

Brydon, L. (2006) 'Ethical practices in doing development research'. In V. Desai and R.B. Potter (eds), *Doing Development Research.* London: SAGE.

Bullard, J. (2010) 'Health and safety in the field'. In N. Clifford, S. French and G. Valentine (eds), *Key Methods in Geography* (2nd edn). London: SAGE.

Bunge, W. (1979) 'Perspective on theoretical geography', *Annals of the Association of American Geographers, 69* (1): 169–174.

Burch, J. (1995) 'An account of some experiential derive in Newcastle', *Transgressions, 1,* 29–32.

Burgess, J. and Jackson, P. (1992) 'Streetwork: an encounter with place', *Journal of Geography in Higher Education, 16* (2): 151–157.

Burgess, R.G. (1984) *In the Field: An Introduction to Social Investigation.* London: Routledge.

Burgess, R.G. (1991) 'Access in educational settings'. In W.B. Shaffir and R.A. Stebbins (eds), *Experiencing Fieldwork: An Inside View of Qualitative Research.* London: SAGE.

Cahill, C. (2007) 'Participatory data analysis'. In S. Kingdon, R. Pain, and M. Kesby (eds), *Participatory Action Research Approaches and Methods.* London: Routledge.

Chacko, E. (2004) 'Positionality and praxis: fieldwork experiences in rural India', *Singapore Journal of Tropical Geography, 25*(1): 51–63.

Chalkley, B. and Waterfield, J. (2001) *Providing Learning Support for Students with Hidden Disabilities and Dyslexia Undertaking Fieldwork and Related Activities.* The Geography Discipline Network (http://www.glos.ac.uk/el/philg/gdn/disabil/hidden/toc.htm).

Chaplin, E. (2004) 'My visual diary'. In C. Knowles and P. Sweetman (eds), *Picturing the Social Landscape: Visual Methods and the Sociological Imagination.* London: Routledge.

Chuan, G.K. and Poh, W.P. (2000) 'Status of fieldwork in the geography curriculum in South East Asia'. In R. Gerber and G.K. Chuan (eds), *Fieldwork in Geography: Reflections, Perspectives and Actions.* Dordrecht, Boston and London: Kluwer Academic.

Clegg, S. and Hardy, C. (1996) 'Some dare call it power'. In S. Clegg, C. Hardy and W. Nord (eds), *Handbook of Organisational Studies.* London: SAGE.

Clifford, J. (1997) *Routes: Travel and Translation in the Late Twentieth Century,.* Cambridge, MA: Harvard University Press.

Clifford, N., French, S. and Valentine, G. (eds) (2010) *Key Methods in Geography* (2nd edn). London: SAGE.

Cloke, P., Cook, I., Crang, P., Goodwin, M., Painter, J. and Philo, C. (2004) *Practising Human Geography.* London: SAGE.

Cochrane, A. (1998) 'Illusions of power: interviewing local elites', *Environment and Planning A, 30*: 2121–2132.

Coe, N.M. and Smyth, F. (2010) 'Students as tour guides: innovation in fieldwork assessment', *Journal of Geography in Higher Education, 34* (1): 125–139.

Coffey, A. (2005) 'The sex(ual) field: sexual activity, desire and expectation impact upon the lived reality fieldwork'. In C. Pole (ed.), *Fieldwork.* London: SAGE.

Cohen, S. and Lashua, B.D. (2010) 'Re-mapping the precinct: music, the built environment and urban change in Liverpool'. In M. Leonard and R. Strachan (eds), *The Beat Goes On: Liverpool, Popular Music and the Changing City.* Liverpool: Liverpool University Press.

Cook, I. (1995) 'Constructing the exotic: the case of tropical fruit'. In J. Allen and C. Hamnett (eds), *A Shrinking World?* Oxford: Open University Press.

Cook, I. (2005) 'Participant observation'. In R. Flowerdew and D. Martin (eds), *Methods in Human Geography.* Harlow: Pearson Education.

Cook, I. and Crang, M. (1995) *Doing Ethnographies.* Norwich: Environmental Publications.

Cooke, B. and Kothari, U. (eds) (2001) *Participation: The New Tyranny?* London: Zed.

Cosgrove, D. (1984) *Social Formation and Symbolic Landscape.* London: Croom Helm.

Crang, M. (2003) 'Qualitative methods touchy, feely, look-see?', *Progress in Human Geography, 27*: 494–504.

Crang, P. (1994) 'It's showtime: on the workplace geographies of display in a restaurant', *Environment and Planning D, Society and Space, 12*, 675–702.

Cupples, C. (2002) 'The field as a landscape of desire: sex and sexuality in geographical fieldwork', *Area, 34*(4): 382–390.

Daniels, S. (1993) *Fields of Vision: Landscape Imagery and National Identity in England and the United States.* Cambridge: Polity.

Davies, A.D. (2009) 'Ethnography, space and politics: interrogating the process of protest in the Tibetan Freedom Movement', *Area, 41*(1): 19–25.

DeLyser, D. and Starrs, P.F. (2001) 'Doing fieldwork: Editors' Introduction', *Geographical Review, 91*(1–2): iv-viii.

Desai, V. and Potter, R.B. (2006) *Doing Development Research.* London: SAGE.

DfES (1999) Skills Task Force Employer Skills Survey, 1999. Department for Education and Skills, London. Available from: http://skillsbase.dfes.gov.uk/Narrative/Narrative.asp?sect=7 (last accessed 1 January 2010).

Dodge, M. and Kitchin, R. (2006) 'Net:Geography fieldwork frequently asked questions'. In J. Weiss, J. Nolan, J. Hunsinger and P. Trifonas (eds), *The International Handbook of Virtual Learning Environments.* Dordrecht: Springer.

Dodman, D.R. (2003) 'Shooting in the city: an autophotographic exploration of the urban environment in Kingston, Jamaica', *Area, 35*(3): 293–304.

Dowling, R. (2005) 'Power, subjectivity and ethics in qualitative research'. In I. Hay (ed.), *Qualitative Research Methods in Human Geography.* Melbourne: Oxford University Press.

Driver, F. (2000) 'Editorial: Field-work in geography', *Transactions of the Institute of British Geographers, 25*(3): 267–268.

Dummer, T.J.B., Cook, I.G., Parker, S.L., Barrett, G.A. and Hull, P.A. (2008) 'Promoting and assessing "deep learning" in geography fieldwork: an evaluation of reflective field diaries', *Journal of Geography in Higher Education, 32*(3): 459–479.

Duncan, J.S. (1990) *The City as Text: The Politics of Landscape Interpretation in the Kandyan Kingdom.* Cambridge: Cambridge University Press.

Duttro, K. (1999) 'Comments at Career Development Strategies II: E-tools and techniques'. AAG Conference Workshop, Honolulu, 25 March.

Elwood, S. and Martin, D. (2000) '"Placing" interviews: location and scales of power in qualitative research', *Professional Geographer, 52*: 649–657.

Ephross, P.H. and Vassit, J.V. (2005) *Groups that Work: Structure and Process* (2nd edn). New York: Columbia University Press.

Fishwick, M. (1995) 'Ray and Ronald girdle the globe', *Journal of American Popular Culture, 18*(1): 13–29.

Flowerdew, R. and Martin, D. (eds) (2005) *Methods in Human Geography: A Guide for Students Doing a Research Project* (2nd edn). Harlow: Prentice Hall.

Foskett, N. (1997) 'Teaching and learning through fieldwork'. In D. Tilbury and M. Williams (eds), *Teaching and Learning Geography*. London: Routledge.

Fuller, I., Edmonson, S., France, D., Higgitt, D. and Ratinen, I. (2006) 'International perspectives on the effectiveness of Geography fieldwork for learning', *Journal of Geography in Higher Education, 30* (1): 89–101.

Gandy, M. (2008) 'Landscapes of disaster: water, modernity and urban fragmentation in Mumbai', *Environment and Planning A, 40*: 108–140.

Geikie, A. (1887) *The Teaching of Geography*. London: Macmillan

Geographical Association (1995) *Geography Outside the Classroom* (pamphlet). Sheffield: Geographical Association.

Geography Collective (2010) *Mission:Explore*. London: Can of Worms Kids Press.

Gerber, R. and Chuan, G.K. (eds) (2000) *Fieldwork in Geography: Reflections, Perspectives and Actions*. Dordrecht, Boston and London: Kluwer Academic.

Glassie, H. (1982) *Passing the Time in Ballymenone: Culture and History of an Ulster Community*. Philadelphia: Wiley.

Gleeson, B. (1998) *Geographies of Disability*. London: Routledge.

Glynn, P. (1988) *Fieldwork Firsthand: A Close Look at Geography Fieldwork*. London: Crakehill.

Goh K.C. and Wong P.P. (2000) 'Status of fieldwork in the geography curriculum in Southeast Asia'. In R. Gerber and G.K. Chuan (eds), *Fieldwork in Geography: Reflections, Perspectives and Actions*. Dordrecht, Boston and London: Kluwer Academic.

Gold, J.R., Jenkins, A., Lee, R., Monk, J., Riley, J., Shepherd, I. and Unwin, D. (1991) *Teaching Geography in Higher Education: A Manual of Good Practice*. Oxford: Blackwell.

Grady, J. (2004) 'Working with visible evidence: an invitation and some practical advice'. In C. Knowles and P. Sweetman (eds), *Picturing the Social Landscape: Visual Methods and the Sociological Imagination*. London: Routledge.

Guardian (2003a) 'Memories caught on the brink of extinction', 3 January, p. 17.

Guardian (2003b) 'Online archive brings Britain's migration story to life', 30 July, p. 7.

Hall, T., Healey, M. and Harrison, M. (2004) 'Fieldwork and disabled students: discourses of exclusion and inclusion', *Transactions of the Institute of British Geographers, 27*: 213–231.

Hamlyn, N. (1989) 'Those tricky situationists', *Guardian*, 4 July.

Harris, R.C. (2001) 'Archival fieldwork', *Geographical Review, 91*(1–2): 328–335.

Healey, M. and Healey, R.L. (2010) 'How to conduct a literature search'. In N. Clifford, S. French and G. Valentine (eds), *Key Methods in Geography* (2nd edn). London: SAGE.

Heath, S. and Cleaver, E. (2004) 'Mapping the spatial in shared household life: a missed opportunity?'. In C. Knowles and P. Sweetman (eds), *Picturing the Social Landscape: Visual Methods and the Sociological Imagination.* London: Routledge.

Heron, J. and Reason, P. (2006) 'The practice of co-operative enquiry: research "with" rather than "on" people'. In P. Reason and H. Bradbury (eds), *Handbook of Action Research.* London: SAGE.

Herrick, C. (2010) 'Lost in the field: ensuring student learning in the "threatened" geography fieldtrip', *Area, 42* (1): 108–116.

Hoggart, K., Lees, L. and Davies, A. (2002) *Researching Human Geographies.* London: Arnold.

Hope, M. (2009) 'The importance of direct experience: a philosophical defence of fieldwork in human geography', *Journal of Geography in Higher Education, 33*(2): 169–182.

Hopkins, P. (2006) 'Youth transitions and going to university: the perceptions of students attending a geography summer school access programme', *Area, 38*(3): 240–247.

Hopkins, P. and Hill, M. (2006) 'This is a good place to live and think about the future': the needs and experiences of unaccompanied asylum-seeking children and young people in Scotland. Glasgow: Scottish Refugee Council.

Hume-Cook, G., Curtis, T., Woods, K., Potaka, J., Tangaroa Wagner, A. and Kindon, S. (2007) 'Uniting people with place using participatory video in Aotearoa/New Zealand'. In S. Kingdon, R. Pain and M. Kesby (eds), *Participatory Action Research Approaches and Methods.* London: Routledge.

Jackson, J.B. (1984) *Discovering the Vernacular Landscape.* New Haven: Yale University Press.

Jackson, P. (1988) 'Definitions of the situation: neighbourhood change and local politics in Chicago'. In J. Eyles and D.M. Smith (eds), *Qualitative Methods in Human Geography.* Cambridge: Polity.

Jackson, P. (1989) *Maps of Meaning: An Introduction to Cultural Geography.* London: Unwin Hyman.

Jacobs, J. (1962 [1961]) *The Death and Life of Great American Cities.* London: Jonathan Cape.

Jacques, D. and Salmon, G. (2007) *Learning in Groups: A Handbook for Face-to-Face and Online Environments* (4th edn). London: Routledge.

Jazeel, T. and McFarlane, C. (2007) 'Intervention: responsible learning: cultures of knowledge production and the north-south divide', *Antipode, 39*(5): 781–789.

Jazeel, T. and McFarlane, C. (2009) 'The limits of responsibility: a postcolonial politics of academic knowledge production', *Transactions of the Institute of British Geographers, 35*: 109–124.

Johns, J. (2004) *Tracing the Connections: Manchester's Film and Television Industry.* PhD thesis, School of Geography, University of Manchester.

Johns, J. (2010) 'Reconceptualizing the film and television production system: relational networks and "project teams"', *Urban Studies, 47* (5): 1059–1077.

Johnsen, S., May, J. and Cloke, P. (2008) 'Imag(in)ing "homeless places": using auto-photography to (re)examine the geographies of homelessness', *Area, 40*(2): 194–207.

Jones, R. (2000) 'Marking closely or on the bench? An Australian's benchmark statement', *Journal of Geography in Higher Education, 24* (3): 419–421.

Katz, C. (1994) 'Playing the field: questions of fieldwork in geography', *Professional Geographer, 46*(1): 67–72.

Kearns, R. (2002) 'Back to the future/field: doing fieldwork', *New Zealand Geographer, 58*(2): 75–76.

Kearns, R. (2005) 'Knowing seeing? Undertaking observational research', In I. Hay (ed.), *Qualitative Research Methods in Human Geography.* Melbourne: Oxford University Press.

Kesby, M. (2000) 'Participatory diagramming: deploying qualitative methods through an action research epistemology', *Area, 32*(4): 423–435.

Kindon, S. (2003) 'Participatory video in geographic research: a feminist practice of looking?', *Area, 35*(2): 142–153.

Kindon, S. (2005) 'Participatory action research'. In I. Hay (ed.), *Qualitative Research Methods in Human Geography.* Melbourne: Oxford University Press.

Kindon, S., Pain, R. and Kesby, M. (eds) (2007) *Participatory Action Research Approaches and Methods.* London: Routledge.

Knapp C. (1990) 'Outdoor education in the United States'. In K. McRae (ed.), *Outdoor and Environmental Education.* Melbourne: Macmillan.

Knight, P. and Yorke, M. (2004) *Learning, Curriculum and Employability in Higher Education.* London: Routledge.

Kobayashi, A. (ed.) (1994) *Women, Work and Place.* Montreal: McGill-Queens University Press.

Kubler, B. and Forbes, P. (2006) *Student Employability Profiles: A Guide for Employers.* London: CIHE.

Kumar, N. (1992) *Friends, Brothers and Informants: Fieldwork Memoirs of Banaras.* Berkeley: University of California Press.

Kwan, T. (2000) 'Fieldwork in geography teaching: the case in Hong Kong'. In R. Gerber and G.K. Chuan (eds), *Fieldwork in Geography: Reflections, Perspectives and Actions.* Dordrecht, Boston and London: Kluwer Academic.

Lai, K.C. (2000) 'Affective-focussed geographical fieldwork: what do adventurous experiences during field trips mean to pupils?'. In R. Gerber and G.K. Chuan (eds), *Fieldwork in Geography: Reflections, Perspectives and Actions.* Dordrecht, Boston and London: Kluwer Academic.

Lashua, B.D. and Cohen, S. (2010) 'Liverpool musicscapes: music performance, movement and the built urban environment'. In B. Fincham, M. McGuinness and L. Murray (eds), *Mobile Methodologies.* London: Palgrave.

Latham, A. and McCormack, D.P. (2007) 'Digital photography and web-based assignments in an urban field course: snapshots from Berlin', *Journal of Geography in Higher Education, 31*(2): 241–256.

Laurier, E. (2003) 'Participant observation'. In N. Clifford and G. Valentine (eds), *Key Methods in Geography.* London: SAGE.

Laurier, E. and Philo, C. (2006) 'Possible geographies: a passing encounter in a café', *Area, 38*(4): 353–363.

Layton, E. and Blanco White, J. (for the Association for Education in Citizenship) (1948) *The School Looks Around.* London: Longmans, Green and Co.

Lee, J. (2007) 'Languages for learning to delight in art'. In G. Beer, M. Bowie and B. Perrey (eds), *In(ter) Discipline: New Languages for Criticism.* Oxford: Legenda.

Lee, R.M. (1995) *Dangerous Fieldwork.* London: SAGE.

Le Heron, R. and Hathaway, J.T. (2000) 'An international perspective on developing skills through geography programmes for employability and life: narratives from New Zealand and the United States', *Journal of Geography in Higher Education, 24* (2): 271–276.

Levin, P. (2003) 'Running group projects: dealing with the free-rider problem', *PLANET, 5*: 7–8.

Levin, P. (2005) *Successful Teamwork.* Maidenhead: Oxford University Press.

Lewis, P. (1979) 'Axioms for reading the landscape: some guides to the American scene'. In D.W. Meinig (ed.), *The Interpretation of Ordinary Landscapes.* New York: Oxford University Press.

Ley, D. and Cybriwsky, R. (1974) 'Urban graffiti as territorial markers', *Annals of the Association of American Geographers, 64*(4): 491–505.

Leyshon, A., Matless, D. and Revill, G. (eds) (1996) *The Place of Music.* New York: Guilford.

Linton, D. (1960) 'Foreword'. In G.E. Hutchings (ed.), *Landscape Drawing.* London: Methuen.

Little, B. (2003) *International Perspectives on Employability.* Enhancing Student Employability Co-ordination Team (ESECT) & Centre for Higher Education Research and Information (CHERI) at the Open University. Available at www.ltsn.ac.uk/genericcentre/index.asp?id=18285 (last accessed April 2003).

Livingstone, I., Matthews, H. and Castley, A. (1998) *Fieldwork and Dissertations in Geography.* Cheltenham: Geography Discipline Network.

Lonergan, N. and Andersen, L.W. (1988) 'Field-based education: some theoretical considerations', *Higher Education Research and Development, 7* (1): 63–77.

Longhurst, R. (2010) 'Semi-structured interviews and focus groups'. In N. Clifford, S. French and G. Valentine (eds), *Key Methods in Geography* (2nd edn). London: SAGE.

Longhurst, R., Ho, E. and Johnston, L. (2008) Using 'the body' as an 'instrument of research': kimch'i and pavlova. *Area* 40(2) p. 208–217.

Low, J. (1996) 'Negotiating identities, negotiating environments', *Disability & Society, 11*(2): 235–248.

Low, K.E.Y. (2005) 'Ruminations on smell as a sociocultural phenomenon', *Current Sociology, 53*: 397–417.

Lykes, M.B. (2006) 'Creative arts and photography in Participatory Action Research in Guatemala'. In P. Reason and H. Bradbury (eds), *Handbook of Action Research.* London: SAGE.

Maddrell, A. (2010) 'Academic geography as terra incognita: lessons from the "expedition debate" and another border to cross', *Transactions of the Institute of British Geographers, 35*: 149–153.

Madge, C. (1993) 'Boundary disputes – comments on Sidaway (1992)', *Area, 25* (3): 294–299.

Maguire, S. (1998) 'Gender differences in attitudes to undergraduate fieldwork', *Area, 30*(3): 207–214.

Malbon, B. (1999) *Clubbing: Dancing, Ecstasy and Vitality.* London: Routledge.

Marsden, B. (2000) 'A British historical perspective on fieldwork from the 1820s to the 1970s'. In R. Gerber and G.K. Chuan (eds), *Fieldwork in Geography: Reflections, Perspectives and Actions.* Dordrecht, Boston and London: Kluwer Academic.

Maskall, J. and Stokes, A. (2008) *Designing Effective Fieldwork for the Environmental and Natural Sciences.* GEES Subject Centre Learning and Teaching Guide. Available at www.gees.ac.uk/pubs/guides/fw2/GEESfwGuide.pdf (last accessed 13 April 2010).

Mason, J. (2002) *Qualitative Researching* (2nd edn). London: SAGE.

Mathewson, K. (2001) 'Between "in camp" and "out of bounds": notes on the history of fieldwork in American geography', *Geographical Review, 91*(1–2): 215–224.

McCaffrey, K., Holdsworth, R.L., Clegg, P., Jones, R. and Wilson, R. (2003) 'Using digital mapping tools and 3–D visualisation to improve undergraduate fieldwork', *Planet,* Special Edition, *5*: 34–36.

McCulloch, G. (2004) *Documentary Research in Education, History and Social Sciences.* London: RoutledgeFalmer.

McDowell, L. (1992) 'Doing gender: feminisim, feminists and research methods in Human Geography', *Transactions of the Institute of British Geographers, 17* (4): 399–416.

McDowell, L. (1997) 'Women/gender/feminisms: doing feminist geography', *Journal of Geography in Higher Education, 21*(3): 381–400.

McEwan, C. (2006) 'Using images, films and photography'. In V. Desai and R.B. Potter (eds), *Doing Development Research*. London: SAGE.

McFarlane, H. and Hansen, N.E. (2007) 'Inclusive methodologies: including disabled people in participatory action research in Scotland and Canada'. In S. Kingdon, R. Pain and M. Kesby (eds), *Participatory Action Research Approaches and Methods*. London: Routledge.

McGuiness, M. and Simm, D. (2005) 'Going global? Long-haul fieldwork in undergraduate geography', *Journal of Geography in Higher Education, 29* (2): 241–253.

Meinig, D. (1983) 'Geography as an art', *Transactions of the Institute of British Geographers, 8*(3): 314–328.

Miéville, C. (2009) *The City and the City*. London: Pan Macmillan.

Miles, M. (1964) *Innovations in Education*. New York: Teachers College Press of Columbia University.

Miles, M. and Huberman, A. (1984) *Qualitative Data Analysis*. London: SAGE.

Mistry, J., Berardi, A. and Simpson, M. (2009) 'Critical reflections on practice: the changing roles of three physical geographers carrying out research in a developing country', *Area, 41*(1): 82–93.

Mitchell, D. (2000) *Cultural Geography: A Critical Introduction*. Oxford: Blackwell.

Mitchell, W.J. (2003) '*Wunderkammer* to World Wide Web: picturing place in the post-photographic era'. In J.M. Schwarz and J.R. Ryan (eds), *Picturing Place: Photography and the Geographical Imagination*. London: I.B. Tauris.

Momsen, J.H. (2006) 'Women, men and fieldwork'. In V. Desai and R.B. Potter (eds), *Doing Development Research*. London: SAGE.

Monk, J. (2007) 'Foreword'. In S. Kingdon, R. Pain and M. Kesby (eds), *Participatory Action Research Approaches and Methods*. London: Routledge.

Mowforth, M. and Munt, I. (1998) *Tourism and Sustainability: New Tourism in the Third World*. London: Routledge.

Mullings, B (1999) 'Insider or outsider, both or neither? Some dilemmas of interviewing in a cross-cultural setting', *Geoforum, 30*: 337–350.

Myers, G. A. (2001) 'Protecting privacy in foreign fields', *Geographical Review, 91*(1–2): 192–200.

Nairn, K. (1999) 'Embodied fieldwork', *Journal of Geography, 98*(6): 272–282.

Nairn, K. (2003) 'What has the geography of sleeping arrangements got to do with the geography of our teaching spaces?', *Gender, Place and Culture, 10*(1): 67–81.

Nairn, K., Higgitt, D.L. and Vanneste, D. (2000) 'International perspectives in fieldcourses', *Journal of Geography in Higher Education, 24* (2): 246–254.

Nast, H.J. (1994) 'Women in the field: critical feminist methodologies and theoretical perspectives', *Professional Geographer, 46* (1): 54–66.

Nelson, A., Hiner, C. and Rios, M. (2009) 'Book review forum: participatory action research', *Area, 41*(3): 364–367.

Ogborn, M. (2010) 'Finding historical sources'. In N. Clifford, S. French and G. Valentine (eds), *Key Methods in Geography* (2nd edn). London: SAGE.

Ostuni, J. (2000) 'The irreplaceable experience of fieldwork in geography'. In R. Gerber and G.K. Chuan (eds), *Fieldwork in Geography: Reflections, Perspectives and Actions*. Dordrecht, Boston and London: Kluwer Academic.

Pain, R. and Francis, P. (2003) 'Reflections on participatory research', *Area,* 35(1): 46–54.

Palriwala, R. (1991) 'Researcher and women: dilemmas of a fieldworker in a Rajasthan village'. In M.N. Panini (ed.), *From the Female Eye: Accounts of Fieldworkers Studying their own Communities.* Delhi: Hindustan.

Parfitt, J. (1997) 'Questionnaire design and sampling'. In M. Flowerdew. and D. Martin (eds), *Methods in Human Geography.* Harlow: Addison Wesley Longman.

Parr, H. (1998) 'Mental health, ethnography and the body', *Area, 30*: 28–37.

Parsons, T. and Knight, P. (1995) *How To Do Your Dissertation in Geography and Related Disciplines.* London: Chapman and Hall.

Pawson, E. and Teather, E.K. (2002) '"Geographical expeditions": assessing the benefits of a student-driven fieldwork method', *Journal of Geography in Higher Education, 26*(3): 275–289.

Perec, G. (1997[1978]) *Species of Space and Other Pieces* (trans. J. Sturrock). Harmondsworth: Penguin.

Peterson, J. and Earl, R. (2000) 'Trends and developments in university level geography field methods courses in the United States'. In R. Gerber and G.K. Chuan (eds), *Fieldwork in Geography: Reflections, Perspectives and Actions.* Dordrecht, Boston and London: Kluwer Academic.

Phillips, R. (2010) 'The impact agenda and geographies of curiosity', *Transactions of the Institute of British Geographers, 35*: 447–452.

Pinder, D. (2005a) *Visions of the City: Utopianism, Power and Politics in Twentieth-Century Urbanism.* Edinburgh: Edinburgh University Press.

Pinder, D. (2005b) 'Arts of urban exploration', *Cultural Geographies, 12*(4): 383–411.

Ploszajska, T. (1998) 'Down to earth? Geography fieldwork in English schools, 1870–1944', *Environment and Planning D, 16*: 757–774.

Plummer, K. (2001) *Documents of Life 2: An Invitation to A Critical Humanism.* London: SAGE.

Powell, R.C. (2002) 'The sirens' voices? Field practices and dialogue in geography', *Area, 34*(3): 261–272.

Powell, R.C. (2008) 'Becoming a geographical scientist: oral histories of Arctic fieldwork', *Transactions of the Institute of British Geographers, 33*(4): 548–565.

Pratt, G. (2007) 'Working with migrant communities: collaborating with the Kalayaan Centre in Vancouver, Canada'. In S. Kingdon, R. Pain and M. Kesby (eds), *Participatory Action Research Approaches and Methods.* London: Routledge.

Priestnall, G. (2009) 'Landscape visualization in fieldwork', *Journal of Geography in Higher Education, 33*(1): 104–112.

Quality Assessment Authority (QAA) (2007) 'Benchmark statement for geography'. Available at: http://www.qaa.ac.uk/academicinfrastructure/benchmark/statements/Geography.asp (last accessed March 2010).

Reason, R. and Bradbury, H. (eds) (2006) *Handbook of Action Research.* London: SAGE.

Reich, R.B. (2002) *The Future of Success.* New York: Vintage.

Robson, C. (1993) *Real World Research.* London: Blackwell.

Robson, E. and Willis, K. with Elmhirst, R.E. (1997) 'Practical tips'. In E. Robson and K. Willis (eds) *Postgraduate Fieldwork in Developing Areas.* Monograph no.9. Developing Areas Research Group. London: RGS-IBG.

Rodaway, P. (1994) *Sensuous Geographies: Body, Sense, Place.* London: Routledge.

Rose, D. (1987) *Black American Street Life: South Philadelphia 1969–71.* Philadelphia: University of Pennsylvania Press.

Rose, G. (1993) *Feminism and Geography: the Limits of Geographical Knowledge.* Cambridge: Polity.

Rose, G. (1997) 'Situating knowledges: positionality, reflexivities and other tactics', *Progress in Human Geography, 21*(3): 305–320.

Rose, G. (2001) *Visual Methodologies: An Introduction to the Interpretation of Visual Materials.* London: SAGE.

Royal Geographical Society (2008) Fieldwork safety: a resource briefing on BS8848. Available at http://www.rgs.org/NR/rdonlyres/D93E45F0–68A4–430B-BC8F-DD0DEEB6D0FA/0/GEES8848Brief.pdf (last accessed 12 May 2010).

Rubenstein, S. (2004) 'Fieldwork and the erotic economy on the colonial frontier', *Signs: Journal of Women in Culture and Society: 29*(4): 1041–1071.

Rundstrom, R.A. and Kenzer, M.S. (1989) 'The decline of field work in human geography', *Professional Geographer, 41* (3): 294–303.

Sauer, C. (1956) 'The education of a geographer', *Annals of the Association of American Geographers, 46*: 287–299.

Schensul, S.L., Schesul, J.J. and LeCompte, M.D. (1999) *Essential Ethnographic Methods: Observations, Interviews and Questionnaires.* London: SAGE.

Scheyvens, R., Nowak, B. and Scheyvens, H. (2003) 'Ethical issues'. In R. Scheyvens and D. Storey (eds), *Development Fieldwork: A Practical Guide.* London: SAGE.

Scheyvens, R. and Storey, D. (eds) (2003) *Development Fieldwork: A Practical Guide.* London: SAGE.

Schwarz, J.M. and Ryan, J.R. (eds) (2003) *Picturing Place: Photography and the Geographical Imagination.* London: I.B. Tauris.

Scott, A.J. (2000) 'French cinema: economy, policy and place in the making of a cultural products industry',. *Theory, Culture and Society, 17* (1): 1–38.

Scott, A.J. (2002) 'A new map of Hollywood: the production and distribution of American Hollywood pictures', *Regional Studies, 36* (9): 957–975.

Scott, S., Miller, F. and Lloyd, K. (2006) 'Doing fieldwork in development geography: research culture and research spaces in Vietnam', *Geographical Research, 44*(1): 28–40.

Shaffir, W.B. and Stebbins, R.A. (eds) (1991) *Experiencing Fieldwork: An Inside View of Qualitative Research.* London: SAGE.

Shah, S. (2004) 'The researcher/interviewer in intercultural context: a social intruder!', *British Educational Research Journal, 30* (4): 549–575.

Shiel, M. and Fitzmaurice, T. (eds) (2001) *Cinema and the City: Film and Urban Societies in a Global Context.* Oxford: Blackwell.

Sidaway, J.D. (2002) 'Photography as geographical fieldwork', *Journal of Geography in Higher Education, 26*(1): 95–103.

Silverman, D. (1985) *Qualitative Methodology and Sociology.* Aldershot: Gower.

Silverman, D. (2000) *Doing Qualitative Research: A Practical Handbook.* London: SAGE.

Silvey, R. (2003) 'Gender and mobility: critical ethnographies of migration in Indonesia'. In A. Blunt, P. Gruffudd, J. May, M. Ogborn and D. Pinder (eds), *Cultural Geography in Practice.* London: Arnold.

Smith, K. (2008) *How to be an Explorer of the World.* New York: Penguin.

Smith. M. (1996) 'The empire filters back: consumption, production and the politics of Starbucks Coffee', *Urban Geography, 17*(6): 502–524.

Smith, S.J. (1994) 'Soundscape', *Area, 26*: 232–240.

Solnit, R. (2006) *A Field Guide to Getting Lost*. Edinburgh: Canongate.

Spronken-Smith, R.A. (2005) 'Implementing a problem-based learning approach for teaching research methods in Geography', *Journal of Geography in Higher Education, 29*: 203–221.

Spronken-Smith, R.A. and Hilton, M. (2009) 'Recapturing quality field experiences and strengthening teaching-research links', *New Zealand Geographer, 65*:139–146.

Staeheli, L.A. and Lawson, V.A. (1994) 'A discussion of "Women in the field": the politics of feminist fieldwork', *Professional Geographer, 46*(1): 96–102.

Staeheli, L.A. and Mitchell, D. (2005) 'The complex politics of relevance in geography', *Annals of the Association of American Geographers, 95*(2): 357–372.

Stanley, L. and Wise, S. (1993) *Breaking Out Against: Feminist Ontology and Epistemology*. London: Routledge.

Stevens, S. (2001) 'Fieldwork as commitment', *Geographical Review, 91*(1–2): 66–73.

Stoddart, D.R. (1986) *On Geography and its History*. Oxford: Basil Blackwell.

Suchar, C. (2004) 'Amsterdam and Chicago: seeing the macro-characteristics of gentrification'. In C. Knowles and P. Sweetman (eds), *Picturing the Social Landscape: Visual Methods and the Sociological Imagination*. London: Routledge.

Thorndycraft, V.R., Thompson, D. and Tomlinson, E. (2009) 'Google Earth, virtual fieldwork and quantitative methods in physical geography', *Planet, 22*: 48–51.

Thrift, N. (2000) 'Dead or alive?'. In I. Cook, D. Couch, S. Naylor and J. Ryan (eds), *Cultural Turns/ Geographical Turns: Perspectives on Cultural Geography*. Harlow: Prentice Hall.

Times (2009) 'Geography outdoors' , 1 May, p. 2.

Times Higher Education Supplement (2009) 'Letter from philosophers: only scholarly freedom delivers real "impact"', 5 November.

Tolia-Kelly, D.P. (2007) 'Capturing spatial vocabularies in a collaborative visual methodology with Melanie Carvalho and South Asian women in London, UK'. In S. Kingdon, R. Pain and M. Kesby (eds), *Participatory Action Research Approaches and Methods*. London: Routledge.

Tuan, Y.F. (2001) 'Life as a field trip', *Geographical Review, 91*(1–2): 41–45.

Valentine, G. (2005) '"Tell me about …": using interviews as a research methodology'. In R. Flowerdew and D. Martin (eds), *Methods in Human Geography: A Guide for Students Doing a Research Project* (2nd edn). Edinburgh Gate: Addison Wesley Longman.

West, M. (1994) *Effective Teamwork*. Leicester: British Psychological Society.

West, R.C. (1979) *Carl Sauer's Fieldwork in Latin America*. New York: Department of Geography, Syracuse University.

Whitehead, T.L. and Conway, M.E. (eds) (1986) *Self, Sex and Gender in Cross-cultural Fieldwork*. Urbana: University of Illinois Press.

Whyte, W. F. (1955) *Street Corner Society: The Social Structure of an Italian Slum*. Chicago: Chicago University Press.

Williams, R. (1961) *The Long Revolution*. London: Chatto & Windus.

Wilson, C. and Groth, P. (eds) (2003) *Everyday America: Cultural Landscape Studies after J. B. Jackson*. Berkeley: University of California Press.

Wilson, D. (1990) 'Comments on "The Decline of Fieldwork in Human Geography"', *Professional Geographer* , 42 (2): 219–221.

Winchester, H.P.M. (1996) 'Ethical issues in interviewing as a research method in human geography', *Australian Geographer, 2*(1): 117–131.

Winchester, H., Kong, L. and Dunn, K. (2003) *Landscapes: Ways of Imagining the World*. Harlow: Pearson Education.

Wooldridge, S.W. (1955) 'The status of geography and the role of fieldwork', *Geography 40*: 73–83.

Wolcott, H.F. (1990) *Writing up Qualitative Research*. London: SAGE.

Yeung, H.W-C. (1995) 'Qualitative personal interviews in international business research: some lessons from a study of Hong Kong transnational corporations', *International Business Review, 4* (3): 313–339.

Young, L. and Barrett, H. (2001) 'Adapting visual methods: action research with Kampala street children', *Area, 33*(2): 141–152

Zelinsky, W. (1985) 'The roving palate: North America's ethnic cuisines', *Geoforum, 16:* 51–72.

Ziller, R.C. (1990) *Auto-Photography: Observations from the Inside-Out*. Newbury Park, CA: SAGE.

INDEX

Page references to Figures are in *italics*